THE POWER GAME

*An Examination of Decision-making
in Government*

JOCK BRUCE-GARDYNE

and

NIGEL LAWSON

ARCHON BOOKS

HAMDEN, CONNECTICUT

© Jock Bruce-Gardyne and Nigel Lawson 1976

First published 1976 by
The Macmillan Press, Ltd., London and Basingstoke
and in the United States of America
as an Archon Book, an imprint of
The Shoe String Press, Inc, Hamden, Connecticut

Library of Congress Cataloging in Publication Data

Bruce-Gardyne, Jock.
The power game.
Bibliography: p.
Includes index.
1. Great Britain—Politics and government—1945–1964. 2. Great
Britain—Politics and government—1964–   . 3. Decision-
making in public administration—Case studies. 4. Power (Social
sciences)—Case studies.
I. Lawson, Nigel.   II. Title.
JN234.1976.B78 1976   320.9'41'0856   76-6971
ISBN 0–208–01598–1

Printed in Great Britain

To Samuel Brittan

CONTENTS

CONTENTS

1 Introduction

This is a book about political power in Britain – where it lies and how, in practice, it is wielded.

In our approach to this question, however, we have deliberately refrained from joining the swelling ranks of latter-day Bagehots, rewriting Britain's unwritten constitution, dissecting its institutions and advancing some new theory of government. Instead, we have chosen to examine in some detail a small number of key political decisions of the recent past, analysing the relative power of the various conflicting forces at work in each case, and attempting to discover how and why it was that one particular outcome prevailed.

These case histories form the main body of the book. In an extended concluding section we draw the threads together and, leaning heavily although not exclusively on the evidence revealed by our case studies, suggest some tentative conclusions about the real distribution of power in the modern British political system. Is the power of the Prime Minister such that we now have a presidential system in all but name? Or are all ministers, the Prime Minister included, merely puppets of the bureaucracy, masking the reality of civil service rule? Or is power slipping away from Whitehall and Westminster altogether, and passing into the hands of the great interest groups, the CBI and the TUC? How, if at all, does public opinion make itself felt? How large a role in our affairs is played by sheer chance? All these questions, and many others, are, we feel, most usefully answered by taking a close look at how, in practice, a number of specific decisions, recognised at the time as being of undoubted importance, actually came to be taken by governments of both parties.

We then had to decide which decisions, and how many of them, to put under the microscope. To do the job in sufficient depth and still keep the book within a reasonable length, we have felt obliged to limit ourselves to four case histories: (i) the decision by the Macmillan government in 1962 (and reluctantly endorsed by the Wilson government in 1964) to build Concorde; (ii) the decision by the Douglas-Home government in 1964 to abolish resale price maintenance; (iii) the decision by the Macmillan government in 1961 and again by the Wilson government in 1967 to apply for membership of the Common Market; and (iv) the decision by the Wilson government in 1964, and again in 1966, *not* to devalue the pound – together with a postscript on the eventual acceptance of *force majeure* in 1967.

Our criteria for selecting these particular decisions we explain below; but it will be noted that each of them fell, in the broadest sense, within the sphere of economic rather than social policy. This may be justified by the undoubted fact that economic policy has been the main preoccupation of successive British governments for the past thirty years or more; none the less, we would hope to redress the balance by subjecting a rather different set of decisions to a similar scrutiny in a subsequent volume.

In a shrinking world, however, with Britain's autonomy shrinking within it, the international repercussions of economic policy choices can rarely be ignored. One of our four case histories, it is true, was a matter of purely domestic concern. But in the others the British government was far from being a self-sufficient power centre. Concorde was a joint venture with France; accession to the Common Market required the assent of the existing members, and profoundly modified our relationships with the rest of our trading partners; devaluation of what was still one of the world's major trading and reserve currencies in the context of a system of ostensibly fixed parities was bound to have far-reaching repercussions of legitimate concern to other governments. So much was inescapable. But some believed at the time – and some have continued to believe ever since – that over and above the legitimate representation of interests by allies and trading partners, more dubious and devious pressures were applied. So we shall need to consider the interaction of these international pressures and domestic policy priorities, and to assess the extent to which they did, or did not, go beyond the normal commerce of governments.

We have deliberately selected decisions taken during a single decade: the 1960s. Our credentials for undertaking the task of writing this book in the first place are that, as journalists, we wrote about these events when they were happening, and discussed them with many of the leading participants at the time. (As practising politicians, we have also been able to add a parliamentary perspective to our perception of events; but it is as journalists that we have written this book.) When we then came to do the research for this volume, which involved a very large number of (for the most part non-attributable) conversations with the principal actors in the case histories chosen, we were thus able to check the accounts we were given, not merely against each other and against published sources, but also against our own contemporary notes. This proved a useful corrective: human memory, even of relatively recent events, can be surprisingly fallible.

But the sixties are a convenient decade for a number of reasons. It was a period more or less equally divided between years of Conservative and Labour rule (and one which saw three Prime Ministers of very different character at contrasting stages of their careers). It is sufficiently distant to allow a measure of historical perspective, while sufficiently close to ensure that the personal witness of most of those most intimately involved in the decisions under scrutiny was still available to us.

It is, of course, a commonplace that we live in a rapidly changing society, and that our constitution is constantly evolving to accommodate itself to new political realities. But while the distribution of political power in the 1970s may be different from what it was in the 1960s (and different from what it will be in the 1980s) we see no reason to believe that it has changed beyond recognition from the disposition that emerges from our case histories. The most obvious change to have occurred since the decade under scrutiny has been the increase in the power of the trade unions – or, at the very least, the heightened awareness of that power throughout the political system, and a greater readiness to use it on the part of the unions themselves. But it is important to be clear what is meant by this. The trade unions undoubtedly exercise great power over a narrow range of decisions: namely, those which directly affect the conditions in which they conduct their everyday business, whether it be in the field of industrial relations legislation as such, or the suspension of free collective bargaining by means of an incomes policy of one kind or another. They are also alleged by many to have the power – a great power, if it be true – to make and (more particularly) break governments; although the smoke has not yet sufficiently cleared to enable the real lesson of the general election of February 1974 to be drawn with any degree of confidence. But it is far from obvious that the trade unions have enjoyed any great accretion of power in the sense in which this book is concerned with it: the power to determine major government decisions over a wide range of issues.

This may be tested against the four case studies chosen for this volume – all of which, as has already been noted, belong at least partly to the economic dimension of government, and which therefore might be expected to be of interest to the TUC. It is not too difficult to imagine that each of them – Concorde, resale price maintenance, the Common Market and devaluation – might have come to the point of decision, not in the sixties, but today. If so, the outcome, in some or all of the cases, might well have been different.

But it is inconceivable that any such difference would be due to the enhanced power of the trade unions: indeed, there is little reason to suppose that the role of the unions in the context of these decisions would be significantly different from what it was in the 1960s, when they were actually taken.

We discuss further the direction in which the British political system may be shifting at the end of the concluding section of this book. But it is worth emphasising here that, had we chosen for our case histories events and decisions of the early seventies instead of those of a few years earlier, it is inevitable that our witnesses would in very many cases have felt far more inhibited and would have spoken to us far less freely than in fact they did.

It is perhaps appropriate to acknowledge at this point our gratitude to the large number of actors in the dramas about which we have written – ministers and ex-ministers (both Labour and Conservative), civil servants and ex-civil servants, and many others – who, in the words of the police, have helped us with our inquiries. To list them all might be tedious: it would certainly (for some) be embarrassing. To list a few of them would be invidious. We therefore name none. (However, Nigel Lawson acknowledges a special debt of gratitude to the Warden and Fellows of Nuffield College, Oxford, who, in their generosity, elected him in 1972/3 to a Research Fellowship, of which his share in this book is the belated fruit.) But without their help this book could not have been written.

Inevitably, our many witnesses spoke to us on a non-attributable basis. One consequence of this is that we are unable to quote a source for much of the material included in our case histories; and this applies in particular to the not inconsiderable amount of evidence of a sensitive nature which has not hitherto been published. But the absence of any quoted source for a particular assertion should not be taken to imply that it is less reliable than evidence drawn from published accounts for which we do provide references. Indeed, it is our experience that non-attributable evidence is frequently more reliable than published sources in general, and political memoirs in particular. Where published sources (which themselves often conflict, as a series of articles in the *Sunday Times* in the summer of 1975 usefully demonstrated) give an account which differs from that given in this book, this is because we have reason to believe that our own version is closer to the truth; but on the whole we have not felt that it would serve any worthwhile purpose explicitly to point out the errors in others' accounts. For those who wish to compare and contrast, we include a select bibliography.

Since this is a book about political power, the case histories we have chosen are in no sense meant to represent 'typical' government decisions. To understand the power of a man's mind, or the strength of his spirit, you do not observe him ordering fish and chips. No more do typical, everyday, government decisions shed much light on the true distribution of power in a political system. Instead, we have chosen four decisions which, while reflecting different facets of the role of modern government, all satisfy three essential criteria.

In the first place, we have chosen decisions which were recognised at the time as being important, either in themselves or by virtue of the controversy which surrounded them: thus we see the political process at its most heightened, when those who enjoy power may be expected to exert it. Second, we have avoided decisions that stemmed from electoral commitments, since such commitments tend to be entered into in opposition, as a result of forces very different from those which operate in government: decisions of this kind are some-thing of a special case, and tell us little about where power normally resides, and how it is wielded. Finally, we have rejected the very much wider range of decisions – perhaps in themselves more 'typical' – which appear to have been either inexorably determined by the series of decisions which preceded them, or else forced upon a government as an inevitable response to the pressure of events. In short, each of our chosen decisions could well have gone the other way: all of them represented conscious choices, consciously made.

It goes without saying that we reject the view, ably refuted by Nelson Polsby in *Community Power and Political Theory*, but still fashionable among some radical American academic writers, that it is not decisions at all, but rather 'non-decisions' that illustrate the nature and distribution of political power in a society. Nor for the purposes of this inquiry, is it of any concern to us whether the de-cisions made were right or wrong.

Within this common framework, the four decisions scrutinised in depth in the pages that follow presented the governments concerned with different sorts of choices and display different arrays of forces at work. Taken together they involved Prime Ministers and Cabinets of both parties, the Treasury, the Foreign Office, the old Board of Trade and Ministry of Aviation, the TUC and the CBI, the Bank of England and the National Farmers' Union, the aircraft industry and the retail trade, American, Continental and Commonwealth govern-ments, parliament, the press and public opinion.

In the first case study, that of the decision to build Concorde, we have an instance of that modern phenomenon, the state as entre-preneur. More specifically, we see the power of a determined spend-ing department supported (although not pushed) by a powerful industrial lobby, the importance of chance, the strength of the *zeitgeist* (it was not only Wilson who was bewitched by 'the white

heat of the technological revolution'), the insidious momentum
acquired by any public project once it has started, the notable weakness of the Treasury (whose opposition to a massive government
spending commitment was as total as it was futile: a foretaste of the
wider loss of control of public expenditure that was to follow in the
1970s), the key role of the external dimension – in the shape of relations with France – and the significance of a Prime Minister with
a deep-seated hostility to the Treasury.

The second case history, that of the decision to abolish resale price
maintenance, is, by contrast, concerned with what might appear to be
a narrow commercial dispute, but one which stirred up acute political
controversy – for the most part within, rather than across, party
lines. Here we see the persistence of a strong departmental policy over
a still longer period of time, its power when – but only when –
harnessed by an ambitious and heavyweight departmental minister,
the failure of a potentially strong and wealthy commercial pressure
group, the importance of a change of Prime Minister, the significance
of the economic consensus, an attempt by parliament to assert itself,
and profound party sentiment overridden in a most unusual way.

Our third story, of the launching of the two abortive attempts to
join the European Community, in 1961 and 1967, concerns what was
regarded as the great issue of the decade. Whether it will stand up to
that contemporary billing will be for future historians to decide.
But at the time it was inevitable that such a seemingly traumatic
choice should have engaged the attention of Prime Ministers and all
their Cabinet colleagues, a galaxy of Whitehall departments –
Foreign Office, Treasury, Board of Trade, Ministry of Agriculture –
backbenchers of the Government Party, the Opposition, the great
industrial lobbies, the press and elite opinion. Yet it is also a story
full of surprises: the leading influence of the city and industrial
lobby, contrasted with the relative aloofness of the TUC; the hesitancy of a Prime Minister with impeccable 'European' credentials,
contrasted with the zeal of a Prime Minister with none; the impact
of a single determined civil servant in a key position; the inability
of the Treasury to halt an adventure which it viewed with mounting
apprehension, contrasted with the ease with which the Foreign
Office was able to set a course which it knew – none better – was
headed for the rocks, in furtherance of a departmental policy.

Finally, in the decision not to devalue the pound, a decision lying
at the heart of what is arguably the crucial area of success or failure
for modern government, the management of the economy, we have
an example of Prime Ministerial power exercised through the
technique of 'divide and rule'. We see the impotence of the Cabinet,
the astonishing unimportance of the big pressure groups, no real

'public' opinion yet a keen anticipation of such opinion, the undoubted importance of elite opinion, the power of the Whitehall
machine to neutralise 'outsiders', the significance of external forces,
the ambivalent (yet crucial) role of the Treasury, and the ultimate
sovereignty of events.

It is, incidentally worth noting that each of the four decisions we
have placed under the microscope seems, in retrospect, surprising, not
to say mysterious. How was it that governments of both parties became committed to a massive spending project for which there was
neither public demand nor the prospect of commercial or electoral
dividends, and which has remained a matter of permanent controversy? How was it that a Conservative government came to introduce a Bill that was bound to split the Party on the eve of a General
Election when the need for party unity might be thought to be paramount? How was it that, on an issue as momentous as Common
Market membership, both a sceptical Conservative administration
and a hostile Labour one successively and without much warning
applied for entry – and yet escaped the traumas associated with many
a lesser *volte-face*? How was it that a Labour government, after
thirteen years in the wilderness, came to sacrifice all its most cherished
plans and objectives, and ultimately even its own survival, for something as technical as a particular external parity for the pound? In
addition to showing the various political forces at work, our four
case histories provide the answers to these conundrums.

Not even the stoutest defenders of the constitutional proprieties
about ministerial responsibility would deny that the overwhelming
majority of decisions in government are in practice taken by the
civil service machine. This is true of any complex modern industrial
state: it is the inescapable consequence of the vast range of responsibilities assumed by the state for the well-being of its citizens. At the
other end of the spectrum, even those who – like the late Mr Crossman – are most suspicious of the erosion of political control by the
might of the bureaucracy, concede that an incoming government with
a strong sense of mission can, at least temporarily, impose decisions
on a reluctant civil service. The disputed territory lies between these
two extreme positions, in the area of major choices with far-reaching
and indisputably political consequences, yet which flow neither from
electoral mandates nor inexorably from previous decisions. All our
case histories fall into this category, and help to shed light on where
the line might be drawn and what sort of line it is.

Similarly, our case studies help to illuminate the nature and extent of the power of the Prime Minister. Not the least of the attractions of the 1960s as a decade for inspection is that it displayed a
Prime Minister on the wane, a Prime Minister who was widely re-

garded by contemporaries as a stand-in co-opted to enable the cast
to complete its run, and a Prime Minister flushed with the authority
of electoral triumph after a long sojourn in the wilderness. Two of
our case histories relate to decisions which were so crucial to the
whole course of government that the Prime Minister, whoever he
might have been, could not have escaped personal involvement. The
other two decisions were much more peripheral; but in each of them,
as will be seen, the element of controversy within the Cabinet was
sufficient to call for Prime Ministerial arbitration. The conclusions
we draw from this are set out in the final section of the book: at this
stage it is appropriate to sound a note of warning. The danger in the
case-history approach is that, out of a whole range of issues that are
developing more or less simultaneously, a handful are plucked out
and presented in somewhat spurious isolation. Yet not only does the
outcome of one event in practice react both directly and indirectly
upon another, but it is the combined pressure of events on a modern
Cabinet that is, in many ways, the most important political reality
of all. This is particularly true in the case of the Prime Minister, who
– however willing and able – simply cannot control all the big
decisions all the time. By deliberately selecting four of the most
important or controversial decisions taken in the period under
scrutiny, there is a risk that the role of the Prime Minister, who will
naturally have made a similar selection for his attention, may
appear a little larger than life.

Another danger, although for a very different reason, is that the
role of public opinion may appear to be given, in these case histories,
less than its due. The truth is that mass public opinion as a positive
and autonomous force for major change is very rare indeed within the
British political system. The only obvious case of this in the past
twenty years has been the decision to control Commonwealth immigration, which we would hope to examine in a subsequent volume;
yet even in this instance the most striking fact is the length of time
it took for public opinion to make itself felt. By contrast, the normal
role of mass public opinion (in so far as it exists: opinion polls
rarely show a decisive verdict on one side or the other on any given
issue) is as a force *against* change; and negative government decisions
made in deference to this (such as the Macmillan government's decision not to complete the process of abolishing rent control) inevitably
pass almost unnoticed among the public at large. Yet ministers are
all too well aware of the constraints of real or imagined public
opinion.

These and other aspects of the disposition of political power in
modern Britain are discussed more fully in our concluding section,
immediately after the four case histories. For whatever its incidental

weaknesses, the great strength of the case-study approach is that, more than any other, it is able to illuminate the living reality of a political system. In addition, it provides the raw material from which the reader may draw his own conclusions, irrespective of ours, about the true nature and distribution of power within that system. At the very least, we hope that these four narratives of modern British government in action (or inaction) may be of interest in themselves as a contribution to the history of our time.

2 How Whitehall Grew Wings: The Concorde Saga

Each of the other three decisions examined in the course of this study might have been taken by any government this century. The decision taken by the Macmillan government in November 1962 to build a supersonic transport was different. It would have been unthinkable for a pre-war government to have embarked on a purely commercial venture with an eye to profit for the nation. After the war, however, with the nationalisation of industries such as coal and the railways, the politicians and civil servants were increasingly called upon to exercise what amounted to commercial judgement. Furthermore, following the recommendations of the wartime Brabazon Committee, successive governments had assumed responsibility for financing research and development in the civil aviation industry.

During the 1950s, under pressure from the Treasury, a conscious effort had been made to limit the scale of the commitment of public finance by insisting that the aircraft manufacturing companies themselves should share the cost of developing projects for which state backing was required. In this sense Concorde, although a quintessential example of the post-war phenomenon of state entrepreneurship, was a return to the earlier pattern of the late 1940s; for in this instance the advance into the uncharted territory of supersonic civilian travel was reckoned from the start to be beyond the resources of private enterprise.

The year 1954 was a disastrous one for the British aircraft industry. The Comet had represented a dramatic breakthrough which had put the industry a lap ahead of the international competition. The Comet order book from the airlines of the world was, in the words of a contemporary civil servant, 'stretching out of sight' at the beginning of 1954. Then, suddenly, in the blue sky over the Mediterranean, the glittering prospect dissolved in an explosion.

This was the moment at which the Royal Aircraft Establishment at Farnborough received a new Deputy Director, Mr (later Sir) Morien Morgan. On 25 February Morgan summoned a meeting of the heads of departments at Farnborough. Up to that time, he told them, the RAE's research work had been 'overwhelmingly military'.

Perhaps the time had come 'to try and redress the balance a little by giving more consideration to civil aircraft'. Paradoxically the RAE was about to be absorbed with a civil aviation project of great urgency: the piecing together of the minute pieces of debris from the Comet crash to discover its cause. But on that morning in February 1954 Morgan was looking further ahead. The generation of aircraft coming off the production lines at that time, he pointed out, would fly at high subsonic speeds. 'The question arose whether their successors should fly at slightly higher subsonic speeds, or at supersonic speed.' It was desirable, he concluded, according to the minutes of the meeting (quoted by Morgan in the *Aeronautical Journal*, January 1972) that the RAE should now give 'some serious thought' to this question.

So a 'working group' was set up, and spent the next fourteen months analysing the various alternative shapes, sizes and speeds for a supersonic airliner. It came to conclusions which were to turn out prophetic: it opted for Mach 2 because this was the highest speed at which conventional light alloys (as opposed to titanium, a wildly expensive metal whose qualities were then untested) could be used; and it singled out the North Atlantic as the essential market – the only one, in Morgan's words, 'with a bag of gold at either end'. But unfortunately what emerged was an aircraft with a take-off weight of 300,000 lb which would carry just fifteen passengers, which meant direct operating costs at least five times as heavy as those of contemporary long-range carriers. Understandably, enthusiasm waned.

But it did not die. At first Farnborough decided to lower its sights and investigate whether an aircraft travelling at Mach 1.2 might be a more practical proposition. The head of RAE's Aero Division, Philip Hufton, became the principal protagonist of the Mach 1.2 scheme. The Mach 2 alternative was not abandoned, however, and when in early 1957 one of the technicians at Farnborough, W. E. Gray, demonstrated with the aid of a simple wooden model released from the top of a step-ladder that the belief that it would be uncontrollable at a flight angle of more than 20 degrees was unfounded, it reverted to the position of Farnborough's first preference.

Meanwhile the RAE's parent department, then the Ministry of Supply, was alerted to what was going on. During the summer of 1956 Hufton succeeded in winning the support of the RAE's Director, Sir George Gardiner, for the work which his Division was doing; and it was Gardiner who decided that the time had come to set up a broadly-based technical committee, including representatives of the aircraft industry, the airlines and the civil service, to 'explore the possibility of economic supersonic transports'. Just as the Anglo-French expeditionary force was disembarking at Suez, on 5 November

1956, the Supersonic Transport Aircraft Committee (STAC) held its first meeting. In retrospect the timing seems remarkably appropriate. The gestation period had begun.

Morgan was put in charge of the STAC. He has since described it as a 'most satisfactory and rewarding assignment' [*Aeronautical Journal*, January 1972]. Membership of the committee included technical directors from most of the aircraft and aero-engine companies, plus representatives from BOAC, BEA, the Registration Board and the Ministry of Supply. There were, in Morgan's phrase, 'no hangers-on'. Understandably, perhaps – but also ominously for the future – there were no watchdogs of public expenditure either.

Three months later the Macmillan government's first Defence White Paper, with its emphasis on the nuclear deterrent and economies in conventional defence, involved a drastic scaling-down of the aircraft industry's expectations of future military orders. The profitability of the industry soon began to slide (a slide which was to continue until by 1961 it was earning less than 6 per cent on capital employed). In May 1957 the Minister of Supply, Aubrey Jones, told the aircraft companies that government finance for research and development work on civil aircraft would be forthcoming. As an earnest of his good intentions he promptly approached the Treasury for £700,000 'on account' towards the cost of research into the supersonic aircraft project. The Treasury duly obliged.

It took the STAC more than two years to produce its report, which was delivered to the Ministry of Aviation (successor to the Ministry of Supply) in March 1959. Its central recommendation was that the aircraft companies should be invited to submit 'brochure studies' for two alternative models of supersonic transport: a medium-range version, to carry one hundred passengers over journeys of 1500 miles at a speed of Mach 1.2; and a long-range version, to carry one hundred and fifty passengers at a speed of at least Mach 1.8. It also made a stab at the cost of the venture, which, it suggested, might amount to some £175m over ten years.

These, it is worth recalling, were the assessments of a group including representatives of the potential manufacturers and customers. Yet the Ministry of Aviation had other ideas. It was symptomatic of the highly speculative nature of the whole venture at this stage that the feasibility studies it decided to commission from the manufacturers in the autumn were more ambitious than those suggested by the STAC, while its estimate of cost was apparently considerably more modest. Two airframe companies, Bristol Aeroplane and Hawker Siddeley, were each invited to prepare a blueprint of a different version of a Mach 2.2 aircraft; while both were to try their hand at a Mach 2.7 model. Yet the new Deputy Secretary at the Ministry who took up office at the beginning of April 1959, Mr Denis Haviland, found that the cost-estimate for the SST waiting on his desk amounted to no more than £60m – an estimate to which, in agreement with the departmental Financial Secretary, he added an extra £40m 'for the sake of not getting things wrong'. (The original estimate was intended to cover research and development up to the production of the first prototype. It was the Ministry's normal practice to draw the line under its cost-estimates at this point even when, as in this case, it was apparent that the Exchequer would have to foot the bill, if it were decided to proceed that far, at least up to the completion of all prototypes.)

Haviland could perhaps fairly be described as the anchor man for the Concorde project throughout the crucial three-year period which divided the 1959 General Election from the final decision to proceed in November 1962. A pre-war engineer with the old LMS railway, he had come to the Ministry of Supply via wartime service in the Engineers and a stint with the Army Control Commission in Germany, and by this time he was an experienced and undazzled veteran of numerous conflicts with the Treasury. He was to remain as Deputy Secretary at the Ministry of Aviation until his departure for private industry in 1964, serving under three ministers – Duncan Sandys, Peter Thorneycroft and Julian Amery. For some time he had been worried about the long-term viability of the British aircraft industry; back in 1954 he had written a memorandum calling for rationalisation into fewer and larger units. By the autumn of 1959 the senior echelons at the Ministry had come to accept that rationalisation was overdue, and at this point it received a new political boss, Duncan Sandys, who had already earned a formidable reputation for despatch as a marriage broker (hitherto of regiments, subsequently of colonies), and who came endowed with a brief to knock the aircraft companies' heads together. Within two months, on 16 December 1959, the merger of Hawker and Armstrong Siddeley to form Hawker Siddeley was announced; and this was followed in January 1960 by the formation of the British Aircraft Corporation by the merging of the airframe interests of Vickers, English Electric and the Bristol Aeroplane Company.

It has been suggested that Government backing for a British SST was the dowry which Duncan Sandys was authorised to offer. Denis Haviland denies this: rather, the SST was held out as a 'makeweight sop' – i.e. the companies were warned that there was little prospect of encouragement for the supersonic project *unless* they agreed to rationalisation. As it was, the government officially welcomed the mergers, but it did not refer specifically to the possibility of support for the SST. On 12 January Sandys acknowledged that there was 'a case for making some increase in the assistance [from the government to the aircraft industry] on the civil side' following the reduction of expenditure on defence equipment; and on 15 February he told the Commons that the government 'may be prepared to contribute to-wards the cost of proving a new type of civil aircraft and of introduc-ing it into regular airline service ...' Cross-questioned a week later about the SST project, he was non-committal; but already there was press speculation that it would cost £200m spread over a ten-year period.

During the ensuing nine months the two newly-formed companies worked hard on their feasibility studies. There was a feeling in the aircraft industry (whether justified or not) that all this was something of a charade, and that the Ministry had in reality made up its mind in advance that the design-study contract – the next stage of the preparatory work – should go to BAC. It was reckoned that Hawker Siddeley was much better endowed with existing military contracts than was BAC; furthermore the old Bristol design team, under Dr Russell, which had done much of such early research work as had been undertaken on supersonic civilian aircraft within the industry, was now part of BAC, and the Ministry was thought to be anxious that this team should not be dispersed for lack of work. There was therefore little surprise when the design-study contract, worth £350,000, was indeed awarded to BAC in the autumn of 1960.

While BAC and Hawker Siddeley prepared their plans, however, the Ministry of Aviation was also looking for partners overseas. The concept of 'interdependence' had figured largely in the vocabulary of the Macmillan government ever since Suez; and while estimates of the likely cost of bringing a supersonic airliner into production varied widely, it was already apparent that it would be a task of for-midable magnitude for the British aviation industry to tackle single-handed.

In practice there were only two possible partners available. The German aircraft industry was still in its infancy; and while it was soon to become apparent that the Russians had the will and the know-how to launch into supersonic civilian transport the obstacles to a co-operative venture with them were so self-evident that the pos-sibility was never discussed. This left the French and the Americans.

The French aircraft industry had enjoyed its first major com-mercial success with the Caravelle short-haul jet in the 1950s; and towards the end of the decade Georges Hereil, the formidable ex-receiver in bankruptcy who presided over Sud-Aviation, the state-controlled manufacturer of Caravelle, had made overtures to the British with a view to co-operation on a supersonic 'Super-Caravelle'. He was firmly (and in his own estimation none too politely) rebuffed. Notwithstanding the success of the Caravelle the British air-craft industry still regarded the French as parvenus. If it was a question of international collaboration the automatic preferred choice was bound to be the United States. Admittedly there was wide-spread suspicion in the British industry of what were regarded as unscrupulous sales methods employed by the giant American firms: it was even rumoured that BOAC's frequent reluctance to 'buy British' was attributable to the fact that a senior executive of BOAC was on Boeing's payroll. Still, the arguments in favour of an Ameri-can partnership were held to be overwhelming. The United States was, after all, the largest commercial airline market in the world, and the one to which access was essential if the SST were to achieve viability. There were no language barriers. Moreover the American airframe companies had been studying the feasibility of supersonic passenger transport throughout the 1950s; and now a formal pledge of support for an American SST from the Eisenhower Administra-tion was thought to be imminent.

During his brief nine-month tenure of the Aviation Ministry Dun-can Sandys initiated preliminary soundings of American intentions. The response to these was adjudged sufficiently favourable to justify a visit to Washington by his successor, Peter Thorneycroft, within weeks of Thorneycroft's appointment in July 1960.

The outcome of Thorneycroft's Washington journey was not en-couraging. The big snag was that the American industry was think-ing in terms of an SST travelling at three times the speed of sound, using titanium as the key material—an approach which the British had already rejected as being too costly and complex. Nevertheless, after his return, Thorneycroft wrote to the American Secretary for Defence, Robert Macnamara, suggesting a joint feasibility study to assess the rival merits of Mach 2 and Mach 3. If this showed that Mach 3 was the speed to go for, then the American industry would be overwhelmingly the dominant partner. If, on the other hand, it showed a better profile for Mach 2, then the American industry would still be the dominant partner, but the British would play a much more significant part.

The Americans did not turn Thorneycroft down out of hand. In-deed in September 1960 the Ministry of Aviation put out a statement to the effect that following negotiations with the Administrator of the Federal Aeronautics Administration the two parties had agreed 'in principle that co-operation in the development of an SST aircraft could be of mutual advantage' and that 'further consideration should be given to how this might be achieved'. But in reality by the autumn of 1960 the British knew the Americans were not interested.

Thorneycroft himself attributes this negative response to the fact that 'the US system is not designed to have a chosen instrument': the US Government 'couldn't pick on Douglas without provoking Boeing, and vice versa'. Yet eventually the FAA did indeed pick Boeing and General Electric, respectively, to build the airframe and the engine of the abortive American SST. Rivalry between the two leading airframe manufacturers may have been *a* factor in 1960, but it was hardly decisive. Much more important was the fact that the Americans had already more or less decided to go for Mach 3; and – according to one authoritative source – above all an erroneous belief in Washington that even a Mach 2 aircraft would require the use of titanium.

Disbelief about the practicality of the British approach was compounded by scepticism about the seriousness of British intentions; and this not least for a reason which had been so much a fact of life of the British SST project from the very start that it would never have occurred to Thorneycroft or his officials as an obstacle. Five years later the Plowden Committee, which surveyed the future of the aircraft industry, drew attention to the fact that Concorde was the one major exception to the rule that 'the initiative in formulating requirements for new civil projects had rested entirely in the hands of the industry and the airlines'. In this case, as already explained, it was the Ministry of Aviation which went to the industry with a suggestion which had emanated from its own research establishment. And the response of the industry was notably detached throughout: Sir George Edwards, managing director of BAC from its inception, points out that 'we were attuned to civil aeroplanes we could see right through, identifying the markets and having a pretty clear idea of the prospects for both short and long-term customers', and this was just not possible with the SST. Hence 'if the aircraft industry had been asked to put up cash for the R and D, the answer would have been "no"'.

The detached attitude of the aircraft industry was to play a significant part in the whole history of Concorde. At this stage it may well have been decisive in ruling out the possibility of an Anglo-American joint venture. The American aircraft industry was well accustomed to close partnership with government; but co-operation with an overseas aircraft industry on a project where all the initiative, and all the cash, came from the state, was a rather different matter.

In retrospect Haviland regards the American rebuff as 'a world tragedy in aviation'. Yet although the Americans had been the Ministry's (and still more the industry's) preferred choice of partners, parallel overtures had also been made to the French. And here the extent of governmental involvement on the British side was, if anything, a positive advantage. For no Western country has a longer history of state *dirigisme* than France, and to the French aircraft industry governmental supervision and control was a fact of life.

In point of time, indeed, the first overtures were made to the French before any formal approach had been made to the Americans. Visiting the Paris air show in June 1959 the Minister of Supply, Aubrey Jones, had taken the opportunity to envisage the possibility of Anglo-French collaboration on an SST; and before the end of that summer Sir George Edwards, then still with Vickers, recalls receiving an inquiry from Sir George Gardiner of the RAE about his views on the scope for a joint venture with the French.

Edwards' response was bleak. The RAE was not put off, however: in the autumn of 1959 ONERA, the French aeronautical research establishment, was invited to send a delegation to Farnborough. There was talk about the idea of an SST, but the visitors showed themselves highly sceptical about the practicability of the whole idea. At this point chance played a hand. It so happened that during the winter of 1959 Sud-Aviation was short of work. The French company was therefore happy to undertake sub-contract work for Vickers on the VC 10. In retrospect Edwards reckons that 'there never would have been an Anglo-French Concorde unless we had gone through this ritual' – what he calls 'finding out at the sharp end' about the practicalities of working with the French.

Six months later, in the summer of 1960, the RAE paid a return visit to ONERA. The British found the attitude of their hosts towards the whole notion of an SST radically transformed. The scepticism of 1959 had given place to enthusiasm. Indeed so radical was the transformation at ONERA that a rumour has persisted in the British aircraft industry of a simple, but Machiavellian, explanation. The Ministry of Aviation, it is suggested, stilled the doubts at ONERA about the practicality of supersonic civilian travel by passing to the French a copy of the STAC report.

Those who were involved at the British end at the time express incredulity when challenged with this story: 'hardly the way to launch a delicate commercial negotiation'. Yet it dies hard. The *Sunday Times* (8 February 1976) reported categorically that Geoffrey Rippon, then Parliamentary Secretary for Aviation, authorised transmission of the STAC report in the early summer of 1960. Whether or not there was a leak from Whitehall, it seems likely that the logic of events would have drawn the French and British together. Perhaps the most significant aspect of the rumour of collusion is the evidence it offers of the extent to which the Ministry of Aviation was seen, throughout the aircraft industry, as completely dedicated to Concorde at this stage.

Once ONERA's initial scepticism had evaporated, for whatever reason, Duncan Sandys lost no time. One of his last actions before departing for the Commonwealth Relations Office in the summer of 1960 was to 'agree informally' with his French opposite number that there were no insuperable objections to Anglo-French co-operation on an SST. To his colleagues in Cabinet he is reported to have argued that 'if we are not in the big supersonic airline business, then it is really only just a matter of time before the whole British aircraft industry packs up'; and 'if we miss this generation, we will never catch up again. We will end up making executive aircraft' [*Battle for Concorde*].

The arrival of Peter Thorneycroft to replace Duncan Sandys in July 1960 nevertheless caused some anxiety. Thorneycroft had, after all, been in the wilderness since he had resigned in 1957 in protest at the excessive level of public expenditure. There were fears that he was being put into the Ministry of Aviation to do a 'hatchet job'. Such fears soon proved unfounded. Within weeks of his appointment he was rhapsodising to a senior civil servant: 'Oh what a lovely Ministry!' He became a vigorous champion of the SST, in Cabinet and out, and his past advocacy of Gladstonian restraint in public spending did not appear to inhibit his enthusiasm for his new task. (It is not only ministers who tend to adapt to the priorities of the departments with which they happen to be associated. Later in the 1960s it was noted how Sir Richard (Otto) Clarke, a formidable critic of the SST in his days as Deputy Secretary at the Treasury, became an enthusiastic advocate for Concorde when he moved to the Ministry of Technology as Permanent Secretary.)

Another anxiety about Thorneycroft's appointment within his new ministry was that he was thought to be much keener on co-operation with the French than on co-operation with the Americans: 'he was rumoured to have had a French nanny', one senior official recalls. He was also identified with the 'European' wing of his Party; though this was even more conspicuously true of his immediate predecessor. The Ministry, on the other hand, was still at this stage pinning its hopes on co-operation with the Americans. Here, too, fears were unfounded. French nanny or no, Thorneycroft espoused his new department's courtship of the American aircraft industry, and it was only when this proved a blind alley that he turned wholeheartedly to the French.

Gradually the battle-lines were beginning to emerge across Whitehall. Ostensibly the Ministry of Aviation's attitude was the one of detachment appropriate to a sponsoring department. In reality it was wholly committed, and with each change of minister its commitment only deepened.

At the other end of the spectrum was the Treasury. Anxiety about the extent of the government's commitment to the SST seems to have been slow to build up in Great George Street. It was not until the summer of 1960 that the Treasury began to show signs of wanting to drag its feet. A turning-point was the virtual abandonment of the idea of partnership with the US aviation industry. The Treasury had been insistent that if the venture were to be attempted, it should be done in conjunction with the Americans. It evidently hoped that the Americans would carry the major share of the cost; furthermore the 'environmentalist' opposition to supersonic travel was already vocal in the United States, and the attractions of an American partner were not diminished by the prospect that it might ultimately get cold feet. (The Treasury's calculation of the strength of opposition to the SST in the US turned out to be well founded on this occasion. But there was a departmental propensity to underestimate the political muscle of the American aviation lobby. Thus in 1971 it was assumed that Congress would never agree to guarantee the solvency of Lockheed as the price of continued UK official financial support for the RB-211. This proved to be an expensive error.)

Once the Ministry of Aviation had turned decisively towards France, the Treasury became more vocal. It did not argue about the technical feasibility of the SST: it was in no position to do so. But it had the strongest reasons, founded in bitter experience, to treat the cost-estimates of the aviation industry with reserve. And it also argued forcibly that by the time the SST was due to come into service in the later 1960s the world's airlines would still be struggling to finance the latest series of subsonic airliners, and in no condition to take on the SST.

Two other departments with a share of responsibility for civil aviation, the Ministry of Transport and the Board of Trade, tended to side with the Treasury rather than with the Ministry of Aviation at this time. They shared the doubts about the marketability of the SST. By 1962, because of the concurrent negotiations for Common Market entry, the Foreign Office lined up with the Ministry of Aviation. But at this stage it showed little evidence of interest either way. The Ministry of Defence was careful to keep its distance, because it was anxious lest a portion of the burden of financing the SST programme might be loaded on to its departmental budget. But it was not unaware that the SST and its own TSR 2 project shared an engine; and hence that an axe for the one was likely to mean a similar fate for the other. In the recollection of one senior minister (a Concorde enthusiast) it was 'totally untrue to say that Defence Ministers were not interested, in Cabinet terms'.

   Last, but most important of all, there was the attitude of the Prime
Minister. One of his colleagues recalls that it was Macmillan's technique to 'hold his hand until very late in the day'; and this was
certainly his response to the SST. He was drawn briefly into the controversy between the Ministry of Aviation and the Treasury in the
summer in 1961; but he did not really throw his weight into the
balance until the last few days before the signing of the agreement
with the French in the winter of 1962. It is noteworthy that Concorde
does not rate a mention in his memoirs.

   During the early months of 1961 BAC and Sud were working in
parallel, but quite separately, on their respective design studies: it
was not until June of that year that Edwards and Georges Hereil of
Sud had their first formal meeting in Paris. Meanwhile the threat of
a British balance of payments crisis was building up; and the unborn
SST faced the first hazard of its existence. Economies in public expenditure were under review, and the SST was high on the Treasury's
list for the axe. The outcome of this preliminary passage of arms between the Ministry of Aviation and the Treasury was highly reassuring for the aviation lobby, and correspondingly ominous for the
Treasury.

   The Ministry of Aviation rested its case on two lines of defence. It
argued that as BAC's design-study contract was virtually complete it
would save little or nothing to cancel it – indeed it might undermine
confidence at home and abroad by suggesting panic. Furthermore it
reminded the Treasury that the major reorganisation of the aircraft
industry carried through in the winter of 1959–60 had been lubri-
cated by the promises of financial support for civil aircraft projects:
it would therefore call in question the entire relationship between
government and industry if the SST were now to be jettisoned. So the
Treasury was effectively told that it had a tiger by the tail, and then
driven to accept that this was not the moment to let go.

   It remained a reluctant passenger; but it may be that it had now
missed the last chance to get off. By the autumn of 1961 Mr Heath
had launched the first British bid to enter the community, and when
the officials of Great George Street made a move to persuade Thorney
croft to cancel a visit by the French Transport Minister, Buron, to
London in October to discuss Anglo-French co-operation on the SST
they were sharply reminded that this would have a deplorable effect
on Anglo-French relations at a most inopportune moment. The visit
went ahead. (There is an interesting and instructive contrast with the
behaviour of the Foreign Office in the spring of 1958. Notwithstanding the fact that Reginald Maudling and a team of officials were
engaged in delicate negotiations to overcome French resistance to the
British plan for a free trade area embracing most of Western Europe

the Foreign Office had no hesitation in aligning itself outspokenly with the Americans in condemnation of infringement of the Tunisian frontier by the French army in Algeria, and in supplying arms to the Tunisians to ward off such infringements. The French were furious.)

Immediately after Buron's visit, in November 1961, BAC and Sud submitted to their respective governments two design-studies each, one for a medium and one for a long-range SST; and on 22 November the French government announced that it had authorised Sud to start work on the construction of a prototype medium-range supersonic, to be ready to fly by 1965, with the first commercial model for delivery in 1968.

On 22 March 1962 there was a further meeting between Buron and Thorneycroft in London, after which it was announced that the two ministers had 'agreed on the principles which might govern a cooperative programme on a fifty-fifty basis ... the two companies would be invited jointly to undertake a design study' [Hansard]. Nothing was said about the fact that the French and the British had their eyes on different – and to a large extent mutually incompatible – markets. The French were thinking in terms of intra-European and Euro-African routes; the British were convinced that the North Atlantic route was the one that mattered.

Nevertheless Thorneycroft did not underestimate the strength of the opposition which he still had to overcome. 'It was always obvious,' he recalls, 'that Concorde would be very expensive and therefore very difficult to sell to the Cabinet.' In the spring of 1962 he decided to play what may well have been a master-stroke. He asked for the establishment of a special technical Committee of the Cabinet, to assess the advantages and disadvantages of proceeding with a SST, under the chairmanship of Lord Mills.

The choice of Lord Mills for the chairmanship of this committee was crucial. Mills was a successful entrepreneur who had originally impressed Macmillan as a wartime recruit to the Ministry of Supply when the future Prime Minister was Parliamentary Under-Secretary in that department. When, following the 1951 General Election, a far from elated Macmillan was shunted by Churchill into the Ministry of Housing, he insisted on having Mills beside him as his personal adviser. The Ministry then went on to fulfil the Tory pledge to build 300,000 houses a year, and when Macmillan reached No. 10 six years later he had some reason to feel that he owed his preferment to Mills. 'Wise old Percy' became the new Prime Minister's personal troubleshooter, and schemes which passed the litmus-test of Mills' scrutiny could usually count on the Prime Minister's benevolence.

The vital meeting of this committee took place on the morning of

13 July 1962. Edwards and Sir Arnold Hall of Hawker Siddeley were bidden to attend. Edwards remembers being 'told to behave myself – it had never been done before'. The Ministry of Aviation made what a member of the committee describes as 'a massive presentation – payloads, noise levels, the lot'. The Treasury made a rival presentation, emphasising the economic imponderables, and calling in question cost-estimates and marketability.

It is possible to piece together, without benefit of too much hindsight, the main elements in the dossier which confronted Lord Mills and his colleagues. On the potential market for the SST, there was the authoritative survey carried out on behalf of the airlines by IATA in 1960 ['Technical Economic and Social Consequences of the introduction into commercial service of supersonic transports']. This concluded that the volume of passenger traffic was likely to double between 1960 and 1967, and thereafter to grow by at least 5 per cent per annum until 1975 (in a 1962 addendum to the survey it was stated that 'the United Kingdom felt that the forecast of a decline in the annual growth rate to around 5 per cent by 1967 was pessimistic'). On this basis it was reckoned that there would be a market for 188 Mach 2 SSTs, almost half of them for the North Atlantic route, or around sixty-three entering service annually from 1967 on. But it was acknowledged that there was a 20 per cent margin of error either way.

A major question-mark hung over the ability of the airlines to finance the purchase of SSTs in the later 1960s. The IATA survey predicted that by 1967 'the state of airline indebtedness will have fallen to the point where it should pose no serious problem to the purchase of supersonic equipment'. Yet Sir William Hildred, the Secretary-General of IATA, in his report to that body's annual conference in Sydney in October 1961 warned that 'if the jet has produced overcapacity, the SST could flood the world with it'.

This led directly to the question of the fare structure of supersonic travel. The 1962 addendum to the IATA survey, referred to above, stated that 'it still seems generally estimated that SST air services will be able to be offered to the public at about the same price as subsonics or at ... a small premium of about 10 per cent ... the demand for SST air services at fares of more than 10 per cent above other services would be small'. But according to Sir William Hildred these estimates were based on the assumption that the governments of the producer countries would bear the whole cost of research and development. 'If the governments are going to make a prestige thing of this, let them pay for it and not load it on the airlines.'

There were also serious doubts about the noise factor. At IATA's spring conference in Montreal in 1961 J.R.D. Tata of Air India argued strongly that this would oblige an SST to fly subsonic half the time; and technical representatives of Sud agreed that on this basis the aircraft could not be viable.

However, the evidence of the airlines was to some extent discounted. As Sir Richard Way, Permanent Secretary at the Ministry of Aviation, told the Estimates Committee, 'I believe it to be true that the airlines have always resisted the introduction of new aircraft ...' Furthermore the customer-resistance of BOAC was particularly suspect: the airline had, in the words of Denis Haviland, 'burnt its fingers badly' with the Comet, and as Sir Richard Way (subsequently a director of BOAC) recalls, the corporation's chairman in 1962 was worried by its commitment to buy the VC 10. The result was, according to Sir Morien Morgan, that BOAC had a 'propensity to suggest that Concorde was a load of old rubbish they'd be made to buy whenever they wanted some cheques signed for other aircraft'.

Yet if the airlines were playing hard to get, it was difficult to deny that there was a good deal of speculation about the presentation of the Ministry of Aviation. It was very much a gut feeling that, in the words of Sir Morien Morgan, 'if you look at the way aviation's developed, you can see that in twenty years' time the cheapest way of shifting a body across the Atlantic will be at Mach 2'. Equally hard to quantify in terms that would impress the Treasury was the evidence that the British and French aircraft industries had always struck gold by striking first, with models like the Viscount, the first short-haul turbo-prop, and the Caravelle, the first medium-range jet. And if the Treasury recalled the sad story of that other 'first', the Comet, the answer was likely to be: 'from a world angle it's a terribly weak-kneed argument for a country with our traditions to say "let it be someone else".'

Two other ancillary considerations which were subsequently to be dismissed by the Plowden Committee as largely irrelevant were those of employment and technological 'spin-off'. The aircraft industry had reached a post-war employment peak of 312,000 in 1957, and in the early 1960s it was fluctuating around the 300,000 mark. Later on, the fortuitous circumstance that the ministers responsible – Wedgwood Benn and his successor, Frederick Corfield – represented constituencies in the Bristol area no doubt enhanced their enthusiasm for Concorde. But at this period there is little tangible evidence to show that constituency considerations quickened ministerial enthusiasms. It is true that Julian Amery, who had a highly marginal constituency in Preston, and who succeeded Thorneycroft in the summer of 1962, had a large number of constituents working on the TSR 2, whose fate was intimately connected, by way of a common power-unit, with that of the SST. Senior civil servants insist that they never saw signs that constituency considerations influenced Amery's views over the SST. But perhaps it would not be unfair to conclude that Preston would have been an uncomfortable base for a minister who shared the Treasury's view of the aircraft industry.

The Plowden Committee would come to the conclusion [para 154] that 'for the kind of workers employed in the aircraft industry it is not jobs, but men, that are scarce'. Nevertheless this was not strictly true of the sophisticated design teams, which could easily have been lost without the prospect of continuity of employment. At any rate the general impression is that the issue of employment was one which the industry found it profitable, in Morgan's phrase, to 'peddle up' in Whitehall.

The committee was equally unimpressed by the argument about 'technological fall-out'. It concluded [para 172] that this considera-tion 'could not be advanced as a major justification for support at any particular level' by the government for the aircraft industry. Still, it was 'probable that no other single industry would have such a pervasive effect on the technical progress of the nation' [para 165]. Denis Haviland reckons that the 'fall-out' was regarded as a con-sideration of decreasing validity from 1959 on. Morien Morgan describes it as 'an awful lot of poetry'. That certainly summed up the way it was viewed by the Treasury.

That leaves the most contentious matter of all – that of costs. Already, by early 1962, the escalation of cost-estimates had been im-pressive. The earliest estimate to come from the Ministry of Supply back in 1959 had been £60m. One year later the Treasury was ex-pressing considerable dubiety about an estimate of £175m. By the time the Mills Committee was set up this figure had been revised up-wards to £200m.

When the Commons Committee came to review the decision to embark on Concorde programme in the 1963-4 parliamentary session it was extremely scathing about the 'contrast between the careful consideration ... paid to the technical aspects ... and the lack of de-tailed study given to the financial aspects' of the project [para 84]. And one of the later critics of Concorde [Edwards, *Concorde: a cost-benefit analysis*] has argued that scant attention had been paid to the work of a research team set up by the Ministry of Supply in 1958, which had shown that 'over a range of about a hundred projects, the average ratio of final costs to initial estimates was about 2·8' Edwards points out that contemporary US studies suggested an even larger margin of error – something in the region of a 6·5 ratio between initial estimates and final costs. He draws the conclusion that the research and development estimates laid before the Cabinet when it came to take its decision in the autumn of 1962 should have been revised upwards to £450m. (The Treasury, in its evidence to the 1971–2 Expenditure Committee, commented that '... if the technicians say the cost will be £Ym, we probably say £5Ym'. [Report, para 285].)

It is difficult to avoid the conclusion that there is an element of hindsight in all this. Haviland argues that the Ministry of Supply's own studies on which these criticisms are based were 'valid in the broad, but not in a particular statistic'; and Sir Richard Way, who was at the Ministry when these studies were carried out, points out that they found an enormous range of variables – in the case of the Seaslug, for example, final cost exceeded initial estimates by a factor of nineteen. So much depended on the time-scale. As Raymond Bell, the Treasury official who had chaired the committee of officials steering the early stages of the project on both sides of the Channel, told the Public Accounts Committee in the 1964–5 Parliamentary session, 'this is obviously a speculative project ... pushing development well into the unknown, and you're bound to take some risks ...'. In other words the cost-estimates were hardly worth the paper they were written on; and it is only fair to add that the higher echelons of Whitehall were well aware of the fact at the time. Davis, in *The Concorde Affair*, quotes one Cabinet minister as saying that 'we all thought it would cost much more than the original estimates, but I don't suppose anyone would have imagined it would have cost as much as it has'.

Evidently the arguments placed before the Mills Committee were finely balanced, and although the Ministry of Aviation had out-pointed the Treasury all along to this stage, Thorneycroft and his officials were by no means confident about the way 'wise old Percy' would jump. However he too came down on their side; and from that moment there was a feeling that the SST was in the clear.

There was a macabre postscript to that vital confrontation on the morning of 13 July. That afternoon Macmillan's 'night of the long knives' began with the abrupt dismissal of Selwyn Lloyd as Chancellor of the Exchequer. Before it was over Thorneycroft had moved to the Ministry of Defence, handing over to Julian Amery, who came from the Air Ministry.

Thorneycroft had been a member of the Cabinet; Amery was not. Senior civil servants attach great importance to Cabinet status for their minister, which alone enables him to 'fight his corner' as of right at the Cabinet table. Furthermore Thorneycroft was widely regarded at the time in Whitehall as a potential future Prime Minister; and Amery was not in that class. At the Treasury Selwyn Lloyd and his Chief Secretary, Henry Brooke (who had been brought into the Cabinet specifically to strengthen control of public expenditure)

were replaced by Reginald Maudling and John Boyd-Carpenter respectively. From the point of view of Concorde's prospects these
changes were finely balanced. Lloyd was a very senior member of the
Cabinet, with a considerable personal standing in the Parliamentary
Party (as the strength of reactions to his abrupt dismissal clearly
showed); Maudling was relatively junior. Furthermore Lloyd was
strongly identified with the Treasury's growing unease about the
rising tide of public expenditure, whereas Maudling owed his ad-
vancement, at least in part, to the Prime Minister's (justified) belief
that he was a good, expansionist neo-Keynesian. Against this Lloyd
had already largely forfeited his leader's confidence, and he was showing signs of exhaustion. Maudling was fresh, and there was a feeling
that the new Treasury leadership had the edge over the old in intellectual calibre. Perhaps most important of all was the fact that the
'night of the long knives' had seriously weakened the Prime Minister's hold on his Party: if the new Chancellor were to treat the endorsement of Concorde as a resigning matter, Macmillan was in no
position to dismiss a second Treasury rebellion as 'a little local
difficulty'.

On balance, therefore, the ministerial reshuffle seemed to go
against Concorde. That ministerial anxieties about the level of
public expenditure were not confined to the outgoing Chancellor
was shown by the establishment, at about this time, of a 'Ministerial
Action Group on Public Expenditure' ('Magpie'), with Iain Macleod
as a prominent member. But its life seems to have been short, and its
influence minimal. As Maudling himself reflects, when the Chancellor is resisting pressures for more spending he is always 'a pretty
lonely man'. Most Chancellors would say 'Amen' to that.

In the case of Concorde, moreover, the new Chancellor faced two
additional obstacles. One was Europe. By the summer of 1962 the
Heath negotiations appeared to be reaching a crucial stage. It was
hardly a propitious moment for the abandonment of the most spec-
tacular instance of Anglo-French co-operation to date. The other
factor was the relationship between the new Minister of Aviation
and the Prime Minister. Julian Amery might lack Cabinet status. But
he was Macmillan's son-in-law. In the words of a colleague (a self-
confessed neutral on Concorde) the Minister of Aviation 'abused his
relationship a bit'.

Amery had prepared the ground for his new assignment. Before
'clearing his desk' at the Air Ministry he had dictated a memorandum
to himself in his new capacity, emphasising the vital importance for
national defence of three continuing programmes: the TSR 2, the
P 1154 and the HS 681. As already noted, the TSR 2 and the SST
shared the same engine design: the two 'marched in step'.

At this point the promoters of the SST had a major stroke of luck.
Georges Hereil was replaced as chief executive of Sud by General
André Puget. There are many in the aircraft industry who believe
that if Hereil had stayed at Sud Concorde would never have been
built, such was the incompatibility of temperament between him and
Edwards of BAC. Edwards does not exactly dissent. Puget, by contrast, was a former French military attaché in London, and a strong
anglophile. He and his British counterpart established a remarkable
rapport from their very first meeting.

It was now apparent that the moment of decision was close. Amery
was due to meet Buron on 7 November and the Aviation Ministry
was pressing for a green light from the Cabinet in advance of this
meeting. The penultimate scrutiny now rested with a Cabinet committee chaired by R. A. Butler. This witnessed one more clash between the Ministry of Aviation and the Treasury; and once more the
Ministry of Aviation won.

A senior member of this Cabinet committee sums up its conclusions like this: 'even then we thought it was going to ruin us; but
also that you can't control the march of science'. There was, he recalls, a 'strong tendency to sit on the fence', and he believes that if
the passenger capacity of the eventual aircraft had been accurately
predicted, that would have finished it. As it was, the committee, like
the Mills committee before it, came down on Concorde's side.

As the conflict between Treasury and Ministry of Aviation was
still unresolved, however, the issue now moved at last to the Cabinet
itself. The first discussion occurred on 5 November. It was indecisive.
One of those present (favourable to Concorde) describes the line-up as
follows: the Treasury was solidly opposed; so, broadly speaking,
were the 'social' ministers, who resented the order of priorities which
massive expenditure on Concorde seemed to imply. On the other side
were ranged the 'Europeans' (i.e. the Foreign Office ministers and
Christopher Soames, Minister of Agriculture), and the 'technologic-
ally-minded' – Sandys, Thorneycroft, Marples (Transport). Overall
there was a 'solid basis of informed opinion and the politically
weighty' in favour: also those who 'spoke for the House of Commons'.
The critics, by contrast, firmly believe that at this first Cabinet they
were in a majority. On one point, though, both camps agree: the
Prime Minister himself was apparently non-committal. Thus he
argued on the one hand that it was essential to get the aircraft industry itself to contribute to the cost of R and D if they were to go
ahead (an opinion which certainly bore witness to a degree of Prime
Ministerial aloofness from the history of the project from its inception); but on the other that if we pulled out the French were likely to
go ahead without us.

The outcome was that while Amery was authorised to proceed with his imminent meeting with Buron, he was not to enter into any commitments, and would be invited to report back to a second Cabinet meeting at which the decision would finally be taken. Macmillan [*Pointing the Way*, p. 34] tells us that 'if there was a clear difference of view between two or more sections of the Cabinet, it was my practice, after a kind of second reading debate, to postpone the decision for a further meeting ... agreement was invariably reached. So it was on this occasion.

In the interval between the two Cabinets Macmillan seems to have been discreetly busy. The spending department ministers were summoned in one by one and reassured that the green light for Concorde would not mean the axe for their pet departmental spending plans. (Perhaps it was not too difficult. One of those who was most closely involved argues that the notion that cash for Project X means less cash for everything else is a civil service concept. Ministers, by contrast, look upon a commitment to a large spending programme in another department as strengthening, not weakening, their departmental hands in claiming their place in the sun.) At any rate by the time the second Cabinet met the Treasury had been virtually isolated.

The story of the second and final Cabinet has passed into Whitehall folklore. The Prime Minister was in reminiscent mood. He told his colleagues about his great aunt's Daimler, which had travelled at 'the sensible speed of thirty miles an hour', and was sufficiently spacious to enable one to descend from it without removing one's top hat. Nowadays, alas! people had a mania for dashing around. But that being so Britain ought to 'cater for this profitable modern eccentricity'. He thought they all really agreed. No one seriously dissented. It was all over in a few minutes.

There was still one more battle for the Treasury to fight – and lose – before Julian Amery signed the Concorde agreement with the French Ambassador, Geoffroy de Courcel, in London on 22 November: this concerned the inclusion of a 'break clause' to enable either party to withdraw. The following year the Treasury was to argue that the failure to write a break clause into the Anglo-French agreement was hardly a matter of significance: 'the financial consequences of a situation in which one Government might wish to withdraw', it told the Commons Estimates Committee, 'would depend upon the circumstances obtaining at the time, and the abandonment of the project by either party would be a matter for discussion between them.'

That had not been the departmental view in the winter of 1962. Then it had argued strenuously for the inclusion of a clause stipu-

lating that if one side decided to withdraw it would have no responsibility for costs incurred by the other to that point. The
Ministry of Aviation argued that, on the contrary, it would be the
height of irresponsibility for the Government to commit large sums
of the taxpayer's money to a project from which our partner might
subsequently be able to withdraw and leave us in the lurch. Amery
feels in retrospect that it is too often overlooked that, at the time,
the French were by no means too keen to proceed (a hesitancy of
which, it seems, his father-in-law was not informed).

The Treasury was thus neatly out-manoeuvred. Its transparent
purpose was to provide a bolt-hole for the future reversal of the
decision which the Cabinet had just arrived at. Yet this was a purpose
it could hardly avow. So it found itself unable to answer the charge
that it was seeking to give our partners an excuse for the betrayal of
the British taxpayer, whose interests it was the Treasury's primary
departmental responsibility to defend.

Fifty-two days after Amery and de Courcel signed in London,
de Gaulle summoned his press conference in Paris and terminated
the Common Market negotiations. Protagonists of Concorde doubt if
the decision would, in practice, have been different if de Gaulle had
interposed his veto three months earlier. In Haviland's words, 'the
European argument would still have been there for next time round'.
Perhaps the fairest conclusion is that Macmillan would have needed
rather more than his great aunt's Daimler to swing the doubters
away from the Treasury position if the door to Europe had already
been barred.

Epilogue – Labour's attempt to withdraw

On Monday 26 October 1964, just ten days after taking office, the
Labour government announced that it was asking the French for 'an
urgent review' of the Concorde project. Three months later, after a
number of acid exchanges with the French government, and much
agonising by the British government's legal advisers, Roy Jenkins, the
Minister for Aviation, told the Commons that although he and his
colleagues 'still retain some doubts about the economic and financial
aspects of the project' they had decided to press ahead and hope for
the best. Concorde has survived numerous crises on its way to full
production. But this was the only occasion on which one of the two
partner-governments embarked on a full-blooded attempt to scrap it.
So although it was an attempt which failed, it forms an interesting
appendage to the original decision to embark on the aircraft in
1962.

Two misconceptions have gained some credence. These are that the Labour Party had taken a decision to axe Concorde before it came to power; or, conversely, that the decision was imposed by the US administration on the incoming government as a condition for financial support.

The attitude of the Labour Party in Opposition towards Concorde had been one of polite scepticism. Amery was one of the most combative members of the last Macmillan and subsequently Douglas-Home administrations, and in his own words the Opposition front bench had 'done me the compliment of building me up into a target of Tory extravagance'. Thus the fact that Concorde had become closely identified with the personality of Amery was not calculated to dispose the Labour Party in its favour. Moreover George Wigg, a close confidant of the new Prime Minister, was a fierce opponent of the TSR 2, Concorde's stable-mate, and he had recruited Richard Worcester as a special adviser to the Labour Party in opposition. Worcester was a leading critic of 'extravagance' in Government support for the aircraft industry, and his name was – and still is – sufficient to provoke cries of rage and pain in the industry. All this past history, coupled with the speed with which the decision was taken to ask the French for a 'review' of Concorde after the October 1964 election (extensive soundings were taken in Whitehall before anything was said about the possible cancellation of the TSR 2) led some civil servants (outside the Treasury) to conclude that Labour had decided to axe Concorde before ever taking office.

This was not, in fact, so. As Amery points out, the Labour aviation spokesman in opposition, John Cronin, was a well-known francophile who, while he had certainly queried the Tories' figuring on Concorde, had never divided the House against it. Wigg himself is categoric: there was 'no hard and fast decision' to cancel in advance of the election.

The second, more conspiratorial, theory – according to which the American government obliged the incoming Labour administration to seek to withdraw from Concorde as the price for its financial backing – is based on the reported evidence of an anonymous civil servant, and the circumstances surrounding the communication of Labour's decision to the French. It is said that a senior civil servant who saw the first draft of the so-called 'Brown Paper' (the document which set out the Government's plans for dealing with the balance of payments situation, and which included the call for the Concorde review – see Chapter 5, on devaluation) recalls no reference in it to the SST. This was the draft, so it is said, which was taken to Washington during the week following the election by Sir Eric Roll, Economic Minister in Washington and Permanent Secretary-designate of the new Depart

ment of Economic Affairs. Concorde – it is alleged – was mysteriously
appended following this visit.

There is no doubt that the Whitehall wires got somewhat tangled
about the decision to ask for a Concorde review. Part of the trouble
arose from the fact that Roy Jenkins, the new Minister of Aviation,
like his Tory predecessor, was not a member of the Cabinet. Concorde was on the Cabinet agenda for Friday 23 October; but whether
by inadvertence or intention, Jenkins had not been bidden to attend.
(Non-Cabinet Ministers are summoned to attend Cabinet by the
secretariat when matters relating to their departments are on the
agenda.) However, officials at the Ministry of Aviation learnt belatedly on the Whitehall grapevine what was in store, and Sir
Richard Way, the Permanent Secretary, secured confirmation from
the Treasury. He fortunately managed to run his minister to ground
in the bar of Brooks's Club.

There followed a hectic weekend during which the Foreign Office
was trying to contact the British Ambassador in Paris to forewarn the
French government of what was to be announced on Monday 26
October. By an agreeable chance the Ambassador was shooting with a
French aircraft manufacturer and entertaining Jenkins's predecessor,
Amery. Eventually the Ambassador was alerted, and managed to
inform the French Foreign Minister hours before the announcement
in London. Amery made a hasty, but diplomatic, departure.

The fact that both the Ministry of Aviation and the French
government were kept in the dark until a very late stage does not
prove that the decision to try and axe Concorde was an afterthought
appended to the 'Brown Paper' in response to American pressure.
Crossman recorded in his diary (see Chapter 5 below) how even those
who were in the Cabinet were not consulted about the contents of
the economy programme. As for the French, there was little doubt
what their reply would have been to advance warning of a request
for 'urgent review' of Concorde. Ministers and civil servants anxious
to commit the British government publicly to the possibility of Concorde abandonment had every reason to delay informing the French
until the last possible moment.

In fact, not only had the Concorde 'review' featured in the very
first draft of the 'Brown Paper', but it had done so as a direct result
of the Treasury's inclusion of a recommendation to scrap Concorde
in its general economic brief to the incoming Government (see
Chapter 5). The Treasury had never been reconciled to its multiple
defeats in 1961–2. It had now to deal with a new and inexperienced
government which had something of a vested interest in maximising
the horrors of its financial inheritance and the severity of the medi-
cine needed to deal with it. The opportunity was too good to miss.

This does not mean to say that many influential Americans were not anxious to see Concorde scrapped. They were; and they had not been slow to question the wisdom of the Anglo-French project in conversations with ministers and senior officials during the Douglas-Home administration. Understandably, perhaps, the British SST lobby believed that they were hell-bent on killing Concorde in order to leave the field clear for its eventual American rival. It seems just as likely that some, at least, of the visiting critics were motivated by the desire to kill the American SST, and the conviction that there was no chance of doing that so long as Concorde was on its way.

Be that as it may, the Treasury had an ample dossier to show the incoming government, anxious to establish its *bona fides* with Washington, that the cancellation of Concorde, quite apart from its other merits, would be very well received by the Americans. This was an important argument; but it is almost certainly the full extent of the American influence on the framing of the 'Brown Paper'.

Sir Richard Way, as the senior civil servant responsible for the Concorde programme, was aghast. No doubt he had a departmental interest to defend. But he also felt that the manner of the announcement could not have been better calculated to provoke French resistance. He believed that there was a chance (maybe not a very strong one) that the French could have been brought to agree to cancellation after three months of discreet bargaining – after all, the Ministry of Finance in Paris was no more enthusiastic than our own Treasury. As it was, they would fight it all the way.

It was later suggested [*Sunday Times*, 2 March 1969] that the incoming government did not grasp the implications of the absence of the break-clause from the original agreement. This overlooks the fact that most contemporary comment regarded the absence of the break-clause as somewhat academic from the point of view of withdrawal: thus the Commons Estimates Committee in the previous year had denounced the Treasury for failing to include a break-clause not because this would make it difficult or impossible for us to withdraw, but on the contrary because it would make it possible for the *French* to withdraw without specific obligations to reimburse us for what we had spent.

In any case the real threat to the Treasury's plan was arguably not so much the vehemence of the French response as the hesitancy of the new government's commitment to it, although the two were interrelated. The very fact that the 'Brown Paper' called for review instead of cancellation bore witness to this hesitancy. The Foreign Office was alarmed from the start by the prospects of months of angry wrangling with the French. The aircraft industry was quick to flex its muscles: Sir George Edwards warned the Government early in

November that cancellation would oblige BAC to close down its Filton factory. Frank Cousins, the former General Secretary of the TGWU, who had just become Minister of Technology, lost no time in voicing his disquiet. Even George Brown, originally an enthusiast for cancellation, soon began to have second thoughts about the impact of a stand-up row with the French on his ambition to nudge his colleagues towards the European Community.

It was Patrick Gordon Walker, the Foreign Secretary, who probably played the decisive card. He persuaded the Cabinet to obtain the views of the law officers and the legal advisers about the possible consequences of unilateral withdrawal. The Attorney-General, Sir Elwyn Jones, was responsible for presenting his colleagues with this assessment.

He and his staff concentrated on the passage in the original agreement which pledged the two governments to make 'every effort to ensure that the programme is carried on'. Could it be shown that 'every effort' had indeed been made, but alas! in vain? In view of the escalation of costs since the agreement was signed, and growing doubts about the acceptability of sonic boom, was there a possible loophole under the *rebus sic stantibus* rule (i.e., could it be said that circumstances had changed)?'

However, since this was an international treaty, registered with the International Court at the Hague, the Attorney-General's department felt it advisable to consult the legal advisers to the Foreign Office, who were the official Whitehall experts on international law. The Foreign Office lawyers delivered their verdict at a meeting in the Foreign Secretary's room. It was that the French government would certainly be entitled to compensation amounting to at least £100m. In the words of one of those present, it was a verdict which 'certainly did not fall on unwilling ears'. Sir Elwyn Jones duly passed it on to the Cabinet. As one of the senior civil servants closely involved comments 'a new government will blench more easily at legal advice'. They blenched; and Concorde was saved.

Not all the members of the Cabinet were immediately convinced. The Chancellor fought a rearguard battle; but he was up to his neck in the government's first big run on the pound, and his thoughts were elsewhere. Denis Healey, the Minister of Defence, was the most outspoken campaigner for cancellation. He did not dispute the verdict of the lawyers: he simply doubted whether the French would actually be prepared to take us to law [Andrew Wilson, *The Concorde Fiasco*].

According to one report Healey subsequently secured confirmation for his view. It is said that he was told by his French opposite number, Messmer, that if only the British government had held out for cancellation a week or two longer the French, under pressure from their Finance Ministry, would have given in.

So much is speculation. Even if M. Messmer did confirm Denis Healey's suspicions, he could have been wrong. The fate of Concorde would have been decided, on the French side, in the Elysée Palace, and General de Gaulle was not in the habit of informing his ministers as to his intentions.

This is why the verdict of those who argue that it was a fatal error – from the Treasury's point of view – to announce the demand for the 'review' in the 'Brown Paper' is suspect. In all probability the combination of French indignation and cold feet at home would have been more than a match for the Treasury in any case. But it might have had a better chance if instead of securing Ministerial commitment to a 'review' – which, after all, could go either way – it had gone for a commitment to outright cancellation, abandonment of which would have involved serious ministerial loss of face. There would have been a battle with the French, and ministers might still have blenched at the consequences. But at least there would not have been an easy escape route for the doubters in the Cabinet.

The early history of Concorde is full of paradoxes. At every stage there seems to be an inevitability about the next phase of commitment: it would be folly to stop when the design-study contract is almost complete; financial support which was originally supposed to be peripheral to the 'rationalisation' of the aircraft industry is transformed in time into the pledge which alone made it acceptable; to withdraw would wreck the attempt to enter Europe, and the French would proceed without us anyway. And yet on numerous occasions the whole venture was only saved by chance: the determination of one technician at Farnborough not to be baulked by the abortive result of the first SST study; the growing impatience of Harold Macmillan with Selwyn Lloyd at the Treasury; the backing of Percy Mills; the family link between Macmillan and Amery; perhaps most striking of all, the replacement of Hereil by Puget at Sud-Aviation; the timing of the General's first veto.

There is the revealing contrast between the Treasury's reluctant acceptance in 1962 of the proposition that neither government could in fact impose financial penalties on its partner for unilateral withdrawal, and the verdict of the civil service lawyers, just two years later, that indeed one of them could – and would. There is the reversal of roles whereby the Chancellor who had resigned in protest at the growth of public expenditure in 1957 became one of the leading architects of a programme that was to cost the taxpayer many hundreds of millions of extra expenditure only five years later.

Right from the start Concorde was the brainchild of government. It was conceived at Farnborough, and subsequently became the chosen vehicle for public financial support for the aircraft industry on the civil aviation side, to make good the run-down of military procurement. At no time was it actively promoted by the industry itself: whereas MPs were vigorously lobbied when various military aircraft were threatened with cancellation, Sir George Edwards cannot recall a single occasion when it was necessary – during the period covered by this account – to recruit parliamentary support for Concorde, for the government itself was leading the way. Yet within ten days of the signature of the agreement with the French the Prime Minister was talking in terms of a financial contribution towards the cost of research and development from the industry as a precondition for government approval.

It is noteworthy that the two occasions when Concorde was most at risk were both occasions when there were acute alarms about the balance of payments: July 1961, and October 1964. Despite its strenuous efforts the Treasury never looked like succeeding in its attempts to avert the decision to go ahead in the autumn, not only because of the coincidence of the Common Market negotiations in Brussels, but also because at that time all the comment in the press and in parliament was about the need to 'reflate' the economy and counteract a post-war peak in unemployment which duly materialised the following spring.

Yet anything less suited to the purposes of economic fine-tuning would be hard to imagine, with the demand-effects of the research and development programme gradually building up over five years or more. One of those closely involved in advising governments about demand management during these years comments that 'governments are sometimes in an expansive mood, and sometimes in a state of panic'. (Some might add that the panic is not always on the side of retrenchment.)

No one now really disputes that the decision to go ahead was taken on other than hard commercial grounds. The conviction that we faced a choice between a supersonic aircraft industry and none at all; the conviction that here was an area of advanced technology where we actually had a chance to 'lick the Americans'; the conviction that supersonic travel must logically be the next stage in man's progress; the conviction that this was the way for Britain to prove her European credentials – these were the ingredients in the final choice.

Indeed there is an air of lightheartedness about the entire history

of Concorde up to the moment of decision. Nobody on either side
of the argument took the cost estimates seriously. The failure to include a break-clause in the agreement with the French was supposed
to reflect the anxiety that they would take advantage of such a clause
to pull out and leave us in the lurch; yet at the same time the Cabinet
was warned that if we pulled out the French would go ahead without
us. The two partners were thinking in terms of completely different,
and incompatible, markets. One member of the November 1962
Cabinet cites this as a textbook example of the Parkinson Law that
the time taken by any committee to come to a decision varies in
inverse proportion to the amount of money involved. It has even
been said that the memory of the Concorde decision was a major
factor in Edward Heath's thinking when he set up the Central Policy
Review Staff to present ministers with the implications of their
choices a decade later. Yet there is something peculiarly appropriate
about the way in which the great venture was launched with the
tale of Macmillan's great aunt's Daimler. Nostalgia – even inverted
nostalgia – is a more likely motivation for state entrepreneurship
than a pretence of market forecasting.

The consequences of embarking on a joint venture with another
government have been the subject of much controversy. In 1963 the
Estimates Committee was still worrying about the possibility that
Britain would be left to pick up the bills following a French withdrawal. Nowadays, by contrast, it tends to be assumed that it was the
entanglement with the French which wrecked the Labour Government's attempt to pull out. Yet there are grounds for doubting
whether the French could or would have prevented cancellation if
the Labour Government had been sufficiently determined to go
through with it; and perhaps even whether that Government would
have faced up to the consequences of cancellation in the absence of
the partnership complication.

The final surprise about the launching of the Concorde programme is the apparent helplessness of the Treasury. Back in the
early 1960s, when Great George Street still dispensed the patronage
at the topmost echelons of Whitehall, it was almost axiomatic that
the wise department would not push its luck when the Treasury was
adamant. On this occasion the Treasury wanted to be adamant, but
its view was consistently ignored. The explanation is to be found in
the preconceptions of the Prime Minister.

The Prime Minister could have drawn the opposite moral from
the story of the Daimler. He did not do so, not because he was pres-
surised by his son-in-law, nor because he regarded Concorde as
Britain's passport to the European Community (even if these were
supporting considerations). He opted for Concorde precisely because

it did involve a large commitment of future resources. By the autumn of 1962, as the last volume of his memoirs makes clear, he was convinced that the Treasury was going to spark off another world slump. The fact that the Treasury was counsel for the prosecution was the strongest reason why judgement was given for the defence.

3 Doomed Departures: Common Market Approaches, 1961 and 1967

The story of Britain's long and hesitating advance to full membership of the European Community has been told and retold. It is not the intention of this analysis to retread the ground in detail. Rather the purpose is to review the motives and the influence of some of the individuals, institutions and forces which shaped the decision of the Macmillan government to open negotiations with a view to possible entry in 1961, and of the Wilson government to apply for membership in 1967.

First, however, a brief recapitulation of the course of events leading up to each of these decisions may be useful for ease of reference.

As soon as the Second World War was over public debate about the need to integrate the nation states of Western Europe in order to avoid a repetition of conflict between them began. In 1946 Winston Churchill, leader of the Opposition in Britain, called in Zurich for the establishment of 'a kind of United States of Europe'. It took the Continental politicians several years to grasp the unpalatable fact that the 'kind of United States' which the British war hero had in mind was not one which embraced the United Kingdom. In 1949 the Council of Europe was assembled, consisting of members of parliament from most of the democratic nations of Western Europe. It lacked all executive power, and has never amounted to anything more than a talking-shop.

In 1951 France, Germany, Italy and the Benelux countries set up the European Coal and Steel Community to integrate their markets for these two basic industrial materials. Britain was invited to join, but declined to do so. There followed a period of wrangling about the establishment of a European Defence Community in which Britain again declined to take part. The whole plan had to be abandoned when the French parliament refused to ratify it. Instead the second Churchill administration took what looks in retrospect like the first substantial British commitment to permanent involvement in the affairs of Continental Europe with a pledge to keep British troops in Germany as launching aid for Western European Union, a grouping including the six nations of the European Coal and Steel

Community plus Britain, which was to take over from the defunct Defence Community as the guardian of German rearmament.

Then, in the autumn of 1955, the six Continental countries opened negotiations about the formation of a customs union at Messina. Once again Britain was invited to take part, but refused to do so. Eventually agreement was reached, and in the spring of 1957 it was embodied in the Treaty of Rome setting up the European Economic Community.

The Macmillan government responded with a plan for a free trade area embracing the Six plus the Scandinavian countries, Austria, Portugal, Switzerland and Britain, and involving internal free trade in industrial goods, but no uniformity of treatment of foodstuffs or goods imported from third countries. This was the subject of lengthy negotiations in Paris by a ministerial committee headed by Reginald Maudling, but in December 1958 these negotiations were terminated, without agreement, by France.

Meanwhile Britain and the other countries outside the Community which had participated in the Maudling discussions had prepared a fall-back plan of their own, and this blossomed into the Treaty of Stockholm in the summer of 1959, providing for industrial free trade between the 'outer seven', plus a special regime for certain items of agricultural trade.

The year 1960 was, to outward appearances, taken up with various abortive schemes for 'bridge-building' between the Six of the Community and the Seven of the European Free Trade Association. Meanwhile the British Government was closely re-examining the implications of full British membership. During the early months of 1961 expectation grew that Mr Macmillan and his colleagues would indeed invite the member-governments of the Community to open negotiations; and at the very end of July this is what they did.

Almost eighteen months of laborious and intensely detailed bargaining ensued in Brussels, where the British team was led by Mr Heath. But in January 1963 General de Gaulle announced his conclusion that Britain was not yet ready to assume the responsibilities of membership of the Community, and that further negotiation was therefore pointless. As a decision to widen the membership of the Community requires the unanimous consent of the existing members, his veto was grudgingly accepted.

For three years thereafter the dossier of British relations with the Community was allowed to gather dust. In 1963 and 1964 British politicians were preoccupied with the disintegration of the Macmillan government, and the imminence of the General Election. The hairsbreadth nature of the Labour victory in October 1964 meant that the pre-electoral atmosphere continued in Britain, while the

Community itself passed through a major crisis with the tempor-
ary withdrawal of France from the Ministerial Council following a
dispute about the powers of the Commission and majority voting.

Very soon after the 1966 British General Election, however, the
Labour government, with a secure majority, began to speak with
enthusiasm about the notion of an enlargement of the Community.
In the autumn it was agreed that the Prime Minister and Foreign
Secretary should tour the capitals of the Community to assess the
scope for a new negotiation. Following this tour the government decided to apply for full membership, and this decision was submitted
to, and received the overwhelming endorsement of, parliament in
May 1967.

In the last volume of his memoirs [*At the End of the Day*, p. 15]
Harold Macmillan describes a 'special paper' which he addressed to
Prime Minister Menzies of Australia at the end of June 1961, as the
moment of the decision to launch negotiations with the Common
Market governments became imminent. He explained how

> when we decided at the end of 1955 not to take part [in the
> Messina discussions on the formation of a European Customs
> Union] ... we were influenced by two considerations, in both of
> which we were to be proved wrong. We thought they wouldn't
> succeed – or, if they did, that we could work out a satisfactory as-
> sociation. We realised now that it was all-or-nothing, and, if we
> went ahead, it would be in order to discover what 'all' involved.

In reality the comfortable conviction that the embarrassing spectre
of a European customs union would go away if we left it alone was
not universally shared in the senior echelons of Government, even
before the Rome Treaty was drafted. Jean Chauvel, the French Ambassador in London at the time, recalls a conversation with Harold
Macmillan, then Chancellor of the Exchequer, in the summer of
1956, during which the future Prime Minister talked of the vital need
for Britain to participate in a European customs union, if one were
to materialise. Admittedly Macmillan was always addicted to what
one of his intimates called 'long-range speculation aloud'; yet it is
significant that before he left the Treasury for No. 10 he had appointed the first committee of civil servants, under Richard Clarke
of his own department, to review the options open to Britain if the
Six should go ahead.

Another senior civil servant, Sir Frank Lee, who was later to play
a crucial part in the evolution of Whitehall thinking, summed up

the dilemma facing the British Government with painful clarity, almost before the Messina talks had got under way in the autumn of 1955. According to the then Overseas Director of the FBI (now the CBI), a former diplomat named Peter Tennant, in February 1956 Lee, then Permanent Secretary at the Board of Trade, insisted in conversation that 'we could not possibly afford not to be members of a common market of this importance, but could not see how this could be done without ultimately paying the price of a common currency and considerable merging of political sovereignty' [quoted by Sir Norman Kipping, *Summing Up*].

Macmillan and Lee and others who shared them put such uncomfortable thoughts behind them. In the autumn of 1956 the Clarke committee of officials submitted its assessment of alternative courses open to the British Government. The most radical of these 'even contemplated some degree of supranational management' [Nora Beloff, *The General Says No*]. But neither the civil servants themselves, nor the ministers to whom their report was submitted, seem to have had any doubts that 'plan G' was the one to go for. This was the scheme for an industrial free trade area of Western Europe, which was negotiated at length in 1957 and 1958.

On taking over the Premiership from Eden at the beginning of 1957 Macmillan's first actions – notwithstanding a personal commitment to the notion of European unity dating back to the 1940s – smacked to many continentals of a desire to turn Britain's back on her neighbours. The February 1957 Defence White Paper scrapped conscription and scaled down the commitment of British forces to German soil; and one month later the new British Premier was in Washington repairing the 'special relationship', so badly battered at Suez. Negotiations on 'plan G' were launched in Paris in the early spring; but the background was hardly considered propitious.

As late as June 1957, only weeks before French ratification of the Rome Treaty, the Prime Minister was continuing to express the hope, in memoranda to his Foreign Secretary and Chancellor, that the French Assembly would shy. In retrospect this may sound like the height of wishful thinking. But at the time there were substantial reasons for thinking that French parliamentary approval might not be forthcoming – this after all was what had happened three years earlier with the abortive European Defence Community – or that if it were forthcoming the Fourth Republic would subsequently be obliged to renege. Weighed down with the war in Algeria transitory governments in Paris were increasingly responding to a position of chronic payments deficit with physical controls on imports. In the summer of 1957 it was hard to find industrialists in France who believed, even after ratification of the Rome Treaty, that there was any chance of tariff reductions and trade liberalisation taking place on schedule at the beginning of 1959.

Thus Macmillan's view, expressed in a note to the Chancellor in the summer of 1957, that 'we must take the lead, either in widening their project, or, if they will not co-operate with us, in opposing it', corresponded broadly to informed opinion on this side of the Channel. The free trade area project was endorsed, virtually without dissent, by the press, the FBI, the TUC and the Labour Party, as a sensible defensive mechanism. Nobody, apart from a few dedicated federalists, the numerically insignificant Liberal Party, and a handful of Tory backbenchers (who were soundly berated by their Chief Whip, Edward Heath, for tabling a parliamentary motion calling for British membership of the Community) advocated joining such an apparently ill-omened grouping as the Six then appeared. And although there is sometimes a tendency to suggest that the civil service was being obliged to drag its feet by the politicians at this epoch, there was at the time no evidence of impatience. On the contrary the Treasury and Board of Trade officials who managed the free trade area negotiations in between the ministerial sessions showed no inclination even to consider supranational solutions at this stage. Sir Frank Lee himself, in the recollection of a colleague, was 'deeply offended' by the concept of support buying of foodstuffs which was an essential feature of the still embryonic common agricultural policy. As for the Foreign Office, it was hardly concerned: the negotiations on 'plan G' were handled in Paris by the UK delegation to the OEEC (predecessor to the OECD), not by the Embassy. These were straightforward matters of trade.

By the early spring of 1958, however, it began to look as if 'plan G' was ploughing into the sand. In February the UK Committee of the European Movement organised a gathering of a hundred leaders from both sides of industry in all thirteen countries involved to discuss the free trade area scheme. According to Sir Norman Kipping, the Director-General of the FBI, this meeting 'turned out to mark the realisation' that this scheme was likely to fail [*Summing Up*, p. 160].

What followed was an unusual instance of a pressure group virtually formulating British foreign policy. According to Kipping the FBI drew the conclusion from the London meeting that 'the time had come to strengthen and emphasise the solidarity of the Outer Six' – i.e. Britain, Sweden, Denmark, Norway, Austria and Switzerland. There followed a series of meetings of the national industrial federations, with the Swedes and the British FBI taking the lead.

Meanwhile discussions between ministers and officials on the wider free trade plan meandered on in Paris. The return of de Gaulle to

power in France in May for a time revived hopes of a positive out-
come, for the General had made no secret of his contempt for the
Common Market and its supranational ambitions. Following Harold
Macmillan's first visit to the new French leader in Paris at the end of
June, the British believed that the General was prepared to give his
blessing to the free trade area plan. But after the summer holidays
these hopes rapidly dwindled, and it came as little surprise when the
French brusquely terminated the negotiations in December.

By then the FBI was ready to act. An important factor here was
the decision of the formidable President of the National Farmers'
Union, Sir James Turner, two years earlier, to take his union into
corporate membership of the FBI. Turner enjoyed a close personal
relationship with Kipping, and this was now brought into play.

A major problem in establishing a rival bloc of the 'Outer Six'
(Portugal was to join at a later stage) was that Denmark was primarily
concerned with food exports. Unless she obtained privileged access
to the only major food market outside the Common Market – the
United Kingdom – she was liable to hold out; and without Denmark
the other Scandinavian countries could not move. But such privileged access could only be provided at the expense of other suppliers,
and notably the domestic farm industry.

It so happened that Turner and Kipping were near neighbours in
the suburbs of north London, where both were constituents of
Reginald Maudling, the Paymaster-General, who had handled the
'plan G' negotiations. During the Christmas holidays of 1958 they
paid a call on their MP 'to see if he would mind if we went together
to Denmark to discuss' ways of satisfying that country's needs without unduly upsetting the NFU at home. Maudling gave his blessing,
and an undertaking that 'he would fully consult the FBI before the
Government entered into any commitments' [Kipping, *Summing
Up*].

By the following summer the Stockholm Treaty, setting up the
European Free Trade Area of the 'Outer Seven', had been signed.
The British Government had entered into a commitment which was
to prove a considerable embarrassment when once the decision to
bid for membership of the Common Market had been taken.

The eagerness of the FBI was matched by the determination of
government at the time to oppose the Six if they would not co-
operate with us. At the end of 1958 Macmillan was complaining to
his Foreign Secretary that 'the Germans and the French have made
an unholy alliance against the British'. The mood in Whitehall was
for retaliation; and there was also the fear that unless the 'Outer
Seven' were firmly tied down the Six might begin to pick them off
one by one. So the actual drafting of the Treaty of Stockholm was

handled in the normal manner, by committees of officials. Neverthe-
less there was a feeling in British Government circles that 'Norman
Kipping was somewhat dangerously in the lead' [Lieber, *British
Politics and European Unity*].

During 1959 the Macmillan government continued to treat the
Community as a direct threat to British interests which, since it was
apparently impervious to reasoned argument, must be obliged by
external pressure to sue for terms. This pressure was expected to
come from two directions: from Bonn and from Washington.

Of all the original member-countries of the European Community,
Germany was the one with by far the most important commercial
stake in Scandinavia. So there were hopes that German industry
would pressurise its government to make the rest of the Community
come to terms with EFTA. Particular hopes were placed in the
personality of the German Economics Minister, Dr Erhard. Erhard,
popularly known as 'the father of the German economic miracle',
was a dedicated free trader who had lent his enthusiastic support to
the British 'plan G'. During 1959 he regularly took space in the
German press to promote the equation '$6 + 7 = 1$'.

Throughout the long decade of abortive British attempts to come
to terms with the Community between 1957 and 1967 the Foreign
Office placed exaggerated faith in the willingness and ability of the
Germans to bring the French into line. During the initial negotiations on the wider free trade concept the message from the Bonn
Embassy was that Dr Erhard could be relied upon to see that everything would be all right in the end; and the fact that these expectations were disappointed in December 1958 did not make our
diplomats any less sanguine thereafter.

The Prime Minister, for his part, tended to look more to the
Americans. It had not taken him long to put the estrangements of
Suez behind him, and to establish a close personal rapport with
President Eisenhower, culminating in a joint appearance on British
television in the late summer of 1959 which, in the eyes of the Prime
Minister's critics, looked like a party political broadcast for the
Tories. So when, at the end of March 1960, Macmillan paid one of
his periodic visits to Washington, he used the opportunity to make
an 'impassioned appeal' for US help in preventing 'the *economic*
division of Europe, which *must* involve its *political* and *military*
division'. He talked darkly of 'import controls ... restrictions and
measures of all kinds' and the withdrawal of British troops from
Germany: 'these were not threats, but facts ...' [*Pointing the Way*].

In reality this was something of a last despairing effort. By the end
of 1959 it was already apparent that huffing and puffing against the
Six was going to get us nowhere. After starting from an attitude of

profound suspicion towards de Gaulle on the General's return to power, Adenauer had been wooed and won by the Frenchman in the autumn of 1959, and he had no intention of allowing his Economics Minister to upset his new friend. As for the Americans, their attitude had been made brutally clear by Treasury Secretary Dillon when he crossed the Atlantic to attend the pre-Christmas ministerial meeting of the OEEC in Paris. Four years later Nora Beloff recorded that 'memories of this disconcerting visit still linger in the Treasury' [*The General Says No*, p. 86].

Dillon's message was that while his country was still ready, notwithstanding the unexpected disappearance of the post-war 'dollar gap' and dawning anxieties about the competitiveness of American industry, to support the *political* unification of Europe, it was certainly not going to help the British to construct an enlarged area of discrimination against US trade denuded of political content. This visit in practice extinguished lingering hopes in Whitehall of a compromise settlement between the Six and the Seven.

Meanwhile the Tory government had increased its parliamentary majority at a General Election for the second time in succession. The European dimension had been conspicuous by its absence at the hustings. The manifestos of the two major parties had nothing to say on the subject, and Lieber [op. cit.] calculates that 92 per cent of Tory candidates, and all save half-a-dozen from the Labour side, followed this example (even in the Liberal camp, where Europe was already an article of faith, half the candidates steered clear of it).

Yet attitudes were evolving rapidly. Leading industrialists were growing increasingly restive about British exclusion from the Community, and increasingly inclined to question the assumption that membership was not for us. One of his closer colleagues believes that it was the influence of men like Sir Hugh Beaver, managing director of Guinness and President of the FBI, which converted the worried scepticism of Sir Frank Lee into a burning determination to take Britain into Europe, before he left the Board of Trade for the Permanent Secretaryship of the Treasury at the end of 1959.

Similarly, notwithstanding the fact that he was still to make one more attempt to swing the Americans behind the concept of 'bridge-building' between Six and Seven, the Prime Minister's restless and inquiring mind was already contemplating more far-reaching possibilities. R. A. Butler, who at the time combined the offices of Home Secretary, Leader of the Commons and Chairman of the Tory Party, believes Macmillan 'made up his mind' to go for Europe immediately after the General Election; and there is supporting evidence for this assessment in a long memorandum the Prime Minister addressed to his Foreign Secretary within a week of the victory at the polls.

Certainly there is no sign of a sudden conversion to the Community concept: the memorandum speaks of reviewing the 'means of defence' open to Britain against the 'positive economic grouping' which was facing us across the Channel 'for the first time since the Napoleonic era'. But it also suggests a 'thorough examination' of 'the sort of price which it would be worth paying in order to be economically associated [with the Community] (*something more in fact than just the concept of a free trade area*)' [our italics].

Growing anxiety about the impact of the exclusion of Britain from a Continental customs union, coupled with the realisation that neither the United States nor Germany were going to help us embrace the Community in a European free trade system – these were two factors in the evolution of the Prime Minister's thinking. There was also a third.

In one of the earlier volumes of his memoirs Macmillan recalls a post-war dinner of 'The Other Club' at the Savoy. Churchill returned the pudding to the kitchens, grumbling that 'it lacks theme'. 'Theme' was of great importance to Macmillan himself. Anthony Sampson, in his puzzled character sketch of the Tory Premier [*Macmillan: A Study in Ambiguity*, p. 141], describes him as constantly 'groping towards summits through the seven years of his premiership'. It would be more accurate to say that he spent the first half of his tenure of office trying steadily to assemble a grand conference of the leaders of Russia, the US, Britain and France which he hoped would draw a line under the balance-sheet of the Cold War. Finally, in May 1960, he succeeded – only to watch his achievement promptly turn to dust in the wake of the U-2 spy flight.

This was the great disappointment of Macmillan's premiership, a disappointment which was only partially redeemed by the event which, in retrospect, he probably regards as his greatest achievement: the 1963 Test Ban Treaty. But in the summer of 1960 the Test Ban Treaty was far in the future. When Macmillan returned forlorn from Paris after the abortive Summit, he too, like The Other Club's pudding, lacked a 'theme'.

In the opinion of some of those who were closest to him at the time – Philip de Zulueta, for example, his Foreign Office private secretary – it was the collapse of summitry which finally turned the Prime Minister's attention to the possibilities of the European Community. Here was the new theme he needed.

Yet even in the bitter aftermath of the Summit, Macmillan was by no means willing to accept that full membership of the Community was either necessary or possible for Britain. His own personal preference was for a bilateral deal with General de Gaulle. With de Gaulle's agreement anything would be possible: without it, nothing.

Right from his very first visit to the restored General in June 1958, Macmillan had been groping for an understanding with the Frenchman, based on the satisfaction of two interrelated Gaullist ambitions: what de Gaulle was later to describe as the elevation of France 'out of the common ruck of European countries'; and the endowment of France with a nuclear arsenal. At the first meeting the British Prime Minister had left his host with the impression that Britain 'supported' his nuclear objective. Yet it was significant that the British Foreign Office spokesman, reporting to the press at the end of that meeting insisted that 'support' was not the *mot juste*: 'understanding' was more accurate.

Within three months de Gaulle was to suffer his first rebuff. He wrote to both Macmillan and Eisenhower, calling for a three-power directorate of NATO. 'As I expected', the General records grimly in his memoirs [p. 203] 'the two recipients ... replied evasively'. But neither de Gaulle nor Macmillan gave up hope. When Eisenhower travelled to Paris at the end of 1959 for allied consultations in preparation for the Summit, de Gaulle inveigled him and Macmillan to a special private meeting at his country residence, Rambouillet, at which plans were laid for further tripartite gatherings in the future.

Macmillan was overjoyed, minuting his Foreign Secretary on his return:

> My purpose now must be to support de Gaulle on the political front and his desire to join the ranks of the Great Powers.... In return he must give me the greatest practical accommodation that he can on the economic front ... I am therefore very anxious indeed about how the Rambouillet Agreement is to be handled. We must ... not allow it to be whittled away by the Americans ... [*Pointing the Way*, pp. 112–14].

The British Prime Minister kept at it, writing constantly to Eisenhower in favour of tripartite consultation, and minuting his own colleagues about the need to get the Americans to 'accept France's nuclear achievements and ambitions'. Finally, at the end of March 1961, he plucked up his courage and decided to tackle the Americans direct. But by then Kennedy had succeeded Eisenhower. On his first visit to the new American President, Macmillan suggested that 'perhaps we could study whether he had the power, as President, to allow the British to give either warheads or nuclear information to the French' [ibid., p. 351].

Kennedy was totally non-committal. Yet Macmillan never gave up hope. Indeed, according to one of his closest advisers at the time, he always believed that 'the first negotiations' [the Brussels negotiations of 1961–3] 'would come up against the General. But then in the end he himself would have to negotiate the final hurdle.' And when, in July 1963, after de Gaulle had imposed his veto, and Britain had fallen at 'the final hurdle', President Kennedy, in an effort to persuade the French to sign the Test Ban Treaty, mooted the idea of releasing to them 'the vital nuclear information which had been so long and so jealously withheld', Macmillan's bitter comment was that if the Americans had 'armed me with this powerful weapon six months before, it might have made the whole difference to Britain and to Europe' [*At the End of the Day*, p. 476].

We shall never know now whether Macmillan's scheme could have worked. It was beset with contradictions. The American government was formally precluded by the MacMahon Act from passing nuclear information and materials to its allies. Britain benefited from a special waiver which was ostensibly justified by the fact alone among the allies Britain had already endowed herself with a nuclear capability. By 1961 it would have been technically possible to justify an extension of the exchange of information to include France, on the same grounds. But in reality the Eisenhower administration had been reluctantly induced to grant the British waiver because of the pooling of British and American efforts on nuclear fission during the war. Both the Eisenhower and Kennedy administrations were increasingly conscious of resentment among the rest of the allies about the British pretensions to a 'special relationship', and hence frightened of provoking still greater resentment by extending similar treatment to France. Indeed Eisenhower seems to have felt from the start that he had been tricked into accepting the notion of 'tripartism' at Rambouillet, and that this was something he ought not to have gone along with.

Even so, Eisenhower was susceptible to the techniques of diplomatic leverage which Macmillan was so skilled at applying. Had Macmillan broached the possibility of sharing nuclear know-how with the French before Eisenhower demitted office, it seems conceivable that he might have made headway. He apparently failed to do so. When he did try, in the spring of 1961, the new President had at his side, as Assistant Under-Secretary of State, George Ball. Ball was a former Washington counsel for the Jean Monnet organisation. He shared Monnet's federalist enthusiasms, and his antipathy to de Gaulle; and he passionately believed that the decision to exchange nuclear know-how with the British had been a disastrous mistake. Macmillan eventually concluded that Ball 'seemed determined to thwart our policy in Europe and the Common Market negotiations' [ibid., p. 111].

Macmillan's own attitude was ambivalent. In his memoirs he says that he 'began to suspect that either de Gaulle did not understand

and could not operate on the lines which the President and I had found natural, or else that he preferred to nurse grievances'. But of course the trouble was that de Gaulle wanted what Macmillan already enjoyed: the outward and visible signs of special treatment in Washington. This was just what the Americans found it most difficult to grant; and yet Macmillan himself had commented at the end of 1959 that 'there was no possibility of our agreeing' to the 'elevation' of France 'at the expense of our relations with the Americans'.

There was another snag: the attitude of the Foreign Office. Throughout the period of the Messina negotiations in 1955-6, and on through the attempt to encompass the nascent Community with a wider European free trade system, the Foreign Office had kept its distance from what were regarded as strictly commercial discussions. Its only contribution had been the encouragement, from the Embassy in Bonn, of illusory hopes of what the enthusiasm of the German Economics Ministry might do to circumvent French resistance to the free trade plan. The kernel of post-war Foreign Office tradition was the fostering of the 'special relationship' with the United States. Thus it was still the practice for telegrams, of whatever classification, to British missions overseas, to be marked 'GUARD', if they were *not* to be shown to American colleagues. Similarly, American correspondents, not only in London but also in other capitals, received preferential briefing from British ministers, including the Prime Minister, at every stage of the Anglo-Continental discussions in the 1950s. More seriously, when a diplomatic row exploded between Paris and Washington in the spring of 1958 over the supply of American arms to Tunisia, at the height of the free trade negotiations, the Foreign Office had no hesitation in backing the American position.

The first signs of an evolution in Foreign Office thinking occurred following de Gaulle's return to power. By 1959 the British Ambassador in Paris, Sir Gladwyn Jebb, had become a belated convert to the virtues of British membership of the European Community, and with all the convert's zeal began to bombard the Foreign Office with telegrams and despatches.

Then, in the early spring of 1960, there was an important shift of personnel in the senior echelons of the Foreign Office in London. Sir Evelyn Shuckburgh returned from NATO and Sir Patrick Reilly from Moscow to Deputy Under-Secretaryships: both belonged to the small minority of Foreign Office 'Europeans'. Even more significant was the creation of a new post of Adviser on European Trade Problems for Sir Roderick Barclay, formerly Ambassador in Denmark.

Yet if the Foreign Office had, by the spring of 1960, come to recognise that British relations with the Continent were acquiring new significance, the attitude attributed by Nora Beloff to Sir Derick Hoyer-Millar, the Permanent Under-Secretary from 1957 to the end of 1961, that 'Britain's European links' were far less important than 'our relations with the US and the Commonwealth', still represented mainstream departmental thinking.

It followed that a commercial deal with the European Community – even a bid to test the possibility of full British membership – was one thing, a deal with the French involving satisfaction of de Gaulle's aspirations to parity of status *vis-à-vis* Washington and the exchange of exclusive nuclear information, quite another.

Macmillan records that when eventually, in 1963, Kennedy momentarily flirted with the notion of supplying the French with nuclear know-how, he felt 'in almost total disagreement with the Foreign Office point of view'. Why be so cautious, when the President was so imaginative? Why bother about going 'far beyond what his advisers feel' ...? The answer is that whether or not the Prime Minister's plans for an Anglo-French nuclear bargain were ever practicable, the Foreign Office had been determined from the start to frustrate them. As their spokesman had explained back in 1958, 'understanding' maybe: 'support', never.

It was not only at the Foreign Office that the spring of 1960 marked a changing of the guard. At the Ministry of Agriculture Eric Roll, a former academic of central European origins, returned from the International Sugar Council to become Deputy Under-Secretary; at the Board of Trade Sir Frank Lee gave place to Sir Richard Powell from the Ministry of Defence; and at the Treasury Lee succeeded Sir Roger Makins as Permanent Under-Secretary.

A senior minister recalls finding it 'fascinating' at the time how civil servants who had totally rejected the customs union concept in 1957–8 had suddenly become 'mad keen' about it eighteen months later. It is a fair point: within months of assuming their new appointments Roll, Powell and Lee were renowned throughout Whitehall and beyond for the fervour of their commitment to the European adventure, and yet none of them had previously been identified with the tiny band of Community enthusiasts in Whitehall.

The key figure here, without any doubt, was Sir Frank Lee. In the days before the formation of the Civil Service Department the Permanent Secretary to the Treasury was one of the two top men in Whitehall (the other being the Secretary to the Cabinet). Lee's predecessor, Sir Roger Makins, a career diplomat and former Ambassador to the United States, with an American wife, had had no sympathy whatever for closer British involvement with

Europe. As soon as Lee took over it was obvious that times had changed.

Lee was in many respects a most unusual civil servant. Small, stocky, abounding in nervous energy and highly articulate, he had never been overburdened with traditional civil service scruples about the need to offer the politicians a choice of courses of action. He might present the choices; but he also made it plain which way the choice should go. Immediately on his appointment to the Treasury he was put in charge of an inter-departmental committee of officials established to examine the pros and cons of British membership of the Community.

Sir John Winnifrith, the Permanent Secretary to the Ministry of Agriculture, and an undisguised opponent of British membership of the Community, recalls finding it all 'very un-civil service'. Lee 'railroaded it all through' his Committee, making it quite clear that 'he wasn't going to stand any nonsense from us peasants'.

Lee's personal conversion seems to have reflected a combination of pressures. He had sensed the dilemma presented by the establishment of the Community from the start; at the Board of Trade he had felt the anxieties of the leaders of the British industry about the impact of Britain's exclusion from the Market. The mere fact of the establishment of the inter-departmental committee on his arrival at the Treasury was evidently the clincher: Prime Ministers do not set up committees of this kind in the hope that they will confirm the wisdom of the *status quo*.

Yet it would be wrong to give the impression that Lee was picked by Macmillan to carry through the European operation. His main qualification for his new job was almost certainly the fact that he did not come from the Treasury. Macmillan regarded the Treasury as a nest of reaction. His choice of Makins to head it had been unprecedented, and in the eyes of several of his colleagues it had not proved an unqualified success: but the Prime Minister remained determined to look once again outside the ranks of the Treasury knights. That being so, Lee virtually 'chose himself'.

There was no wholesale stampede among the civil servants to board the boat-train for Europe in the spring of 1960. The Foreign Office continued largely aloof; the Treasury establishment was (and remained) perturbed about the balance of payments implications of the adoption of the Community systems of protection; at the Ministry of Agriculture, Sir John Winnifrith, while far too scrupulous a civil servant to allow his own preferences to obtrude, could be relied upon to ensure that the complications of the Community's apparent intentions – they were no more at the time – for farm support policy were taken fully into account. Most civil servants

remained unaware of any impending change of direction. But with
Lee in charge there was never any question about the outcome of the
investigations of the crucial inter-departmental committee.

Following the changing of the guard among the top civil servants
came the first ministerial reshuffle of the 1959 Parliament. Here again
it has sometimes been suggested that the selection of ministers was
'orchestrated' by Macmillan with Europe in mind. George Hutchinson, in his biography of Edward Heath, writes that the effect of the
July 1960 reshuffle was 'to fit "the Europeans" in [the Cabinet] –
mere handful that they were – into spheres of delicate importance
to the development of the policy which [the Prime Minister] was
already contemplating'. That may indeed have been the effect: there
is no evidence that it was the intention.

The key appointments here were the moves of Duncan Sandys
from the Ministry of Aviation to the Commonwealth Relations
Office; of Edward Heath from the Ministry of Labour to be Lord
Privy Seal and spokesman for the Foreign Office in the Commons;
and of Christopher Soames from the War Office to the Ministry of
Agriculture. One does not have to go so far as one of Macmillan's
ministers, who dismisses the notion of orchestration by saying that
'Prime Ministers only conduct reshuffles to plug holes', to see that
the essential change was none of these, but rather the transfer of
Selwyn Lloyd to the Treasury. At the Foreign Office Lloyd had
proved generally amenable to a fair measure of intervention by
No. 10; and this was what Macmillan now wanted at the Treasury.

Lloyd's successor was Lord Home. Home was not identified in
the minds of his colleagues with Europe; and after he had gone to the
Foreign Office his most apparent personal concern was with the
global threat of Russian expansionism. This inclined him to favour
the elimination of divisions in Western Europe; but that was about
as far as his own preference was to go. However, being in the Lords,
he needed a senior colleague to represent his department in the
Commons. Hence the appointment of Edward Heath.

Heath was highly ambitious, and it was no doubt improbable
that he would be content with a subordinate role for long: he would
need a sphere of action of his own. But although he had used his
maiden speech ten years before to call for British participation in
the European Coal and Steel Community, he had spent almost the
whole of the intervening period in the Whips' Office. Not very
surprisingly, therefore, one of his Ministerial colleagues says that
'we didn't really know much what he thought about anything'. But
as the same witness comments, 'he comes late to everything – but
makes up with enthusiasm when he's got there'. Thus it was to be
with Europe.

The two appointments which, with benefit of hindsight, might be seen to have pointed to what lay ahead were those of Sandys and Soames. Perhaps no member of the Macmillan government had better European credentials than Duncan Sandys; and here he was, moving to the Commonwealth Relations Office, where he would be responsible for winning the acquiescence of Commonwealth leaders for a European initiative – an acquiescence which was of vital importance if a revolt on the Tory back benches was to be avoided. Soames's advance to the Ministry of Agriculture was, in the eyes of some of his colleagues, even more important. As one of them puts it, 'here was a man of outstanding ability and a convinced European' going to the department which would have to make the crucial assessment of the likely impact of the Community's agricultural system on the British farming industry, with its strong hold on the Tory back benches. A senior civil servant closely involved in the Macmillan approach believes, in fact, that Soames was put in to 'find the key' to the enigma of the European agricultural system.

Soames himself refutes this assumption. When the Prime Minister told him of his new assignment, he recalls asking straight out whether it was 'for Europe'; and the answer was that Europe was simply 'not on' for the present. Nor does he recall searching for the 'key' to the common agricultural policy: rather it was the alarming cost of deficiency payments under the British system at a time of very low world food prices which convinced him, during his early months at the Ministry of Agriculture, that it was time for a change in any case.

Perhaps this is a little disingenuous. This was not the first occasion that the deficiency payments bill had soared ahead as world market prices slumped. Soames's predecessors had devised incentives to the orderly market of home-produced foodstuffs, and Soames himself was to lecture the Russian Ambassador on the iniquity of cheap Russian sales of grain. Another minister, more sceptical about the wider attractions of Community membership, would hardly have looked as favourably on the possibilities of the Continental system of farm support. But at the time of his appointment all this was in the future.

As the inner circle of Whitehall was preparing, under the powerful impetus of Sir Frank Lee, for a reappraisal of the Common Market option, so was influential opinion beyond the ranks of government. Prior to the 1959 General Election, calls for a positive approach to Market membership in the press were confined to the letter columns of *The Times*. By the late spring of 1960 the editorial columns began to move with striking unanimity: the *Observer* in April, followed by the *Guardian* in May, the *Economist* in June, and the *Financial*

Times in the autumn. By July the issue had sufficiently impinged on public consciousness to justify the first of a long series of public opinion polls. This showed that almost half those interviewed – 49 per cent – favoured British participation in the Common Market, while only 13 per cent were against.

The movement of opinion in Fleet Street reflected, as much as anything else, the diminished role of the proprietors. The days of campaigning ownership of newspapers were past: even Cecil King, assiduously courted by Harold Macmillan and later by Harold Wilson, did not control the editorial columns of the *Mirror* group. With one major exception, editorial policy was now decided by working journalists. On matters of foreign and economic policy, such as the Common Market, it was the economic, diplomatic and political correspondents who held sway; and they were swift to catch the nuances of changing attitudes in Whitehall. The one exception, of course, was Beaverbrook Newspapers, still dominated by the elderly proprietor. It was no coincidence that this was the only national newspaper group which failed to get the message.

Thus by the autumn of 1960 it could be said that '... the press was squared,/The middle classes quite prepared'. The time had come to test the water. In August Macmillan visited Chancellor Adenauer in Bonn. Adenauer, twice imprisoned by the British, was instinctively anglophobe and particularly distrustful of Macmillan, whom he regarded as dangerously prone to flirtations with Moscow. Great was the surprise of the British, therefore, when he agreed to a series of technical discussions at official level on the scope for special arrangements, within an enlarged Community, for British agriculture and the Commonwealth. Edward Heath, in his Godkin lectures six years later, identified this as the moment when membership first entered the realms of practical possibilities.

This reflects, once again, the strength of the perennial delusion at the Foreign Office about the weight of German influence within the Community. At the time, however, it added powerfully to the pressures mounting on Macmillan to commit himself. During the autumn the two most fervent members of the Cabinet, Sandys and Soames, were in the words of one senior civil servant, 'in and out of Birch Grove' (the Macmillan country house) urging the European case. The fact that both were, or had been, married into the Churchill family no doubt gave added weight to their advocacy in the eyes of a Prime Minister who seasoned his economic radicalism with a romantic respect for dynasties.

Then, in the early months of 1961, the French took a hand. Couve de Murville, de Gaulle's Foreign Minister, was one of those Frenchmen who combined a preference for London tailoring with a pronounced distrust of 'Anglo-Saxon' political influence: he was supposed to have had an unhappy experience tutoring an English family in his youth. So when he took the opportunity of a private lunch with a dedicated Tory backbench European enthusiast, Peter Kirk, to indicate that a British bid for membership of the Market would be well received in Paris, and followed this up with a speech early in March in Strasbourg in which he said that for Britain to join the Community was 'doubtless the only really satisfactory solution', it was understandable that to many in the government and in Whitehall (though not to Macmillan himself) it appeared that the last major obstacle had been removed.

For the Prime Minister there were still three important hurdles to overcome. The first was the Commonwealth. The Commonwealth Prime Ministers were due to meet at Lancaster House in March. This, according to one of Macmillan's most senior colleagues, was 'the big fence'. Sir Robert Menzies, doyen of the club, was 'the only person Harold Macmillan was really frightened of'. Understandably so: for had not Menzies, alone among Commonwealth leaders, stood up for Britain at the time of Suez? A denunciation of the European approach from Menzies would have made a disastrous impact on the Tory back benches.

In the event the Conference could hardly have gone better from this point of view. Certainly there were storms. Keith Holyoake, the newly appointed New Zealand Premier, was, in the words of one of those present, 'most offensive', saying that his country was 'aghast' at the notion of Britain joining the Community. But Menzies was 'softened up' by Macmillan's 'lavish and skilful hospitality'. Moreover the big issue at the Conference turned out not to be the Common Market at all, but the expulsion of South Africa. Nothing could have been more helpful for Macmillan with his own back benches. A club from which South Africa had been ejected was not the sort of grouping to which most of the doubting Tories would feel a sense of overriding loyalty.

The second hurdle was the attitude of the Americans. Since the United States had consistently advocated British participation in an enlarged European customs union, the Prime Minister's anxiety on this score was a little surprising. But the strength of American hostility to 'bridge-building' between Common Market and EFTA had come as a rude shock; and the Minister of State at the Foreign Office, David Ormsby-Gore, a close friend of the new President and his family, had reported after a visit to Washington that 'the new President was no great admirer of de Gaulle's political philosophy . . .' [*Pointing the Way*, p. 328]. Is it even conceivable that Macmillan secretly hoped for an American veto to resolve his own personal doubts? Certainly it would have been unthinkable for him to have gone ahead without first obtaining American blessing.

This was promptly forthcoming. On the first day of his visit to Washington at the end of March, Macmillan asked Kennedy how the United States would view a British bid to join the Common Market. According to Ball [*Discipline of Power*], 'President Kennedy turned to me'. Ball, a long-standing advocate of the need to enlarge the European Community and to terminate the Anglo-American 'special relationship', needed no further prompting. Nothing, he assured the British Prime Minister, would be better received in Washington.

At home, the City was becoming increasingly impatient. Most of the leading merchant banking houses – Rothschilds, Lazards, Schroders, Hambros, Kleinworts, Warburgs – were of Continental origin, and had close links with the Community countries. It was an article of faith in the City, which had highlighted the sluggishness of traditional British markets in the Commonwealth long before this had been recognised in Whitehall – let alone at Westminster – that the scale and sophistication of the London capital market would make it the centre of financial services for an enlarged European Community. Already, by September 1960, *The Director*, the house-magazine of the Institute of Directors, was warning the government that industry had decided to plump for Europe even if it meant leaving Harold Macmillan and his ministers 'waving goodbye from the dock'.

The attitude of the FBI was more ambivalent. The February issue of the *FBI Review* explained editorially that the federation could not act as a pressure group in this situation because 'economic judgement may be coloured, or even overridden, by political considerations'. In truth the FBI was somewhat divided internally. Smaller member firms, and the trade organisations representing them, were worried about the impact of open competition with the Continent, while the large companies were raring to go. The attitude of the FBI central staff seems to have been a good deal less than enthusiastic: the *FBI Review* felt it necessary to remind itself that the Federation had to 'work with the broad mandate laid down by its members, even though the private views of the staff might diverge'. (The nature of those 'private views' was perhaps most clearly demonstrated by a full-page advertisement taken by the FBI in the pages of the *Financial Times* when the Common Market negotiations finally broke down on January 1963. This called upon British industry finally to put the notion of membership of the Community behind it. Edward Heath was not amused.)

For all the major pressure groups the scope for influencing Government policies was radically transformed once it became a matter of choosing for or against membership of the Community. The FBI had taken the lead in the construction of EFTA; and during the earlier negotiations on 'plan G' *The Director* had commented testily that 'the road from the TUC to the Treasury is worn smooth by Union leaders seeking information and imposing conditions which, if conceded altogether, would hamstring negotiations.' But now FBI, TUC and National Farmers' Union were all inhibited. Each of them had been able to take a view about what should, or should not, be incorporated in a strictly trading arrangement. But a stand on the desirability, or otherwise, of British membership of the Community would, in each case, have split the membership.

Instead the TUC and the NFU each concentrated, characteristically, on protecting its own particular *raison d'être*. Thus a major worry for the TUC was the Community's aspirations in the matter of 'social policy'. For if the Community was to lay down centrally the number of paid holidays a year, or the conditions governing the availability of sickness benefit, this would detract from the bargaining role of the British unions. Similarly the NFU was concerned above all to protect its right to conduct an annual price review with the British government; for it was this spring mating display, inaugurated by the post-war Labour Government, which had really put the NFU on the map.

In one important respect the attitude of the two major producer pressure groups seems to have differed. The NFU has never had any qualms about appealing over the heads of ministers to the backbench MPs. Essentially this only operates when a Tory Government is in power, for the number of Labour MPs with a significant farming electorate is too small to matter. But the NFU argues not only that it must lobby backbench MPs to pressurise the government when it cannot get satisfaction from the Minister of Agriculture, but also that the minister is often grateful for such orchestrated backbench pressure to shift his colleagues in Cabinet. The TUC – at least so long as George Woodcock was in charge, as he was throughout the period under review – took the more traditional lobbyist viewpoint that such pressure was liable to be counterproductive, undermining the intimacy of the crucial relationship with ministers and senior civil servants. (Woodcock tends to be critical of the way in which, after his departure, the TUC moved away from such abstemiousness, notably over the Labour Government's 'In Place of Strife' White Paper. Yet it is instructive that the pressure applied at that time by the unions on backbench Labour MPs was effective in securing the abandonment of the White Paper.)

Whatever the merits of these respective approaches to the business of lobbying, there is no doubt that in 1960–1 Macmillan was worried about the attitude of the NFU and its impact on Tory backbench opinion. He was particularly anxious about his third hurdle: the second member of his administration, R. A. Butler. Butler was given to agonising about the welfare of his farming constituents in Saffron Walden. This was a good example of the tendency of all MPs to find constituency justifications for personal prejudice; for there cannot have been many farmers in the United Kingdom who were likely to do better out of the bias which the European Community was already displaying towards cereal production than the barley barons of north-west Essex. (It is only fair to add that one of Butler's Cabinet colleagues recalls hearing at least as much from the Prime Minister himself about the perils of the Community arrangements for the lobster fishermen of the Hebrides, with whom Macmillan liked to claim an ancestral connection, as he heard from Butler about the farmers of Saffron Walden.)

So during the winter of 1960–1 Macmillan invited Butler, in his role as Party Chairman, to tour the country paying particular attention to agricultural opinion. Butler himself says that he 'came round with the farmers'. In any case he would never have led a palace revolution against Europe. He had 'Doubts', very much as Victorian undergraduates had religious 'Doubts': as a colleague comments, 'RAB had doubts about everything.' Maudling, the President of the Board of Trade, also had doubts; and so did Watkinson, the Minister of Defence. Watkinson was a dedicated 'special relationship' man; but he had neither the desire nor the weight in Cabinet to cause serious trouble. Maudling's views reflected in part his commitment to EFTA, of which he had stood sponsor, and in part the Board of Trade's departmental distaste for protectionism in all its forms. His scepticism was more serious, in that it must have played a part in his willing acquiescence in the so-called London Agreement, by which Britain committed herself in July 1961, weeks before the launching of the European negotiation, to an arrangement with EFTA which 'went very near to stating that the UK would not join the Six unless and until the Six agree on a single market of Thirteen' [Miriam Camps, p. 354].

There was, however, never any question of Butler, Watkinson or Maudling leading a revolt against a decision by Macmillan to launch a negotiation with Europe. A more serious candidate, in the eyes of some commentators, was the Lord President, Lord Hailsham. Hailsham had the oratorical power to sway large audiences, and in the words of one ministerial colleague he was 'liable to become impatient'. Nora Beloff [op. cit.] notes that 'all the efforts to harness his oratorical talents to the European chariot were dodged'.

Calculated aloofness is one thing: public hostility quite another

There is no evidence to suggest that at any time during the build-up period prior to the decision to launch negotiations at the end of July was there a serious threat of trouble within the Conservative Party. Sir Michael Fraser, the head of the Party bureaucracy throughout the 1960s, describes the general mood of the party at the time as broadly reflecting the mood of the nation. This was a mood which offered both 'good news and bad news' for the European approach. The nation was 'much more self-confident' than it is today, which was helpful; but by the same token it was 'much more self-reliant', which was unhelpful.

Lieber [op. cit.] calculates that 'perhaps one hundred Tory MPs in all were reserved in one way or another.' Most of these belonged to the 'knights of the shires' category, who were temperamentally strongly disposed to give their leaders the benefit of the doubt at all times. Admittedly if and when they did choose to dig in their heels their collective resistance to the drift of government policy could be formidable indeed. But they were the last people to make trouble over something as tentative as a bid to find out whether it might be possible to refashion the Community to suit our requirements.

At the other end of the scale there was a much smaller group of Tories, mostly from the younger generation of backbenchers, but also including some like Duncan Sandys and Peter Thorneycroft who were senior departmental ministers, who were increasingly impatient with the government's hesitations. Not that backbench pressures were ever likely to jostle the Government into action: as Lord Thorneycroft puts it, 'backbench pressures can stop things, but they can't *do* things'.

The Labour benches were a good deal more reserved. Lieber calculates that around one-third of the 258 Labour MPs were fiercely opposed to any idea of joining the Market; and within an Opposition party it is natural that those who are fiercely critical of a government policy should enjoy the benefit of doubt among their colleagues. Most of the opponents were grouped on the left of the Party, although there were some senior men on the centre or right – Healey, Jay, Gordon Walker – with greater or lesser reservations.

However, this section of the Party was just about balanced by Common Market enthusiasts, primarily from the right (only three left-wing MPs, Robert Edwards, Walter Padley and Fenner Brockway positively supported the Market bid), with a third section willing to follow the line of the leadership, whatever that might be. Given that some of the most senior and influential trade union leaders were at this time strongly in favour of the European approach – Frank Cousins, for example, and Harry Douglass of the Steelworkers, whose executive had in August 1960 urged the Government to seek entry into the Community 'without delay' – the logical course for the Parliamentary Party was to give its blessing to the opening of negotiations, while reserving its position on the substance of the issue until the implications could be more fairly assessed.

This indeed is what it did. Because Hugh Gaitskell was to lead his colleagues into outright opposition to Market entry during 1962, a contrast is sometimes drawn between the all-party support which Harold Wilson enjoyed for his decision to renew the British bid in 1967, and the way in which the Tories in 1961 had to launch their approach in the teeth of Labour resistance. In fact there was no such resistance in 1961. When the Commons was finally invited to endorse the Macmillan Government's decision to open negotiations at the beginning of August, the Labour Party did indeed table a 'reasoned amendment' to the Government motion. But it was so reasoned as to amount to a distinction without a difference.

The government invited the Commons to support the decision to

> initiate negotiations to see if satisfactory arrangements can be made to meet the special interests of the United Kingdom, of the Commonwealth, and of the European Free Trade Association; and further [to accept] the undertaking of Her Majesty's Government that no agreement affecting these special interests or involving British sovereignty will be entered into until it has been approved by this House after full consultation with the Commonwealth countries, by whatever procedure they may generally agree.

Labour sought to substitute 'notes' for 'supports', made a ritual Party point by regretting the weakness of the Government's negotiating position, and concluded that Britain should enter the Community

> only if this House gives its approval and if the conditions negotiated are generally acceptable to a Commonwealth Prime Ministers' Conference and accord with our obligations and pledges to other members of the European Free Trade Association.

At the end of the debate it was reckoned that about twenty-five Tory MPs abstained; and when the Opposition amendment had been voted down the Labour Party abstained on the Government motion, leaving it to five of its left-wingers (Michael Foot, S. O. Davies, Emrys Hughes, Sydney Silverman and K. Zilliacus) plus a somewhat unpredictable Scots Socialist, Willy Baxter, and Anthony Fell from the right wing of the Tory Party, to divide the House.

The real surprise is not that Macmillan should have avoided serious political trouble over a decision to investigate a possibility which, right up until the spring of 1961, had been repeatedly ruled out in public by senior ministers; but that he should evidently have imagined that he would encounter it. After the Commonwealth Conference and the blessing of the new American administration in March four long months were still to elapse before the final decision was taken. By now the whole of Fleet Street apart from the Communist *Morning Star* and the *Daily Express* were campaigning for an early, and positive, decision.* And while the opinion polls were somewhat less favourable than they had been at the start of the series the previous summer, they continued to show that outright opposition was confined to a small minority of the public. Still the government hesitated.

Cabinet Ministers were despatched to the four corners of the Commonwealth to extract grudging acknowledgement of Britain's freedom of action, and the EFTA ministers were summoned to a conference in London. Miriam Camps comments that the result was an 'unfortunate decision to promise too much to too many sectional interests'. Ironically, however, it was not the Commonwealth, with its strong claims on the emotions and loyalty of the Tory Party, but EFTA, with no such leverage, which extracted from the British government the real hostages to fortune. Here perhaps we see the influence of the personal attitudes of the ministers directly respons- ible – Maudling in the one case, Sandys in the other – as well as the reflection of the Board of Trade's sense of obligation to a grouping which it had so recently been instrumental in creating.

Ian Gilmour [*The Body Politic*, p. 244] argues that 'the decision to seek entry into the EEC would have been taken much earlier had it lain with Macmillan alone. It was preceded by seemingly inter- minable Cabinet discussions in which the doubts and objections of many Ministers had to be slowly whittled down before the attempt was made'; and George Ball, in his memoirs [p. 86], comments bitingly that the Prime Minister, 'being much more of a tactician than a strategist ... forswore a frontal assault, preferring to try and move sideways like a crab'. Both these accounts ascribe to the Prime Minister a certainty of intention which was not there. We now know from the last volume of his memoirs that as late as 20 July Macmillan was writing to Sir Edward Boyle, the Financial Secretary, that he did not see 'how the Conservative Party can avoid some sort of a split on this issue'.

---

* Woodrow Wyatt, MP and newspaper proprietor, was to argue in a television discussion four years later that a series of enthusiastic articles in the *Daily Herald* in the summer of 1961 was the 'tip-over factor' which 'caused the Government to stop vacillating'. This exaggerates the influence of the press. It helped to orches- trate the public conversion which occurred in 1960–1. But it did not write the score, nor did it dictate the tempo.

The Prime Minister had not faltered in his conviction that participation in an enlarged Community was right for Britain. His
trouble was that almost alone among ministers and senior officials (Sir
Michael Fraser, the Tory Party research chief, says that he had come
to a similar conclusion) he was deeply sceptical about the likelihood
of obliging de Gaulle to accept us as members on terms which the
Parliamentary Party would swallow.

By the summer of 1961 the conventional wisdom in Whitehall was
that our attempts to come to terms with the Community had failed
to date because we had appeared to be trying to sabotage its objectives. If, instead, we showed ourselves willing to assume the obligations of membership (still in their formative stage), nobody could
keep us out: did not the Treaty of Rome expressly provide for the
adherence of other European countries which accepted its provisions?
Macmillan was unconvinced. And of course he was right.

The Labour bid

The Labour Party had switched in 1962 to outright opposition to
the Macmillan government's Common Market approach, to the
undisguised dismay of some senior members of the Party, including
notably George Brown and Roy Jenkins. A few months later, just a
week before de Gaulle interposed his first veto, Hugh Gaitskell was
dead, and Labour faced a leadership election. By the time this took
place it was already apparent that the Macmillan negotiations were
over, and the Common Market was not by any means the main issue
in the party election.

Nevertheless in one respect it was, arguably, decisive. The two
main contenders were Harold Wilson and George Brown. Wilson
broadly enjoyed the support of the left; George Brown that of the
right. But to win Wilson desperately needed the support of at least a
section of the trade union group,, who regarded him with deep
suspicion; and that he nevertheless collected some vital trade union
MPs' votes was due to the energetic canvassing conducted on his behalf by an elderly and well-respected mining MP, Bill Blyton. Blyton
was passionately opposed to the Common Market, and determined
for this reason to beat George Brown. He never forgave Harold
Wilson his subsequent apostasy.

Not that Wilson was swift to change sides. From the moment that
he succeeded to the Labour leadership the General Election began to
cast its shadow forward. When it eventually came, in October 1964
both the major parties firmly turned their backs on the European
issue, which Sir Alec Douglas-Home dismissed as 'a dead duck'

Lieber has calculated that only one Tory candidate in nine and only one Labour candidate in twelve gave 'attention' to Europe in his election address.

The narrow balance of the 1964 parliament would have made such a potentially divisive issue as Europe difficult for the incoming Labour government to tackle if it had been so minded. In any case it was not. Rather it had high hopes of the Commonwealth. In opposition Wilson had floated the idea of a Commonwealth free trade area; and on gaining office he tried a Commonwealth relief mission for what turned out to be a non-existent famine in Rhodesia, and an abortive Commonwealth Prime Ministers' peace mission to Vietnam. Meanwhile the Common Market itself was plunged in its worst crisis to date, with the decision of the French government to boycott meetings of the Council of Ministers until its partners surrendered the right to impose decisions on France by a majority.

Lord George-Brown tells us in his memoirs [*In My Way*, p. 205] that his leader's attitude 'began to change' from the moment he took office. There was little to show for this at the time. Yet beneath the surface attitudes *were* evolving, as we now know. The Commonwealth failed to live up to expectations. Its share of British trade continued to decline, while the stationing of British garrisons east of Suez was proving difficult to reconcile with Labour's commitment to reduce defence expenditure and the need to correct the balance of payments deficit. The new Prime Minister slipped easily into Macmillan's habit of regular visits to Washington; but President Johnson soon became impatient with what he regarded as Wilson's importuning for help in coping with left-wing Labour Party pressures over Vietnam. (Indeed according to one newspaper report [*Sunday Times*, 7 May 1967] Wilson returned from his very first visit to Washington as Prime Minister in December 1964 and complained to a 'Downing Street aide' that 'Johnson's gone mad: we'll have to find a new ally', and when the aide jokingly suggested de Gaulle, he was taken aback to receive the answer 'that's right'.) As for EFTA, in which Labour in opposition had also placed high hopes, it had been shaken to its foundations by the decision of the incoming government to impose a tariff surcharge on imports into Britain from the other member countries without consultation and in flagrant defiance of the rules.

Meanwhile, for largely fortuitous reasons, the composition of the Labour Government was changing in a 'European' direction. Patrick Gordon Walker, a keen pro-Commonwealth man, had been the Prime Minister's choice for the Foreign Office. But he had been defeated at the General Election, and then again at a by-election. So he had to be replaced by Michael Stewart, the Minister of Education, who in turn was succeeded by Anthony Crosland. A few months later the health of Sir Frank Soskice, the Home Secretary, forced him to withdraw to the Lords, and Roy Jenkins came into the Cabinet as his replacement.

Both Crosland and Jenkins had won their promotion on merit. Both enjoyed the personal allegiance of sections of the new 1964 Labour Commons intake; and both were bound to be influential members of the Cabinet from the start. It also so happened that both were fervent pro-Marketeers: indeed Jenkins's 'European' credentials were second in the Party only to those of George Brown. Stewart was not identified with the pro-European wing of the Party before he went to the Foreign Office; but throughout his ministerial career he showed a marked propensity to adopt the coloration of the department for which he happened to be responsible. It did not take him long to acquire enthusiasm for early renewal of negotiations with the Six: according to some reports he was particularly worried about the prospect of German domination of the existing Community after de Gaulle's death – a prospect to which his officials were quick to draw his attention.

This gradual evolution during the course of 1965 was reflected in the wording of the Queen's Speech at the beginning of the second session of the 1964 Parliament in November 1965. The Commonwealth was relegated to a passing mention: instead the Government pledged itself to 'promote ... the establishment of a wider European market'. (If Crossman is to be believed the intention of those responsible for one draft of the Speech – the officials at the Foreign Office? – had been to carry the Government a good deal further than this: 'I spotted a very sinister phrase about entry into the European Common Market and said it had to go. It did.' [*The Diaries of a Cabinet Minister*, p. 365].)

One month later Wilson dined with a group of younger Labour MPs. According to Nora Beloff in the *Observer* and a later report in the *Sunday Times* he told the pro-Europeans among them to 'stop pushing' because things were going their way anyway, and announced that Labour's long-standing (and plainly unattainable) pre-conditions for membership of the Market had been whittled down to two: food prices, and the common agricultural policy. Meanwhile the Prime Minister's waning enthusiasm for the Commonwealth was, according to some of his colleagues, finally destroyed by two events around the turn of the year: first, the manner in which Pakistan and India turned to Moscow, rather than London, to mediate in their border dispute; and second the furious denunciations of the British Government's failure to use force against Rhodesian UDI at the Prime Ministers' conference in Lagos.

Early in the new year (1966) Cecil King confided to his diary that George Brown had come to lunch with him 'in order to tell me that Wilson is deciding to enter the Common Market'. First he needed to secure a more substantial parliamentary majority. This he duly did at the General Election in March. During the course of the campaign there occurred an incident which attracted considerable attention at the time. At a meeting of the Ministerial Council of the Western European Union (a body whose membership included Britain and all six Community countries) in London the French delegate, a top civil servant from the Quai d'Orsay, uttered what the British Prime Minister was later to describe in his memoirs as 'delphic words which were interpreted by some as a sign that France might be moving towards support for an enlarged Community'.

The leader of the Opposition, Edward Heath, promptly called for a British response. The Prime Minister was due to make a major election speech in Bristol a few days later. According to Cecil King, Callaghan, the Chancellor, told King's *Mirror* colleague, Hugh Cudlipp, that in this speech Wilson would give the 'green light' for a new approach to the Community. In the event he did nothing of the kind. Instead he accused the Leader of the Opposition of 'rolling over like a spaniel' at the least sign of encouragement from General de Gaulle, and roundly reaffirmed the Labour Party's intention to continue to buy Britain's food 'in the cheapest markets in the world'.

As usual with the Labour leader, there were some qualifying phrases in the 'small print' of the Bristol speech; and no sooner was the election won than Wilson himself revealed to the new parliament that he knew how to interpret the 'delphic words' of the French delegate to WEU: it was, after all, right to say that these represented a 'major change' in the French position. In re-forming his government after the election, the Prime Minister seemed to be responding to this.

From the autumn of 1965 George Brown had been working away at his Department of Economic Affairs, in conjunction with his senior civil servant, Sir Eric Roll (a passionate European who, after his involvement at the Ministry of Agriculture in the build-up to the Macmillan government's Market bid, had been a leading member of Heath's team during the long and abortive negotiations in Brussels), on a series of papers setting out afresh the case for British entry. Now Brown was formally designated Minister with overall responsibility for relations with the Community – this was apparently in compensation for the partial withdrawal of the DEA's control of prices and incomes policy – while George Thomson, one of the Foreign Office Ministers of State, was promoted Chancellor of the Duchy of Lancaster with a remit, the House of Commons was told, to 'probe,

in a very positive sense, the terms on which we would be able to
enter Europe' [Hansard, 21 April 1966, col. 90]. Another appointment of considerable significance was that of Michael Palliser as
the Foreign Office representative on the Prime Minister's personal
staff.

There is, however, no reason to think that either Thomson or
Palliser owed promotion to known pro-European views. Indeed
Thomson, a quiet-spoken, popular and respected Scot, had always
been known as a Commonwealth enthusiast, and admits that he
viewed the Common Market with considerable suspicion until well
after he had joined the Foreign Office in 1964 (and that, in the
opinion of some of his civil service colleagues, is 'quite an under-
statement'). Like Stewart, he was quick to assimilate departmental
attitudes: indeed the golden opinions he had earned among the civil
servants probably had as much to do with his new promotion as
anything else. Palliser, in the words of a contemporary colleague,
'virtually picked himself' because of his immediately preceding appointment as head of the Foreign Office long-range planning staff.
Nevertheless he did have wide experience of the Common Market
capitals (especially Paris); he was bilingual in French, and he was
son-in-law to one of the founding fathers of the Community, Paul-
Henri Spaak. From a hostile angle Marcia Williams [*Inside Number
10*] reckoned Palliser had 'great influence in No. 10, particularly on
problems connected with Europe ...'

This influence was 'infinitely strengthened', according to the same
source, by the support which Palliser enjoyed from two other
strategically-placed civil servants: Sir Burke Trend, the Secretary to
the Cabinet, whom Wilson had inherited from Sir Alec Douglas-
Home, and Mr William Nield, who had just joined the Cabinet
Office as a Deputy Under-Secretary from the DEA. Nield, who had
actually started his working life in the Labour Party Research Department ('without', Mrs Williams comments acidly, 'having its
imprint left on him'), did bring a pro-European bias with him from
the DEA. There is no supporting evidence for Mrs Williams's charge
against Sir Burke. He was something of a bogeyman to the left of the
Labour Party, who mistrusted the intimate relationship which he
had undoubtedly established with the Prime Minister. But his reputation in Whitehall was one of magisterial impartiality, on this as on
every other issue.

Nor was the Prime Minister lacking in contrary advice. The
hostility of his personal economic adviser, Thomas Balogh, to the
Common Market and all its works was well known. He and the two
other members of the triumvirate of political recruits, Robert Neild
and Nicholas Kaldor, respectively Economic Adviser to the Treasury

and Special Adviser to the Chancellor, shared Balogh's antipathy to the European Community.

From the election onwards, however, the civil service machine was beginning to move into gear in preparation for a fresh approach to Europe. The *Sunday Times* was to report the following summer that 'the only politicians conversant with the full details of the civil service studies were Wilson himself, Brown, and Douglas Houghton, the Minister without Portfolio and an ardent Marketeer. The Cabinet was not formally consulted.' The operation was master-minded by an inter-departmental committee of top civil servants, from which the political appointees – Balogh, Kaldor and Neild – 'were carefully excluded' (it would have been odd had they not been, since this was a body made up of Permanent Secretaries or their deputies). Sir Eric Roll from the DEA took the chair; the Foreign Office was represented by a Deputy Under-Secretary and former Ambassador to the Communities, Sir Con O'Neill; the Treasury by its Permanent Secretary, Sir William Armstrong, and the Ministry of Agriculture by Sir John Winnifrith (whose own antipathy to Community involvement had not mellowed with time).

This account overstates the hole-and-corner nature of the operation. There was also a Ministerial Cabinet Committee specially set up for the purpose, a committee to which Crossman was apparently invited by mistake, much to the embarrassment of Wilson, who had specifically excluded Jenkins in order to preserve 'balance' [*Diaries*, p. 513].

In other respects the domestic scene looked increasingly propitious for renewed negotiations with the Six. During the summer of 1966 the public opinion polls were showing a more favourable balance of responses towards entry than ever before. Apart from the *Morning Star* and the Beaverbrook papers (which had become much less vociferous since the death of the founder in 1964) Fleet Street was solidly in favour. Industry could hardly wait. Most important of all, the 1966 intake of 65 new Labour MPs was heavily weighted on the European side.

Like the Macmillan government in 1961, the Labour Cabinet had some preliminary hurdles to clear. First there was EFTA. It was evident that the EFTA 'neutrals' – Sweden, Switzerland, Austria and associate Finland – could not be accommodated within the Community corral. So it was going to be necessary to secure for Britain a waiver to the 1961 London agreement, which effectively had meant either 'everybody out' or 'everybody in'.

Fortunately this time round EFTA, although still ostensibly a Board of Trade responsibility, was in the robust hands of George Brown. Arming himself with an assurance that the hated 1964 import

surcharge was to be scrapped forthwith, Brown set off to meet his
EFTA colleagues at Bergen in May. Sure enough, he returned with
what he wanted: a blessing for a unilateral British approach to the
Community.

The second hurdle was much more difficult: the attitude of the
French. Had the veto been withdrawn, or not? Early in July the
French Prime Minister and Foreign Minister, Pompidou and Couve
de Murville, visited London. Wilson subsequently described the visit
as 'agreeable, though of little profit as far as our approach to Europe
was concerned' [Wilson, *Labour Government*, p. 249]. Cecil King,
who lunched with the French Premier, put it less diplomatically.
Pompidou, he recorded in his diary, had 'made it clear that there is
no prospect of admitting Britain to the Common Market at this
stage ... while we're so deeply in hock to the Americans ...'

As soon as the French had departed, the Prime Minister was off to
Moscow, leaving behind an ugly economic crisis. Within a month
Brown was Foreign Secretary. Wilson explains that during July 'we
seemed to be drawing near to the point where we would have to take
a decision about Europe, and George Brown seemed to me the appropriate leader for the task which might lie ahead' [ibid.]. This was
a remarkable over-simplification.

Lord Wigg, still at that time perhaps the Prime Minister's closest
political confidant (and himself a strong anti-Marketeer), in his account [*Memoirs*, pp. 338–9] emphasises the linkage between the
Common Market bid and the financial crisis. 'Wilson's conversion',
according to Wigg, 'flowed from the fact that he had to put Brown
and Callaghan in baulk ...' He concludes that

> The arch-pragmatist had solved the political crisis of the July
> package deal [of economic measures: see Chapter 5] by promising
> to deliver the goods and to float the pound from strength. He could
> not do the first. He had no intention of doing the second. To tour
> Europe was his way out.

The logic of Wigg's account is not wholly apparent. Moreover it
is misleading at several points. It implies that Callaghan was a Market enthusiast, whereas he was nothing of the kind. It also suggests
that Wilson's personal conversion dated from the July crisis, whereas – as we have seen – he had been shifting his ground for several
months, starting even before the March election. It also leaves out of
account one further dimension: the Prime Minister's disillusionment
with his 'special relationship' alternative, stemming from President
Johnson's brusque refusal to save him from the need for another
'July package' of economic measures by offering further financial

assistance as a reward for what he, Wilson, regarded as his good behaviour over Vietnam.

Nevertheless Lord Wigg was right to spot that George Brown's
move to the Foreign Office had much more to do with the outcome of
the financial crisis than it had with any growing sense of urgency
about Europe. The truth, as explained elsewhere, was that the Prime
Minister dared not risk his deputy's withdrawal to the back benches
at this particular juncture, and shrewdly identified the offer of the
Foreign Office as the only one which George Brown would find
irresistible.

From that moment the heat was on. Up to that point the Prime
Minister had gone along with the gathering momentum of events in
Whitehall. Now he himself joined the vanguard. In April Cecil King
had recorded Wilson saying that it would be 'two to three years before we were in' [*Diary*, p. 67]. After the ministerial reshuffle he was
in a hurry.

Little was said about all this at the Labour Party Conference; and
although in his memoirs the Prime Minister made much of the way
in which all levels of government and the whole Parliamentary Party
were drawn into the process of consultation about the Common Market approach, the Cabinet itself was not formally consulted until
after the Party Conference, and by then the Prime Minister himself
was emotionally committed.

There was a difference, indeed, between the Wilson and Macmillan
approaches which struck outsiders. George Woodcock, General
Secretary of the TUC on both occasions, recalls that on the second,
unlike the first, 'there was a quite unmistakable determination to get
in'.

The formal position of the TUC was as it had always been: a
cautious blessing for a voyage of inquiry to find out what would be
involved in membership. In practice there was much less room for
uncertainty than there had been in 1961, because in the interval the
Community had filled in many of the outlines of its ambitions. There
was no longer room for doubt, for example, about the impact of
Community membership on British food prices: and this was one
major factor which had led to a distinct hardening of attitudes among
some of the most powerful trade unions.

George Woodcock described his own attitude towards the Market,
in an article in the *Guardian*, as 'passionless' (to what was it not?).
He had regarded Walter Hallstein, the influential first President of
the Common Market Commission, as a desiccated, nineteenth-century
laissez-faire liberal: by 1966 Hallstein had been eliminated, and the
national governments, directly responsive to national lobbying, were
much more in control. In any case George Brown was skilful at

smothering any potential resistance from the Labour Party's industrial wing. He had set up an Industrial Consultative Committee
under the aegis of the DEA. This had upwards of thirty members,
embracing the TUC, and CBI and the City. 'I always said,' Woodcock
comments somewhat ruefully, 'that if you wanted to avoid consultation you set up the largest possible consultative committee.'

The attitude of the other powerful producer lobby, the NFU, had
evolved significantly since 1961. During the summer of 1966 the fervent anti-market President, Sir Harold Woolley, had handed over to
a moderate from the Welsh borders, Gwilym Williams; and his
prejudice against the Common Market had been a factor (although
not the major factor) in Woolley's departure. For while the Union
could not hope to exercise the influence on a Labour government to
which it could aspire when the Tories were in power, the reality
was that the membership had been leaving Woolley behind. The first
two Labour government farm price reviews had infuriated the rank
and file, and undermined its confidence in the British system of farm
support. Furthermore the realisation had been spreading that the
Community's policy of high protection would be remarkably attractive for most sectors of British agriculture.

In short the Prime Minister and his pro-Market colleagues had
little to fear from the lobbies. The ranks of Government and Whitehall were a different matter. Until the Brussels negotiations had got
well under way in the autumn of 1961 the issue of Europe had been
peripheral to the majority of the thinking public. In the autumn of
1966 this was no longer the case. For the political world – and this
includes the civil servants – Europe was *the* external issue. Attitudes
were, by now, clearly defined.

In Whitehall there were only two Ministries unequivocally in
favour of a fresh approach: the Department of Economic Affairs, and
the Foreign Office. The Board of Trade, now presided over by the
most outspoken anti-Marketeer in the government, Douglas Jay, felt
all its traditional free trade prejudices to be outraged by the *dirigisme* and protectionism of the Community. The Ministry of Agriculture, also now led by a prominent anti-Marketeer, Fred Peart, and
deprived of the influence of Sir Eric Roll, was filled with forebodings.
So was the Treasury, where the Chancellor, Callaghan, was himself
a pronounced sceptic, and where this time round there was no Sir
Frank Lee to silence the doubters.

The line-up in Cabinet in the autumn of 1966 was hardly pro-
pitious. The pro-Europeans numbered nine out of twenty-one:
Wilson himself, Brown, Stewart (now at the DEA), Gardiner (the
Lord Chancellor), Jenkins, Crosland, Longford (leader of the Lords),
Gunter (Labour) and Hughes (Wales). Against them were ranged

Healey (Defence), Ross (Scotland), Jay (Trade), Peart (Agriculture), Greenwood (Housing), Castle (Transport) and Marsh (Power). Wedgwood Benn (Technology) had, until the July crisis, also sided firmly with the opponents, but was now wavering; so was Crossman (Leader of the House). Gordon Walker, now back in the Commons and Minister without Portfolio, Callaghan and Bowden (Commonwealth) were 'don't knows'. Admittedly this crude head-count understates the 'weight' of the pro-European side: among the antis only Healey and possibly Peart ranked as senior members of the Cabinet, and only Castle had a significant following on the back benches. Still, the Prime Minister could hardly be accused of exaggerating when he described the securing of Cabinet approval for the European venture as 'a formidable task' [op. cit., p. 387].

How was it done? John Mackintosh [*The British Cabinet*] implies that the technique of exhaustive discussion was used to stifle dissent:

> A series of papers on the effects of Britain entering the Common Market put before a Cabinet committee would end up as a single memorandum for full Cabinet, and if one of these (i.e. Douglas Jay's at the Board of Trade) was hostile and the others in favour, these would carry the day and Mr Jay's paper would never reach the Cabinet.

Those who were personally involved in the preparation of the paperwork dispute this interpretation. They recall a whole series of papers produced by the officials (and at this stage Balogh, Kaldor and Robert Neild *were* drawn in, unlike what had happened in the summer), designed to assess the short and long-term costs and benefits of entry, together with studies of what might happen to the UK if it 'went it alone', and of the North Atlantic Free Trade Area alternative (embracing the US, Canada and possibly Japan, and the members of EFTA, and any members of the EEC who wanted to join) much favoured by Douglas Jay among others. The 'cost–benefit analysis' was inevitably inconclusive: by this stage the short-term costs were more easily quantifiable than the medium-term benefits of Market membership; but one of those involved recalls that the assessment of splendid isolation 'came to much the same conclusion as Herman Kahn has come to since', while NAFTA was found to exist 'only in the mind' of its leading American protagonist, Senator Javits of New York.

The general impression is left of a skilful hustle, mounted essentially by the Prime Minister himself, in which doubting colleagues were carried along from one stage to the next, 'without commitment', yet at each stage without unnecessary opportunity for contemplation of the extent to which each step implied commitment to the next. As soon as the Party Conference was out of the way Wilson summoned his ministers to Chequers for 'a second debate with no vote' [op. cit., p. 295]. The outcome of this meeting was a decision that the Prime Minister and Foreign Secretary ('Don Quixote and Sancho Panza', as Michael Foot, a persistent critic, was to christen them) would tour the capitals of the Community to test the climate. According to Wilson there was 'a momentary suspicion that [George Brown] would prefer to go alone in the first instance, but ... he suddenly sensed that it was important that I should go too ... to put directly to the European heads of Government the doubts which were still troubling me, and *get them answered* ...' [our italics]. One of the Prime Minister's close confidants gives a somewhat different picture, saying that the Secretary to the Cabinet and he himself tried hard to stop the Prime Minister going. 'We told him if he did he would be committed. But the Prime Minister insisted that he must go too "in order to keep George Brown".'

By November George Brown was confiding to Hugh Cudlipp that 'the juggernaut had started to roll, and nothing could now stop it' [King, *Diary*, 10 November 1966]; while Crossman is reported as telling Cecil King that he was 'trying to persuade the Prime Minister to make a definite commitment at the Mansion House' [at the Lord Mayor's Banquet on 14 November] because 'there is probably more political mileage in being for than against, but none in merely dithering ...' Superficially this was a surprising attitude for one who had, until very recently, been markedly hostile to the whole idea: but it is by no means out of character.

If anything could have 'stopped the juggernaut', it was surely the reception which the British emissaries received from General de Gaulle in January. The Frenchman, by Wilson's own account, informed his visitors with elaborate courtesy that they were wasting their time, and urged them to drop the idea of applying for membership of the Community, and to go for 'either ..."something entirely new", or an agreement for "association" '.

The Prime Minister was not to be put off. His tour completed, ministers were once again summoned to Chequers at the end of March. It appears to have been on this occasion that a curious incident occurred. According to an article by Terry Pitt, a senior member of the Transport House research team, published subsequently in the *Guardian*, ministers should have had before them 'a long paper from Transport House opposing entry, circulated independently to Ministers'; but this was 'withdrawn by despatch-riders at the constitutional directive of the great Sir Burke [Trend]'.

There is a degree of muddled thinking here. It would in fact have been 'unconstitutional' if the document described by Terry Pitt *had* been circulated as a Cabinet paper. But that did not mean that ministers were debarred from having such a paper before them as a Party document; and all those who have worked with him find it inherently implausible that Sir Burke Trend would have taken the initiative in blocking such a document. The logical conclusion seems to be that if ministers did not receive the report from Transport House, that was because their leader did not wish them to do so.

At any rate the meeting proceeded smoothly to the desired conclusion. Patrick Gordon Walker, the Minister without Portfolio, tells us that 'every member spoke, *heads were counted*, and a decision made in effect to apply for entry' [*The Cabinet*, p. 113, our italics]. All that remained was to secure clearance from the back benches.

This was achieved at a series of Party meetings at the Commons in April. Lieber calculates that one-third of the Parliamentary Party was firmly opposed to Market membership, and it was embarrassing that this group included the chairman, the veteran Emanuel Shinwell. Fortunately the Prime Minister had his block vote: upwards of one hundred MPs and peers were members of the government, and whereas in the Tory Party attendance of ministers when the Party is in power is normally banned, in the Labour Party the 'payroll vote', as it was known, was expected to attend and to vote the official ticket. As with the Cabinet, much emphasis was laid on the fact that the government was only seeking endorsement of its decision to open negotiations: it would be time enough to take a decision on the merits of entry when the terms became known. George Brown went out of his way to quash doubts on one score. General de Gaulle, he revealed, had lost the power to impose another veto even if he were of a mind to do so. Would-be rebels also knew that they could only hope to make a gesture, for the Opposition was committed to support the Government (although this knowledge was in practice better calculated to stimulate than to deter rebellion). The Goverment secured what Wilson [op. cit.] called a 'very clear majority'; and when the question was put at the end of the Commons debate at the beginning of May a modest thirty-six out of the 358 Labour MPs joined the small band of Tory anti-marketeers in dividing the House; about another fifty Labour MPs abstained.

Ronald Butt, in *The Power of Parliament*, selects the successive Tory and Labour conversions to the Common Market as classic instances of Prime Ministerial power:

The decision to try to take Britain into the Common Market was essentially that of the Prime Minister, Harold Macmillan. Though

he had the support of important members of the civil service and
of some close colleagues in the Cabinet ... the essential will that
finally determined the decision to negotiate with the Common
Market was that of the Prime Minister ... The decision of the
Labour Government in 1965 [*sic*] to attempt a new approach also
rested ultimately on the Prime Minister, Harold Wilson ... it was
Wilson's will which determined the full Whitehall enquiry into
the consequences of British membership and non-membership
and ... it was the Prime Minister who led the Cabinet into a new
attempt to find a means to entry.

There were indeed, as this account suggests, striking parallels between the two abortive bids to widen the European Community. For
both Prime Ministers Europe was a *pis aller*, resorted to only when
preferred goals had proved unattainable. Macmillan had hoped to
go down to history as the man who healed the breach between east
and west; and as far as Western Europe was concerned he much
preferred the looser, more pragmatic approach of the Treaty of Stockholm. Wilson had hoped to revive the Commonwealth; he clung to
the illusion of British influence in Washington; and he too looked to
the Social Democrat Scandinavians in preference to the Christian
Democrat-inclined members of the Community.

Both Prime Ministers also succeeded in crossing wires with the
Foreign Office. For both instinctively recognised that Gaullist
gradualism suited British requirements and susceptibilities infinitely
better than Monnet-ist fundamentalism. Both men also believed they
knew how to charm de Gaulle, that supreme modern Machiavellian,
into acquiescence. (Macmillan alarmed his Foreign Office advisers
with his penchant for *tête-à-tête* conversations with the Frenchman
conducted in French, a language in which he was fluent but – in the
eyes of his officials – not fluent enough.) Macmillan groped after a
nuclear accommodation with the General. Wilson knew better than
to try that approach, given the susceptibilities of his backbenchers on
the subject of nuclear proliferation. Instead he made a rather forlorn attempt to appeal to de Gaulle's known distaste for 'dollar
imperialism' with imaginative rhetoric about the scope for a 'technological community' once Britain's skills were harnessed to the task.
But the underlying attitude of the two men was the same, and was
well summed up in a comment of Wilson's reported by Cecil King.
He did not wish, he told the newspaper magnate, to take sides between France and her partners, 'particularly as the French are intent
on maintaining a separate foreign and defence policy, which fits in
best with British ... ideas' [*Diary*, p. 67].

To the Foreign Office, by contrast, it is scarcely too strong to say

that de Gaulle represented at this time the incarnation of evil. Crossman [*Diaries*, p. 442] recorded that at the end of January 1966 the
unfortunate Foreign Secretary, Michael Stewart, was persuaded by
his department to circulate a paper to Cabinet denouncing the
General for his plans 'for knocking the supra-national elements out
of the Common Market and for working with the Soviet Union to
get an understanding over Germany's head'. Hardly, one might have
thought, the most persuasive *plaidoyer* to put before a Labour
Cabinet; and sure enough the Foreign Secretary was soundly snubbed
for his pains.

Not that the Foreign Office was staffed with dedicated federalists.
On the contrary, it was as keen on autonomy in matters of foreign
policy as the Quai d'Orsay was. That was just the trouble: the two
professional bodies were old sparring partners for influences in
Europe and beyond. With the return of de Gaulle to power these
ancient jealousies were sharply exacerbated. For the 'special relationship' with Washington lay at the core of British foreign policy
throughout the first twenty-five years of the post-war era; and it was
precisely this 'Anglo-Saxon hegemony' that de Gaulle had vowed to
destroy.

Macmillan's plans for a nuclear entente with France horrified the
Foreign Office because they conflicted directly with Britain's unique
privileges under the MacMahon Acts. By the time the Wilson Government turned towards Europe things had reached the point where
one senior British diplomat, Sir Con O'Neill, was said to have confided to his friends that his aim on the grouse moor was greatly improved if he identified an oncoming bird as the hated General. (The
departmental neurosis may be said to have reached its climax in the
'Soames affair' of the spring of 1969, when a carefully doctored
version of a conversation between the General and the British
Ambassador was leaked by the British diplomatic service to the other
Community capitals in flagrant defiance of all the established canons
of diplomatic behaviour.)

So the primary departmental objective in 1966–7 was not so much
to join the European Community, but to frustrate the General's
plans for turning the Community into a platform for the projection
of French authority. The Foreign Office calculated that so long as the
British candidature for membership was regularly reiterated the
other members of the Community would defer their acquiescence in
the General's schemes. And the record shows it to have been entirely
correct. But it followed from all this that from the moment the
department began to take the Common Market seriously, in 1961, it
consistently looked for support to the 'friendly five'. Macmillan and
Wilson both in turn correctly concluded that it was the French, and

the French alone, who would seal the fate of any application we might make.

Another important similarity between 1961 and 1967 was that on each occasion the decision taken was not to join the Market, but to try and find out whether acceptable conditions for British membership were available (although it is true that the actual format of the Labour application was much more straightforward and unconditional than that of the Conservatives). Time and again it was emphasised, both by Macmillan and by Wilson, that nobody was being asked to endorse the notion of British membership – that would come later, if at all. In reality it is no doubt true that once government had engaged its prestige in a lengthy and detailed negotiation in a blaze of publicity the pressure for acceptance of terms ultimately negotiated was bound to mount. But it takes a remarkably thrawn politician to vote against the decision of his own leaders to investigate a new line of foreign policy – entirely *without commitment*. And if that is true of the back benches it is doubly true of the front benches, where the hazards of ministerial resignation are all too well known.

Yet there are also important, and instructive, differences between the two approaches. Foremost among these is the inherent improbability of the second attempt. In 1961 the commentators were virtually unanimous (one of the present authors was one of the few dissenters) that if only the British Government would pluck up its courage and bid for membership, it could not fail. The Treaty of Rome specifically laid down that membership was available to any Western European democracy which was prepared to accept the conditions of membership; and these were, in 1961, open to a wide variety of interpretations to suit different national tastes. In 1967, by contrast, the conditions of membership were much more precisely and tightly drawn. General de Gaulle had already vetoed one attempt to widen the Community, and the earth had not opened to swallow him up. There was no apparent reason why he should not repeat the treatment: indeed on this occasion he had far stronger justification, in that the state of the British balance of payments cast doubt on the ability of Britain to assume the burdens of membership. The British Government did not even have to speculate about the nature of the French response, as did the Macmillan Government in 1961. It had been told, not once but twice, that there was nothing doing.

So the real mystery about the second attempt is how it ever came to be undertaken. It appears quixotic, to say the least, for a government to embark on a major foreign policy initiative which is known to be doomed to failure before it starts. Admittedly the inherent improbability of the Labour bid could have helped to eliminate some of the obstacles to its launching: ministers and departments with 'doubts' might be discouraged from pressing their misgivings by the calculation that the whole operation was largely academic anyway.

In fact there it little evidence that such calculation played a significant role in the elimination of obstacles to the Labour bid. Among ministers only Denis Healey seems to have reassured himself with the firm belief that membership was not going to materialise anyway. But when he used this argument to dissuade others who shared his antipathy from taking drastic action, the general response seems to have been that the Prime Minister's determination to proceed was such that he would indeed 'not take "no" for an answer'. Evidently neither the Prime Minister nor George Brown was inclined to reveal to colleagues the strength of the warnings uttered by M. Pompidou and his party when they came to London in the summer of 1966, and reiterated by the General himself in Paris at the beginning of 1967.

The key question is how did the Prime Minister and the Foreign Secretary come to show such blithe disregard for the warning signals from Paris? In George Brown's case it is perhaps not unfair to say that, in the words of one senior civil servant, 'he was temperamentally inclined to charge at brick walls'. Nor was this personal predisposition as strongly restrained by departmental attitudes as has sometimes been suggested since by the diplomats themselves.

It is perfectly true that the Foreign Secretary did not take kindly to advice which conflicted with his own intentions. There is evidence that the career prospects of Sir Patrick Reilly, the Ambassador in Paris at the time, were not advanced by the consistency with which he gave forewarning of French opposition to a new British bid to join the Market. George Brown's assurance to the Parliamentary Labour Party in March 1967 that de Gaulle had lost the power to impose a second veto represented a flight of personal fancy rather than a departmental attitude.

Yet at the same time, as already noted, the Foreign Office did have a departmental interest in the renewal of British approaches to the Market however doomed they might be. John Mackintosh quotes the anti-Europeans in the government as feeling that by the spring of 1967 the Foreign Office had become 'a pressure group rather than a Department of State, and that its enthusiasm about the prospect of British entry had outrun its judgement ...' A more revealing comment was that of the Permanent Under-Secretary, Sir Paul Gore-Booth, as recorded by Cecil King in November 1966. King, in conversation with Gore-Booth, had described the Common Market as a red herring intended to distract attention from Rhodesia and troubles at home. 'Gore-Booth and his very attractive wife both said "but the red herring, having been trundled across the stage, cannot be trundled back again".'

Civil servants have a professional interest in political bi-partisan-ship. They hate seeing major policy issues subject to Party conflict. If only a Tory government can be persuaded to espouse prices and incomes legislation, or a Labour government to launch a negotiation with Europe, then when the other side returns to power, as no doubt it will, the front benches will be in accord. In practice it is a strategy which rarely works out – it failed to do so in the case of the Common Market after the 1970 election. But the strong Whitehall instinct remains. Why restrain George Brown from hitting his head against a brick wall if, in the process, he can commit his Party for the future?

When all this is said, however, Ronald Butt is surely right to identify Harold Wilson, and not George Brown or the Foreign Office, as the prime mover in 1966–7. Indeed the evidence of Prime Minis-terial initiative is far stronger in the case of Harold Wilson, the sceptic, than it is in the case of Harold Macmillan, the enthusiast for European unity from back in the 1940s.

No single explanation of Wilson's conversion suffices. There was an element of straightforward Cabinet management about it, as George Wigg suggests; but then there was an element of this about almost all his decisions. The press was overwhelmingly favourable to a bid for entry in the summer of 1966, and Harold Wilson was certainly not averse to being seen in a favourable light in Fleet Street. The public opinion polls suggested a high tide of European enthusiasm in the country, and the Prime Minister paid more attention to opinion polls than he was inclined to admit.

In a contemporary satirical play, *Mrs Wilson's Diary*, based on a popular magazine series of the same name in *Private Eye*, Harold Wilson was depicted as regularly consulting a filing cabinet in which were contained the details of Macmillan's policy initiatives. There was an element of truth about this picture too. Wilson regarded his predecessor as a highly skilful political operator. Furthermore, as one of his senior ministerial colleagues comments, he was 'never averse to pinching the Tories' clothes'; and if he admired Macmillan, he was profoundly antipathetic to the leader of the Opposition, Edward Heath. The fact that a Labour application to join the Community would cause Heath embarrassment with some of his own back benchers was hardly a disadvantage in the eyes of the Prime Minister.

Above all, perhaps, there was the 'better 'ole' syndrome. The Commonwealth had not lived up to expectations; EFTA and the 'special relationship' had gone sour; the 'white heat of the technological revolution' had been virtually extinguished with the tacit abandonment of the National Plan as a result of the July 1966 economic measures. Like Macmillan in 1961, Wilson in 1966 badly needed a new 'theme'.

Nor is the fact that Wilson's determination in 1966–7 was more wholehearted than Macmillan's had been in 1961 really as paradoxical as it appears at first sight. For Wilson is, *par excellence*, the hopeful traveller. Macmillan continued to hesitate about the wisdom of the 1961 approach not so much because – as hostile witnesses like George Ball would have us believe – he was scared of big initiatives, but because he was genuinely sceptical about the chances of overcoming de Gaulle's resistance, and correctly foresaw the disastrous consequences of committing his Government and Party to a flop. Wilson, by contrast, saw little point in losing sleep about the distant scene. The mere fact of launching negotiations would secure impressive headlines and convey a sense of positive action. It would be time enough to worry about the consequences of another rebuff when it happened.

In a way both Prime Ministers were right. De Gaulle's January 1963 veto, when it came, spelled the beginning of the end for the Macmillan Government. His second veto, in the autumn of 1967, was swiftly forgotten in the trauma of devaluation.

4 How the Stern Unbending Tories Bent: The Decision to Abolish Resale Price Maintenance, 1963–4

A decade later it may seem almost bizarre to include in any short list of key political decisions of the sixties the Resale Prices Act of 1964. This unremarkable departmental measure, whose effect was to abolish the right of manufacturers to dictate the prices at which their goods are sold in the shops, earns its place as the occasion of the most serious backbench revolt against a Conservative Government since the war. Moreover this rare form of parliamentary conflict (backbench revolts are customarily reserved for Labour Governments) was parallelled by conflict both within the Cabinet itself and between the Government and a well-organised pressure group. The resolution of conflict sheds most light on the distribution of power in any system, society or polity, and on this score alone the abolition of resale price maintenance (RPM) provides an illuminating case study.

The principal actor in the drama of 1964 was, of course, the Minister responsible for introducing the Bill, Mr Edward Heath, then rejoicing in the somewhat Pooh-Bah-ish title of Secretary of State for Industry, Trade and Regional Development and President of the Board of Trade. But this was only the final act in a play that had been running, with occasional intervals, more or less ever since the war. Continuity on this scale, persisting while individual ministers and governments come and go, can only mean one thing: a Departmental Policy. Such, *par excellence*, was the case with RPM.

Throughout the twenty-five years from the end of the war to its merger with the Ministry of Technology in 1970 to form the Department of Trade and Industry, the Board of Trade was imbued with a strong departmental philosophy of free trade and free competition. RPM was thus anathema, since its avowed purpose was to prevent price competition among retailers over a wide range of branded goods. (The general attitude of the Board of Trade, throughout the RPM affair, is best characterised in the words of Adam Smith [*The Wealth of Nations*, Book 1, Chapter 10, Part 2]: 'People of the same trade seldom meet together even for merriment or diversion, but the conversation ends in a conspiracy against the public, or in some contrivance to raise prices.')

It was in August 1947, with the legislation to set up the Monopolies Commission already in the pipeline, that the Board of Trade turned its attention to RPM for the first time during the post-war period. Labour was in office, Sir Stafford Cripps was President of the Board of Trade, and a departmental committee under the chairmanship of Mr G. H. Lloyd Jacob, K.C., was set up to inquire into the practice. The practitioners, in turn, immediately retaliated by reactivating (on a rather smaller scale) a pre-war pressure group for the defence of RPM, the self-styled Fair Trading Congress; and the broad lines of the battle that finally came to a head with the Act of 1964 were drawn.

The pressure group was an alliance of some of the leading trade associations whose members practiced RPM. Some of them – including the oldest and perhaps the strongest of all, the Proprietary Articles Trade Association, founded in 1896, to which the retail chemists and pharmaceutical companies belonged – had been expressly established to combat price-cutting.

There are (or were) two forms of RPM: individual and collective. In individual RPM, the individual manufacturer lays down a minimum retail price for the goods he supplies, and enforces this by the threat to withhold supplies from any retailer who sells below the minimum price. In collective RPM, the policing and enforcement is carried out by the trade association, and the sanction is considerably greater. Ultimately, any shopkeeper who cut the price of a price-maintained product would risk being the victim of collective boycott which would deny him the whole range of goods with which the trade association is concerned: this could well put him out of business altogether. This extreme penalty was the ultimate deterrent: the normal practice in collective RPM was for the trade association to 'try' any retailer accused of price-cutting, and, if he were found guilty, to fine him for it. Manufacturers who were not members of a trade association would in turn be deterred from flouting the rules of the RPM game by the knowledge that, were they to do so, the shopkeeper members of the relevant trade association would cease to stock their goods.

It was collective RPM that was the predominant form of the practice at the time the Lloyd Jacob Committee was set up in 1947, and the purpose of the pressure group formed by the trade associations responsible for policing and enforcing this practice was principally to organise the giving of evidence to the Committee in favour of RPM.

The Lloyd Jacob Committee reported in March 1949 to Cripps's

successor as President of the Board of Trade, Mr Harold Wilson. So
far as collective RPM was concerned, the Committee's recommendation was unequivocal: the practice should be made illegal. On
individual RPM, however, its finding was more complicated. It was
sufficiently impressed by the evidence in favour of RPM – notably the
'loss leader' argument that, without RPM, experience had shown that
trade would be disrupted by the use of carefully selected massive
price cuts as a form of promotion – to recommend that individual
RPM should *not* be made illegal. On the other hand, it believed that
the practice should not be used 'to obstruct the development of
particular methods of trading ... or to deprive the public of the
benefits of improvements in distribution', and suggested that the
Board of Trade should sit down with the trade associations to work
out an agreed way of making this somewhat imprecise recommendation effective.

The government considered the Lloyd Jacob Report, ultimately at
Cabinet level, and decided that legislation on so controversial an
issue was not practicable – at least, not during that parliament. Accordingly, in June 1949, the President of the Board of Trade published the Lloyd Jacob Report and simultaneously announced the
Government's own 'compromise' proposal. The gist of this was that,
in the light of the evidence produced in the Report, the Government
called on manufacturers and traders to abandon collective RPM
voluntarily, and that in due course, as recommended by the Committee, it would hold discussions with industry to find an agreed way
of tempering the use of individual RPM. This statement was soon
followed by meetings between the Board and the Federation of
British Industries (FBI), the predecessor of the Confederation of
British Industry (CBI) as the principal spokesman of, and officially
recognised pressure group for, manufacturing industry.

The RPM pressure group, which had manifestly failed in its
narrow objective of securing a pro-RPM Report, promptly re-
constituted itself as the Fair Prices Defence Committee, with wider
aims and more open methods. It quickly succeeded, through personal
contacts and some overlap in membership, in influencing the FBI's
stance on RPM, but it was less successful in securing direct access to
the Board of Trade in its own right. It accordingly settled on a policy
of concerted passive resistance. Wilson's optimistic plea for the
voluntary abandonment of collective RPM was simply ignored.
Eventually, in April 1950, he reluctantly agreed to a meeting with
representatives of the pressure group. For his part, he hoped that this
might lead to a more co-operative attitude on the part of the trade
associations. The FPDC's hope was that, as a result of this breakthrough, it would emerge as the officially recognised spokesman for

the RPM interest, an accredited pressure group with an automatic right of access to, and consultation by, the government. Both hopes were to prove unfounded.

Nevertheless, in the eyes of the pressure group it did look now as if the danger to RPM had been averted. In the General Election earlier that year the Labour government had seen its overall majority slashed from 147 to an exiguous six. If Labour had been unwilling to grasp the nettle and legislate during the previous parliament, there could certainly be no question of its doing anything now. It could only be a matter of time before the Conservatives returned to office; and, throughout the Lloyd Jacob debates, Tory backbenchers had demonstrated a heartwarming affection for RPM.

The Board of Trade, however, drew a rather different moral. The Lloyd Jacob episode had demonstrated two things: first, that the notion of ending collective RPM by voluntary means was doomed to failure; and, second, that the Committee's idea of drawing an agreed line between permissible and impermissible forms of individual RPM was equally a non-starter. There was thus nothing for it but to legislate against both collective and individual RPM.

There could have been no clearer earnest of the Department's long-term intentions, nor of its determination to carry them through, than the publication in June 1951 of a White Paper, baldly announcing that the Government proposed to introduce legislation to make both collective and individual RPM illegal – subject only to the somewhat obscure proviso that '... in drafting the legislation the government will take account of any cases where it may be established that exceptional conditions would render the operation of the proposed provisions unworkable or undesirable in the public interest'.

At one level this seemed little more than an anti-inflation public relations exercise. Legislation on this controversial issue at that time was never a practical possibility. The government was manifestly on its last legs – indeed, the White Paper proposals themselves had to be introduced to Parliament by a new President of the Board of Trade, Sir Hartley Shawcross, his predecessor, Harold Wilson, having resigned from the government, along with Aneurin Bevan, only seven weeks previously. Four months after the Shawcross statement, before any Bill could be drafted, Labour was out of office.

But the Board of Trade was not out of office. And for the Board, this curious, last-gasp White Paper was no mere public relations exercise. It was a Declaration of Intent.

Whereas the Labour manifesto for the 1951 General Election contained a more or less explicit pledge to legislate against RPM – 'We shall prohibit by law the withholding of supplies to traders who bring prices down' – the Conservative manifesto was notably vaguer, stating only that: 'We believe in the necessity for reducing to the minimum all restrictive practices on both sides of industry, and we shall rely on a greatly strengthened Monopolies Commission to seek, and enable Parliament to correct, any operations in restraint of trade, including of course those in the nationalised industries.' It was, therefore, natural that, when the Conservatives returned to office in 1951, the Board of Trade – now under Mr Peter Thorneycroft as President – should look to the Monopolies Commission as the key to reopening the issue of RPM. Accordingly, in December 1952, the Department asked the Commission to examine, for the first time, not a specific industry but a specific practice: 'collective discrimination'.

Although, with the Tories now in office, the pressure group felt more confident, it was taking no chances. In January 1952 it sought, and secured, an undertaking from Thorneycroft that he would meet and consult it in advance of any legislation concerning RPM. With this crucial assurance, it sat back and then, following the announcement of the Monopolies Commission inquiry, set out to prepare the ground in other ways. Favourable evidence to the Commission on RPM was carefully co-ordinated. The important link with the FBI, established during the Lloyd Jacob episode, was further cultivated. Through the shopworkers' trade union, USDAW, the TUC was persuaded to take a mildly pro-RPM line which lasted, in fact, throughout the fifties. Overtures were made to the Co-operative movement, important by virtue of its links with the Labour Party and its sponsored MPs, which was badly split over RPM, and something like benevolent neutrality seems to have been secured.

But above all the pressure group set out to build up substantial backbench support for RPM on the Government side of the House. And it found the soil, not surprisingly, fertile. If England is a nation of shopkeepers, the Conservative Party's claim to be a truly national Party can hardly be gainsaid. Not that shopkeepers as such were conspicuously well represented among the Tories in Parliament; but the disproportionate presence of small shopkeepers among the Party activists and supporters in the constituencies was something of which no Conservative MP could be unaware.

By the time the Monopolies Commission Report on 'Collective Discrimination' landed on the desk of the President of the Board of Trade in the early part of 1955, it was clear that the government had an issue of considerable delicacy on its hands. But first, in May, there was the hurdle of a General Election to be overcome. Reference was made in the manifesto to RPM in the most guardedly neutral terms;

and then, a month after the Conservative government had been returned with an increased majority, the Commission's report was published. A fortnight later Thorneycroft announced the government's
intentions to the House of Commons: in the interim he had made
good his promise to initiate consultations with the pressure group.

On RPM the Commission had been unable to reach agreement,
with six members taking a hard line, three a soft line, and a tenth
siding partly with the majority and partly with minority. The
majority called for legislation to abolish, outright, collective RPM
(with all its apparatus of trade courts) and, with provision for individual exemptions, collective agreements to enforce individual RPM
as well. (Individual RPM individually enforced had been outside
the Commission's terms of reference.) The minority, however, recommended that collective arrangements of both kinds should merely
be formally registered and made subject to a detailed, case-by-case
examination to determine whether or not they were in the public
interest.

Accordingly, months of 'consultations' ensued, conducted against
a background of massive backbench pressure on the government.
This was a pressure which was no less formidable for being exerted
largely behind the scenes: it is easy, but mistaken, to allow the open
rebellion of 1964 to eclipse the more conventional opposition of
1956. Mackintosh [op. cit. p. 582] notes that 'some members of the
Conservative Cabinet doubted whether they could persuade the
Party to accept the Restrictive Trade Practices Bill in 1956', and a
former senior Board of Trade official reckons that 'the backbench
fuss about RPM in 1956 was much greater than in 1964.'

Still, in the end, a compromise did emerge on this occasion. The
1956 Restrictive Trade Practices Act banned collective RPM, in the
traditional sense of collective enforcement. Collective agreements to
enforce individual RPM would, like other restrictive trade practices,
have to be formally registered and defended in the newly-created
Restrictive Practices Court. But – and this was the important *quid
pro quo* secured by the pressure group – individual RPM, individually enforced, was given a legal backing it had never hitherto
possessed. Under Section 25 of the Act – the so-called 'non-signer'
clause – any retailer taking delivery of a product which he had been
notified was subject to RPM was legally obliged to sell it at the
maintained price, irrespective of whether or not he had contracted
to do so; and should he sell it below the maintained price the manufacturer could take him to court.

After nine years' continuous work, the pressure group at last felt
able to relax. Yet it had not gone wholly unnoticed that, in introducing the 1956 legislation to Parliament, Thorneycroft had declared

that so far as RPM was concerned, the Bill represented '... the first, although perhaps not the last ... proposals on the matter'. The Board of Trade, having settled for the time being for half a loaf, remained determined to secure the other half as soon as the opportunity arose.

So far as the permanent officials were concerned, that opportunity seemed to come with the result of the General Election of 1959. The government had been returned with a still larger majority, the Board had been given a new President, Mr Reginald Maudling, who, like any new minister, would obviously be looking for something to do, and the first year of a parliament is always the best time to push through any controversial measure. Moreover, since 1956 the tide of events had seemed to be moving still further in a favourable direction. In 1958 the Council on Productivity, Prices and Incomes, better known as the Three Wise Men, a strange triumvirate which had been set up the previous year by the new Prime Minister, Mr Harold Macmillan, in order to provide sage and impartial counsel on the nation's perennial economic problem, produced its first report, in which it suggested, *inter alia*, that the abolition of individual RPM might be worth thinking about. More important, however, the late fifties had seen the irruption in Britain of the so-called 'retailing revolution' – the emergence and rapid growth of self-service stores and supermarkets, as a result of which, by 1959, RPM in the grocery trade had irreparably broken down.

It was against this background that the permanent officials at the Board of Trade presented their new political head, in the winter of 1959, with a formal submission on RPM, giving the arguments on both sides at scrupulous length, coming down unequivocally in favour of abolition, and proposing, in some detail, legislation along the lines that were eventually to be followed to the letter in 1964. As soon as he had considered the departmental submission, Maudling informed his advisers that although he, personally, was 100 per cent in favour of the measure they were suggesting, he saw little point in putting it to the Cabinet since it was bound to be shot down – a view in which it seems he had been reinforced after informal consultations with a number of his colleagues. Although his officials were deeply disappointed at what seemed to them so defeatist an approach at so opportune a time, Maudling was undoubtedly better aware than they were of the change in the climate of top Tory thinking that roughly coincided with the replacement of Sir Anthony Eden by Macmillan in 1957.

Partly, of course, this simply reflected the fact that there had been a considerable rise in unemployment between the two elections; and partly too, the pendulum of intellectual fashion. But there can be little doubt that Macmillan's own personal economic philosophy was also a factor. The Prime Minister had, since the depression years of the thirties, entertained a suspicion of the free market; and in the context of RPM it was of at least equal significance that, as he frequently reminded his Cabinet colleagues, he was a publisher by trade. Nor was he just *any* publisher. The book trade was one whose very survival, so it maintained, depended on RPM, which it religiously practised under the terms of a long-standing collective arrangement (duly registered under the 1956 Act) known as the Net Book Agreement of 1899. And the architect and progenitor of the Net Book Agreement had been Sir Frederick Macmillan, the Prime Minister's uncle, and then head of the family publishing firm. (With a fine sense of irony Sir Frederick chose, in 1890, as his company's first book to be sold under individual RPM, Alfred Marshall's *Principles of Economics*.)

Any Cabinet Minister who contemplates seeking the consent of his colleagues to the introduction of a highly controversial piece of legislation will attach considerable importance to securing the approval, or at least avoiding the disapproval, of the Prime Minister of the day. Not surprisingly, Maudling did not feel confident of obtaining Macmillan's support for an RPM Bill. Personality, too, plays a part. The Board of Trade were delighted that they had a new minister of manifest ability, a man who (although young, and still on the way up) could be expected to carry weight in Cabinet. But what they also had was someone who, in contrast to their own crusading zeal, felt that very few issues indeed were worth a row. And the abolition of RPM was certainly not one of them.

Nevertheless the issue was no longer one that would go away of its own accord. Rumours began to appear in the press that RPM abolition was in the air, and questions were asked from both sides of the Commons about the Government's intentions. Maudling quickly came to the conclusion that his only way out was to buy time by setting up yet another inquiry into RPM. But this one, he explained to the House when announcing the event in March 1960, would be different: unlike its predecessors, it would not be a public inquiry listening to evidence for and against RPM and reaching a verdict; it would be a confidential inquiry, conducted within the Board of Trade, and concerned simply with establishing the facts of the case – the precise extent of RPM, and so on. A decision on whether or not to legislate could then be taken on a more informed basis.

Immediately after Maudling's announcement, the pressure group sought an urgent meeting with him, in an attempt to persuade him that a further inquiry would – in the words of one of the Fair Prices Defence Committee's backbench sympathisers, the then Prime Minister's son, Mr Maurice Macmillan – 'be unnecessary and futile'. A delegation composed of the President of the FPDC (and secretary of PATA), Mrs H. E. Chapman, and representatives of the National Chamber of Trade (a key constituent member of the FPDC) called on the Board of Trade, and was condescendingly granted an audience with the Department's Parliamentary Secretary, Mr John Rodgers.

The pressure group was to have only one further meeting with the Board of Trade – in January 1961, to elucidate one or two points on some questionnaires the department had sent out – before RPM received its sentence of death in 1964. In the meantime, in June 1960, it had undergone yet another change of name, to become the more explicit (if less persuasive) Resale Price Maintenance Co-ordinating Committee, under a new chairman, Mr Leonard Pagliero of the Stationers' Association. But more than a mere change in nomenclature was involved. Although its hard core remained the same group of trade associations, the new RPMCC had more than twice as many members as the old FPDC – an achievement assisted by the pressure group's decision to open its membership, for the first time, to individual companies, in both manufacturing and re-tailing. Tobacco, record, drug and confectionery firms were among those who joined and gave financial support. A full-time public relations team was hired and, in general, the pressure group felt that, stronger than ever before, it was in a position to deal with some confidence with any White Paper and subsequent Bill which it feared would emerge once the Departmental 'fact-finding' inquiry was complete.

By the end of the year, in addition to an abundance of letters, pamphlets and documentary 'briefing' in general, the RPMCC had arranged for a series of small dinners to be held at the House of Commons, under the sponsorship of Mr Robert Carr (then an ex-junior minister and former PPS to the previous Prime Minister), at each of which four backbench MPs and four representatives of trade associations would be able to talk informally about RPM. Carr had earlier agreed to approach the Tory backbench Trade and Industry Committee in the RPM cause. But although the pressure group could feel that it was making useful headway within the governing Party in Parliament, the failure to maintain contact with the Board of Trade was to prove a grave tactical error. Another – albeit lesser – mistake may well have been the ignoring of the Co-operative Movement by the RPMCC. At all events, at the Annual Congress of the Co-operative Union, in May 1961, the movement came out for the first time, and to the dismay of many of its members, unequivocally against RPM.

In October 1961 Maudling was appointed Colonial Secretary, and was replaced as President of the Board of Trade by a newcomer to the

Cabinet, Mr Frederick Erroll, a politician of considerably less 'weight' who had hitherto been Maudling's deputy as Minister of State at the Board of Trade. As with the appointment of Maudling two years earlier, the permanent officials decided that here, once again, with a new minister, was their opportunity to complete the unfinished business of 1956. Accordingly, that winter, they dusted down the formal submission for the abolition of RPM they had previously presented to Maudling and resubmitted it to Erroll. But this time it was accompanied by the long-awaited report of the departmental fact-finding committee (which showed, if it needed showing, that, in general, RPM was certainly not withering away as it had in the grocery trade), together with yet another departmental report on the effects of RPM and its abolition in other countries (which allegedly showed, *inter alia*, that abolition had not meant the demise of the small shopkeeper).

Erroll was quickly convinced, and in January 1962 he duly presented the Economic Policy Committee of the Cabinet with a paper embodying the Board's proposal for the abolition of RPM. In the words of one witness, 'it was torn to pieces'. Erroll's most emphatic opponent was Lord Hailsham (at the time Lord President of the Council), who argued that to try and prevent a manufacturer from making a maintained price a condition of sale was to undermine the sanctity of contract – a topic on which he expatiated at some length and with considerable eloquence. All Erroll could salvage was permission to take the proposal to the Cabinet itself.

It is a convention of the Cabinet Committee system that, if a Minister presents a paper to a Cabinet Committee, and the matter is then referred to the full Cabinet, it is the Chairman of the Cabinet Committee who presents the proposal to the Cabinet, and not the Minister whose paper it originally was. It was Erroll's further misfortune that the regular Chairman of the Economic Policy Committee, the Chancellor of the Exchequer, had not been present at the meeting at which RPM abolition had been proposed, and in his place the chair had been taken by the Lord President. It was, therefore, Hailsham, the dedicated opponent, who presented Erroll's paper to the Cabinet – although Erroll, of course, spoke to it as well.

Not surprisingly, it received short shrift: the consensus of the Economic Policy Committee was confirmed after only the briefest discussion. Most of the senior Ministers, headed by Mr R. A. Butler, the *de facto* deputy Premier, remembering the trouble there had been in 1955/6, and knowing that backbench opinion was in a bad enough state as it was in the aftermath of the pay pause and other economic measures of July 1961, felt that, whatever the economic merits of the proposal, politically it was far more trouble than it was worth. As for Macmillan himself (who had been known to observe, in private, that, because the Net Book Agreement did not operate there, there was no longer a decent bookshop left in America), he was content to comment mockingly that the President of the Board of Trade was a Cobdenite masquerading as a Conservative. According to a senior Board of Trade official, recalling this whole episode, Erroll 'was trounced – there is no other word for it'.

While all this was happening, however, rumours began to spread among Conservative backbenchers and even to creep into the press that something was up. The Trade and Industry Committee asked Erroll to meet them to speak and answer questions on RPM (which he did, giving as little away as he could) and pro-RPM back-benchers began to bombard the Chief Whip, Mr Martin Redmayne – who, as former managing director of the family firm of Redmayne & Todd, the Nottingham-based sports outfitters, was not unsympathetic to their case. Eventually, at the end of January, after his 'trouncing' was completed, to scotch the rumours and end speculation, Erroll announced to the House that he had put in hand yet another de-partmental inquiry – this time to review all aspects of policy and legislation on monopolies and restrictive practices. Meanwhile the Gallup Poll, for the first time, asked people whether they thought it best 'for manufacturers to fix the price of their goods and insist that shopkeepers sell them at the same price', or to 'let shopkeepers fix their own prices and sell their goods below prices recommended by the manufacturer if they want to'. The result was a two-to-one majority against RPM.

Back at the Board of Trade, the officials were deeply disappointed by the whole débâcle, feeling that they had been let down by their minister in both Cabinet Committee and Cabinet. It was only later that they came to feel that they were probably wrong to put Erroll, a Cabinet lightweight, up to it in the first place. As for the pressure group, they should have been as pleased as the Department was disappointed: in fact, they were becoming increasingly out of touch with what was happening in Government and felt distinctly uneasy as a result.

But even if the pressure group had been wholly *in* touch, it could hardly have been expected to foresee the next reapparance of RPM on the agenda. As 1962 went by Macmillan became increasingly de-pressed by the politico-economic situation at home. Thoroughly fed up with the Treasury and all its works, he set to work in the middle of June, as he describes in his memoirs, 'to devise some new treat-ment by my own efforts'. Within a few days he had completed a paper entitled 'Incomes Policy: a new approach'. The 'new approach' had three elements: a non-statutory pay board, to pronounce on the relative merits of different pay claims; and two packages of measures, one designed to give new 'status and security' to the worker, the other to give new protection to the consumer. The consumer package was based on the final report of the Molony Committee on Consumer Protection, which had been set up in June 1959 by Thorneycroft's successor and Maudling's predecessor as President of the Board of Trade, Sir David Eccles. This report was at last in the Government's hands, although it had not yet been published. Its central recommendation was the setting up of a state-financed Consumer Council; but it had also suggested that RPM, although strictly speaking outside its terms of reference, was probably a Bad Thing. Macmillan included both the Consumer Council and RPM abolition in his 'new approach'.

In its original form, the Macmillan plan never reached the Cabinet. The Prime Minister was still at the earlier stage of discussing it with groups of selected Ministers when he decided on the 'night of the long knives' of 13 July 1962, which was scarcely less shattering to Conservative backbenchers than it was to the Cabinet itself. When, towards the end of July, Macmillan put a watered-down version of his 'new approach' to the new Cabinet he was careful to exclude the contentious proposal to abolish RPM. The situation had become quite fraught enough without that.

Nevertheless the momentary relaxation of Macmillan's personal hostility to RPM abolition was not without its consequences. For Erroll, who had survived the purge in which one-third of the Cabinet had perished, felt sufficiently emboldened to try, albeit in a more circumspect way, to return to the subject – particularly since the wholesale reshuffle had removed some of the leading opponents of his earlier attempt, among them Lord Mills and Selwyn Lloyd himself, and brought into the Cabinet such dependable allies of the abolitionist cause as Sir Edward Boyle and Sir Keith Joseph. Moreover throughout the latter half of 1962 Erroll continued to be embarrassed by demands from backbench Tory friends of RPM (and of the pressure group) for a categorical and firm assurance that Government would *not* bring in legislation against RPM – an assurance which, in the circumstances, he was hardly in a position to give.

He therefore decided to suggest, as a compromise situation, that individual RPM as such should be brought within the procedure under the 1956 Act for dealing with collective agreements to enforce individual RPM. Accordingly, during the early part of 1963, Erroll put up a paper to the Economic Policy Committee of the Cabinet, advocating this approach. Maudling, now, as Chancellor of the Exchequer, Chairman of the Economic Policy Committee, suggested, and the Committee agreed, that, before any decision of any kind was taken, it might be wise to discuss the matter with the Prime Minister.

The discussion was not to take place. Macmillan had scarcely recovered from the shock of the breakdown of the Common Market negotiations at the end of January 1963 when he was immersed in the Profumo affair; he had barely emerged from the long-drawn-out disruption of that bizarre scandal when, in October 1963, illness forced resignation upon him. He was succeeded as Prime Minister by the Earl of Home (shortly to re-emerge as Sir Alec Douglas-Home); and with the new administration there came a new man to the Board of Trade – Mr Edward Heath.

Heath had initially been very disappointed to be offered nothing better in the new administration than the Presidency of the Board of Trade, and indeed only accepted after receiving assurances from Home that the job would carry greatly enhanced status and responsibilities, including elevation to the top ministerial rank of Secretary of State. Then, while his senior Cabinet colleagues ruefully licked the wounds suffered in the recent leadership struggle, he busily set about finding something worthwhile to achieve during the brief period – a year, at most – that remained before the next General Election; something that would help erase the memory of the earlier failure of his Common Market negotiations. Moreover Heath was convinced that the government's only chance of winning the election lay in seizing the initiative from the Opposition – something that only action, and dramatic action at that, could achieve. Immediately on arrival at the Board of Trade, therefore, he instructed his officials to forget everything that was in the pipeline (this included Erroll's 'compromise' proposal on RPM) and, in conjunction with the new Minister of State at the Board of Trade, Mr Edward du Cann, to compile a brand new list of measures of the type he sought. A list was duly compiled. Du Cann's preference was for a reform of company law (the Jenkins Report had been published in June 1962, and no action had been taken on it so far); but Heath could not see this setting the heather alight. The Department, more or less as a matter of course, included the abolition of RPM, but they did not press it, assuming that so contentious a proposal was hardly suitable for the last few months before a General Election.

In any event, the Secretary of State had already made up his mind what his dramatic action was to be: a brand new regional policy. 'Plans for comprehensive regional development' were prominently written into the Queen's Speech for the new session of Parliament – its theme was 'the modernisation of Britain' and it contained no mention of competition or monopolies, let alone RPM. Meanwhile the senior Board of Trade officials were beginning to entertain second thoughts. They had, of course, been delighted with Heath's appoint-

ment in October: they had recognised straight away their good
fortune in acquiring a genuinely 'heavyweight' minister who could
be expected to hold his own in Cabinet, and they welcomed the new
responsibilities and importance for the Department. But what they
had not at first appreciated was the strength of Heath's determination to make a real impact during the remaining months of the old
parliament. As they watched their new master in action, it began to
dawn on them that they might have been over-hasty in writing off
RPM abolition during the pre-election period after all.

Moreover a new factor had entered the equation. In 1963, trading
stamps, for the first time in Britain, began to catch on on a large
scale as the aggressive new supermarket chains (notably Tesco and
Fine Fare) vied for a larger share of a booming consumer expenditure. The established retailers were appalled by this surrogate price-
cutting. In July, Lord Sainsbury called on the Government to
control the operation of trading stamp companies. One of Erroll's
very last acts as President of the Board of Trade had been to turn
down, on 7 October, a written request from a Labour Member, Mr
John Stonehouse, for a government inquiry into the effect of stamp
trading on the cost of living.

By the end of October the established retailers had become sufficiently alarmed to set up an *ad hoc* pressure group, the so-called
Distributive Trades Alliance, led by J. Sainsbury and Allied Suppliers, specifically to fight the trading stamp menace: the DTA
claimed to represent over four-fifths of all multiple groups in the
United Kingdom, and its small 'Action Committee' included representatives of such prominent chains as (in addition to the two prime
movers) Boots, Marks & Spencer, W. H. Smith, Macfisheries (the
Unilever subsidiary) and the Victoria Wine Company. And by mid-
November it had become clear what form the 'fight' was to take: in
the words of EMI, the gramophone record company, in its warning to
shopkeepers at the time, 'remedial action will be taken if retailers
give stamps with their products. This action could take the form of
refusing to supply them with goods, or, ultimately, court action.'
The court action referred to was prosecution under Section 25 of the
1956 Restrictive Trade Practices Act – the section that gave legal
backing to individual RPM.

Immediately parliament had reassembled, on 12 November, Com-
mander Kerans, a Tory backbench friend of the RPM lobby, had
given notice of a question to the new President of the Board of Trade
to ask whether the government would introduce legislation to prohibit trading stamps 'in the interests of consumers'. On the evening
of Wednesday 20 November, when the Trade and Industry Committee met for the first of its weekly meetings of the new session, it

was clear that Heath intended to reiterate the *laissez-faire* Board of Trade line previously spelled out by Erroll in reply to Stonehouse. An unusually lively, well-attended and divided meeting of this hitherto rather sleepy backbench committee was almost entirely devoted to the stamp controversy; and, although RPM was not mentioned, one of the Whips present noted at the time that 'I believe we are going to hear a great deal more about this seemingly innocuous domestic issue.'

Then, the following day, came the ballot for Private Members' Bills. First place was drawn by John Stonehouse, then President of the London Co-operative Society and the movement's leading MP; second by Mr John Osborn, a Conservative. Stonehouse's original inclination was to follow up his approach to Erroll and do something about trading stamps; but Osborn had already promised his friend, coeval and fellow Yorkshire Tory MP of the class of 1959, Wilfred Proudfoot, owner of a small chain of (non-stamp-trading) self-service shops, that *he* would bring in a stamp trading Bill. So Stonehouse promised Osborn his (and his friends') support for Osborn's Bill, and decided instead to tackle another consumer issue : armed with the authority of the resolution passed at the Co-op's 1961 Annual Congress, he would introduce a Bill to abolish individual RPM. Within hours of his decision, it was known to the Board of Trade. The senior civil servants there, increasingly impressed by Heath's determination to make his mark in the short time available, and seeing the stamp controversy push RPM to the forefront willy-nilly, were already on the point of presenting him, after all, with the formal submission the department had originally proffered to Maudling, four years earlier. Now they hesitated no longer. The abolition of RPM was about to come before Parliament, in the unlikely guise of an opposition Private Member's Bill, whether the Cabinet liked it or not. The Government would be obliged to express a view on the issue; and it was quite clear, in the Department's eyes, what that view should be.

The pressure group, too, soon heard the news of Stonehouse's intentions, and immediately set in motion plans to circulate to all MPs a broadside attacking the proposed Private Member's Bill and (for good measure) the trading stamp menace as well. For the past two years, in fact, the pressure group had been unwontedly self-effacing. It remained rather puzzled by the lack of any White Paper embodying the findings of the Board of Trade RPM fact-finding inquiry of 1960/1; but, on the basis that no news is good news, mistakenly inferred that this meant that no new Government onslaught was in the offing. The pressure group had felt sufficiently confident, by the end of 1962, to cut back sharply on its annual expenditure, and by September 1963 the RPMCC's estimate of it needs was well below its income, and the surplus was invested with a building society. By that time, in any case, the threat to RPM was coming, as the group saw it, not from potential government action but from the backdoor price-cutting of the trading stamp users. Since January 1961 its political contacts had been exclusively with the backbenchers, where it was taken for granted that RPM legislation was unthinkable in a pre-election year. Nor did the pressure group see any reason to change that expectation in the light of the proposed Private Member's Bill, its broadside against which was little more than a reflex action.

A few days after the result of the private members' ballot had been announced the Board of Trade officials presented to Heath the bulky submission on RPM and its abolition which had been shown to both his immediate predecessors – to Maudling in 1959, and to Erroll in 1961. They had immediately accepted it in principle; Heath was characteristically non-committal, promising only to think about it. Heath was always slow to make up his mind, but also notably reluctant to change it once it was made up. Commitment to a course of action, once decided on, became total.

In this instance he could see quite clearly arguments on both sides. He vividly recalled, from his early days as Chief Whip, the massive Tory backbench pressure in favour of RPM in 1956, and knew well enough that this was a political hot potato which it would be prudent to avoid. On the other hand, there was the Stonehouse Bill. The only practical alternative to, in effect, taking it over himself, was to vote it down in favour of a promise of major legislation against every conceivable form of wickedness (monopolies, undesirable mergers, restrictive practices of all kinds) in the next parliament: this would probably receive a bad press (which had become increasingly anti-RPM) and certainly give Labour valuable electioneering ammunition. Then, more important, there was the trading stamp war. However much stamps might be detested by the traditional trading interest (and disapproved of by the austere, concerned that the – often American-owned – stamp companies were making vast profits at either the shopkeeper's or the customer's expense), they were certainly popular with the consumer: a recent Gallup Poll (privately commissioned) seemed to show that almost one shopper in four was now saving trading stamps. Clearly, the government would do nothing to prohibit them; but, even so, the prospect of an increasing number of manufacturers' boycotts, and threats of boycotts, of retailers who gave (or wanted to give) stamps, was not a happy one.

As for the economic case for the proposal, as set out in the Board of Trade submission, this was clear enough. But politically, too, it was argued the thing could be a vote-winner. Anything that promised to bring prices down was bound to be popular with the voter in general and the housewife in particular; while the fact that the measure would undoubtedly be loudly opposed by the pro-RPM lobby would bring the added benefit of showing the Government to be bold and brave in pursuit of the public interest. Abolition could count on getting a good press – which would, indeed, be a welcome change for the government.

Yet when all was said and done, Heath remained to be convinced that the measure was as important as his advisers seemed to think. A new dynamic regional policy, he suggested to them, was surely of infinitely more significance than the abolition of RPM. The officials pointed out that regional policy, though undoubtedly important, was inevitably a very long-term job: there was no possibility of there being anything in the way of results to show for it this side of the General Election. Abolishing RPM, by contrast, was something that could be done here and now, before the election. Heath replied that he would brood on it.

He was still brooding (a process which included making one or two discreet soundings) when, on 11 December, he met the Conservative Trade and Industry Committee to discuss with them the twin problems of trading stamps and RPM. It was already clear that the question of RPM would shortly have to come before the Cabinet, simply to determine the Government's line on the Stonehouse Bill. The prevailing assumption, however, was still that the government would opt for the wider measure, which would necessarily have to wait until after the election. This was not dispelled by Heath, who told the Committee that a fresh and fundamental re-examination of the whole question of monopolistic practices, mergers and RPM was now in progress; and that they should not expect any decision or statement until January, when the Government would state its attitude to both Stonehouse's and Osborn's Bills. (Osborn's Bill was subsequently supported by the Government and, as the Trading Stamps Act, became law in July 1964.)

At the Board of Trade the officials were beginning to get worried. Over a fortnight had gone by, and still Heath seemed unable to make up his mind. But the Board still had some cards up its sleeve. The Monopolies Commission had at last completed a six-year-long investigation into electrical equipment for motor vehicles, and recommended the abolition of RPM on the whole of the range of goods involved. Moreover in March 1963, following the recommendations of the Molony Committee, the Government had set up the Consumer Council; and the Board of Trade had appointed, as its first Director, one of its own former senior officials, Miss Elizabeth

Ackroyd. Miss Ackroyd, who had left the Board's employ in 1961, had a long involvement in the anti-RPM crusade, and had been intimately concerned with the row over the Restrictive Trade Practices Act in 1956. The department was entitled to feel that it had not so much lost a daughter as gained a son: on 19 December, the day the Monopolies Commission report was published, the Consumer Council publicly recommended that all RPM should be made illegal.

The following day the Commons rose for the Christmas recess. Heath's private office packed his red box with holiday reading. On top of the pile they placed the papers on RPM; and on the front of that file was a note, on blue paper, pointing out that, unless the Secretary of State reached a decision during the recess, it would be too late. Immediately after the New Year Heath returned to the office and summoned his senior officials. He had made up his mind. He would introduce a Bill to abolish RPM. 'From then on,' one of those present recalls, 'it was full steam ahead.'

While the officials set about their work Heath's first task was to inform the Prime Minister of his decision and seek his support. The continuing low standing of the Government (Luton had been lost in a by-election in November, and Dumfries barely held in December), coupled with the strain of the leadership struggle had left Douglas-Home with an unhappy and squabbling Cabinet: he had already become deeply disillusioned by the unpleasantness and intensity of the in-fighting, which he had been unaccustomed to and unprepared for. Indeed, over Christmas he had even toyed with the idea of resigning. The prospect, therefore, of being saddled now with a row over RPM abolition was all the more depressing. On the other hand, he had no wish to alienate Heath, the one senior minister who, having supported him during the leadership crisis, was now wholeheartedly trying to steer the government out of the doldrums and win the election.

Nevertheless, had Douglas-Home wished to withhold his support from Heath's proposal, he could and would have done so. In fact, he had no such wish. The issue was not one in which he had ever taken much interest, nor could he regard it as of great importance, although anything which tended to stop prices rising must be worth considering. But during the months in which Heath had worked with him at the Foreign Office, Douglas-Home had come increasingly to rely, on matters of detail such as the intricacies of the mix-manned nuclear force (MLF) plan, on his industrious colleague, and to respect the younger man's judgement. Heath conceded that RPM would be unpopular with a number of Tory backbenchers, but was able to claim, with the authority and experience of an ex-Chief Whip who had dealt with the unrest over the 1956 Bill, that this should present no insuperable difficulty. But the argument which weighed most with the Prime Minister was Heath's contention that the overriding need was to show the nation that, despite all the setbacks and troubles of the past year, the Government was still capable of taking firm and vigorous action; and the abolition of RPM would prove just that. Douglas-Home gave Heath the green light, and it was agreed that the issue would come before Cabinet on 14 January, the first day of the new parliamentary session.

When, over the next two months, the full extent of the furore caused by the RPM Bill manifested itself, Douglas-Home came privately to regret he had allowed it to happen, and became rather more wary of relying on Heath's advice. But at the time he had found himself in a curiously difficult position: as a Prime Minister who had spent the past twelve years in the House of Lords, the one thing he was least equipped to do was to assess the strength of feeling on this issue of his supporters in the Commons – and the form that feeling might take. And once having given his word, he was not going to rat on it.

But the furore was still in the future when, on Monday, 13 January, Douglas-Home held a preliminary meeting on the proposal with the Chancellor of the Exchequer, Maudling, and the Chairman of the Party, Lord Blakenham. Maudling had, in fact, raised the issue of RPM in Cabinet before the Queen's Speech in November, pointing out that the Government might soon have to choose between the damage threatened by the escalating trading stamp war and the perils of legislation against RPM, but he did not press the matter. Now, asked by the Prime Minister, he agreed that abolition was wholly consistent with the economic policy he was pursuing, particularly the attempt to secure a voluntary incomes policy. Blakenham, however, was against doing anything. For one thing, it put paid to the possibility of holding a March election, which at that time he, personally, favoured; but in any case the timing was disastrous: it would be a tremendous shock to the Party's active supporters in the constituencies, just when he was trying to restore their shattered morale in time for the General Election.

The following day the Cabinet met to discuss Heath's paper on RPM. He proposed the complete and unqualified abolition of the practice, with the possible exception of the net book agreement which was generally conceded to be a special case. However, he had not spent the weary days and nights haggling at Brussels for nothing: knowing the trouble he was bound to run into in Cabinet, the strategy he had agreed with his officials was to present this proposal as an initial negotiating position, while having up his sleeve the original proposal contained in the departmental submission. This suggested that claims for exceptional treatment should be made to the Registrar of Restrictive Trade Practices, who would then refer them to the Restrictive Practices Court, before which the supplicant manufacturers would have the opportunity to demonstrate that, in their case, RPM was in the public interest as defined by certain strict and precise criteria.

As expected, the Cabinet was bitterly divided; nor was the opposition to Heath placated by his fairly swift retreat to his prepared 'compromise' position. As in 1962, when Erroll had unsuccessfully tried to get it through, the strongest opponent was the former Lord Hailsham, Mr Quintin Hogg (once again, mainly on legal grounds, although he was also highly critical of the lack of consultation or political preparation: 'you must always let people see the cat before you let it out of the bag'), followed closely by Mr Selwyn Lloyd. Speaking as Leader of the House of Commons, and the man who, after being sacked by Macmillan in 1962, had made a full investigation of the Conservative Party in the constituencies, Lloyd warned of the havoc the Bill would wreak in both sections of the Party. This was echoed, as to the Commons, by Redmayne, the Chief Whip (the Chief Whip, although not normally a member of the Cabinet, is always present at Cabinet meetings; the convention is that he speaks only when asked to by the Prime Minister, and then only on his own specialist field) and, as to the Party in the country, less stridently by Blakenham. A notably heavyweight, although less outspoken, opponent was Butler.

With opposition on this scale, the normal practice would be for the Cabinet at the very least to postpone taking a decision, one way or the other, in the hope of reaching a consensus at a later date. But this, Heath pointed out, was out of the question in the present case: Stonehouse's Bill was down for its second reading in the Commons in three days' time – Friday, 17 January – and the Government therefore had to make up its mind on RPM abolition before that date.

And so the argument continued. There can be little doubt that, in part, the strength of the opposition was explained by opposition to Heath himself. In the eyes of a number of his colleagues he was foisting this controversial Bill on the Cabinet, at the worst possible time, out of self-importance and personal ambition – a determination to make his name as a man of courage, having failed to carry off the Common Market prize. But opposition to the measure itself – above all, at that time – was real enough. It was argued that Heath was 'throwing the small shopkeeper to the supermarket wolves', that there could be no effect on prices before the election anyway, and that in any case the whole package – monopolies, mergers and all – ought to be done together, after the election, instead of picking on the little man, who looked on the Conservative Party to protect his interests, first.

Heath's political case *for* the proposal has already been outlined. Among his most prominent supporters in Cabinet (apart, of course, from the Prime Minister, whose backing had already been secured, as the colleagues knew) were Boyle and Joseph. Maudling also spoke in favour, emphasising the incomes policy argument, but took little part in the subsequent discussion. This, when it became absolutely clear that Heath was determined to legislate, come what may, revolved around the question of the 'onus of proof'.

Heath insisted that RPM must be presumed to be against the public interest, and thus if any industry claimed exemption from the Bill the burden of proof must be on that industry to prove that, in its case, RPM was in the public interest, by showing that, without it, the consumer would suffer in certain defined and specific ways. Heath's opponents suggested, as a compromise, for which they were prepared to settle, that the onus of proof should be the other way about: the burden should be on the Registrar of Restrictive Practices to prove, in each case, that RPM was against the public interest. Heath refused to accept this compromise; and, in the absence of any agreement between the two sides, the Prime Minister announced that they would continue the discussion and reach a conclusion at a further Cabinet meeting next day.

After the Cabinet, Heath met some of his colleagues privately, to muster support for the following day, and then returned to the Board of Trade, where his advisers reinforced his belief that the onus of proof was crucial: unless the burden remained on the RPM practitioner, and the 'gateways' for exemption were kept narrow, instead of abolition there would (in effect) be a prolonged and indefinite filibuster.

The Cabinet duly met again on the morning of Wednesday, 15 January. This time the argument was entirely over the onus of proof. Heath, in the words of one witness, 'made it eyeball to eyeball'. He refused to budge, and was given full support by Douglas-Home, whose diplomatic skill softened the rough edges of Heath's 'extraordinary resolution'. Eventually after, in all, three hours of Cabinet discussion of this one issue, the opponents conceded: Heath had won. There was to be full-blooded abolition of RPM and legislation to achieve it that session. That afternoon, he made a statement in the House on 'monopolies, mergers, restrictive practices and resale price maintenance'. In it, to the consternation of many of his own backbench supporters, he announced that:

The Government ... have reached the conclusion that resale price maintenance should be presumed to be against the public interest unless in any particular case it is proved to the contrary to the satisfaction of a judicial tribunal. They therefore propose to introduce legislation this Session designed to bring this practice to an end subject to the right to apply for exemption to the judicial tribunal to which I have referred.

In the strict sense, the decision had now been taken; in the British system of government it is in Cabinet that the final stage of the real battle is fought. Once the Cabinet has reached a firm decision and that decision is announced in parliament, the struggle is all over bar the shouting. Just as pressure groups customarily exert their influence through their activities during the period of the *formulation* of a policy, so, too, the power of parliamentary and public opinion is normally evidenced in the weight attached by a government to the anticipated reaction of the public and parliament *before* any major Cabinet decision is taken and promulgated. And, indeed, the measure that Heath announced on 15 January 1964 – and it is immaterial for the purposes of this case study whether that measure was or was not in the public interest – duly came to pass. But in this case, it very nearly did not: the substantive battle continued, in more than merely token form, for a further two months. Before, therefore, drawing conclusions about the distribution of power in the light of the history of the RPM affair, it is necessary to outline the sequence of events during that atypical aftermath, and to analyse why this politically deviant behaviour occurred.

To the RPM pressure group, Heath's statement came as a bombshell, a bolt from the blue as unwelcome as it was unexpected. 'This is an absolutely dreadful statement,' complained a shocked Pagliero, chairman of the RPMCC; and his comrade-in-arms, the secretary of the National Chamber of Trade, warned that 'We shall move heaven and earth to prevent this being adopted.' The pressure group had been outflanked, but at least there was still a few weeks' grace before the publication of the dreaded Bill. Spearheaded by the RPMCC's action committee, from its Wimpole Street headquarters, an all-out campaign was launched – 'the most intensive "lobby" the present Parliament has known', in the words of *The Times*. The National Chamber of Trade was deputed to organise a series of protest meetings throughout the country, culminating in a mass rally at St Pancras Town Hall. A strident pamphlet was circulated to the press and to all MPs. The constituent trade associations, too, agreed to write to the newspapers and Members of Parliament, putting the case for RPM in their own trade; more important, they were roused

to circulate their members, urging each of them to write in protest to
their own local MP. Finally, and more discreetly, the pressure group
made contact with its known 'friends' on the Tory back benches,
whom it had been cultivating so assiduously (and unceasingly) over
the past four years, in order to co-ordinate tactics for the parliamentary battle that lay ahead. Its object was clear: if possible, to
prevent the emergence of a Bill altogether; if – as seemed probable
– that was not possible, to cause sufficient trouble to persuade the
Government to drop the Bill; or, failing that, to persuade Parliament
to draw the Bill's teeth by substantive amendment.

Heath's first encounter with his own backbenchers was on the
evening of the day of his original statement, when (accompanied by
du Cann and Mr David Price, the Board's Parliamentary Secretary)
he attended a meeting of the Trade and Industry Committee. Over
100 Members attended, and Heath was listened to in almost total
silence. When he had finished, it was clear that the overwhelming
majority were hostile. No one actually defended RPM as such:
the complaint was about the timing (to those who maintained that
abolition would be electorally disastrous, Heath pointed out that he
himself had a marginal seat, and was confident of holding it), the lack
of prior consultation, and the onus of proof. Eight days later he met
the much more important 1922 Committee: this time some 200
Members were present. A neutral observer commented at the time
that Heath was impressive in the face of a largely hostile meeting.
(The previous week, when the 1922 Committee had first discussed the
matter, hostility had been even greater.) Once again, although some
defended RPM as such, the opposition was principally directed
towards its timing (shopkeepers alienated before the election but
no effect on prices until after it), the lack of prior consultation with
backbenchers (coupled with in particular, the lack of the customary
White Paper to prepare the ground and allow a pre-legislative debate
on the subject), and the monstrous unfairness of clobbering the small
shopkeeper while leaving the much more serious trade union restrictive practices untouched. By this time Heath was also receiving a
rising tide of representations from individual backbenchers – friends
of the pressure group, ordinary MPs alarmed by letters from their
local supporters and constituents, and officers of the Trade and
Industry Committee.

It was as a result of the Trade and Industry Committee representations that Heath at long last agreed to see, at the beginning of
February, a deputation from the pressure group – its first contact
with the Board of Trade for three full years. For political and public
relations purposes, the pressure group usually liked to present itself
as the defender of the (traditionally small) shopkeeper; but on this

occasion the RPMCC action committee decided to demonstrate it had the big battalions on its side, too, by including in its delegation (led by Sir Richard Glyn, MP, who had briefly been PPS to Maudling's predecessor as President of the Board of Trade, Sir David Eccles) the chairman of Decca (Sir Edward Lewis) and senior directors of both Imperial Tobacco and W. H. Smith. Heath was unimpressed. The FBI, representing manufacturers who both did and did not practice RPM, had already taken a neutral line. Nor was he receptive to the series of demands the deputation made, of which the two key ones were for a White Paper (an obvious ploy to gain time) and for a reversal of the onus of proof.

If Heath's unconciliatory behaviour was largely a matter of personal style, he was undoubtedly reinforced by the reaction of the press and public opinion. With the exception of the *Daily Express*, which had not forgiven Heath for the attempt to join the Common Market, and which ran a vehement anti-abolition campaign, the great bulk of the national press (including all the 'heavies') was strongly abolitionist. (The most enthusiastic of all was *The Economist*, which told its readers, the week after Heath's original statement, that he could 'indeed start rapidly emerging as Sir Alec's heir apparent'.) This was quite a turn-up for a government which had long been considered fit only for satire, and when Wilson was Fleet's Street's blue-eyed boy, Moreover the contentiousness of the RPM affair ensured that it remained worthy of press comment. As for public opinion, this seemed more equivocal, but potentially more favourable than not. A Gallup Poll published shortly after Heath's announcement recorded that 63 per cent approved of the Government's decision (on the understanding that it would enable shops to sell at prices below those fixed by manufacturers) against 18 per cent who disapproved; but if abolition were to mean 'quite considerable hardship for small shopkeepers' then the balance was reversed by a margin of 39 per cent to 43 per cent.

From the constituencies Conservative area agents were already reporting to Central Office an unprecedented volume of critical letters and telephone calls, considerable numbers of resignations among local association office holders, and widespread dissent; but Blakenham, as both Party Chairman and a personal friend of Douglas-Home's, had no wish to add to the Prime Minister's worries by raising such matters now. He had, after all, warned the Cabinet that this sort of thing would happen at the time the crucial decision was taken.

As internal party dissent rumbled on, Douglas-Home firmly came out in support of the proposal in a major speech on 25 January (even Butler, the Foreign Secretary and elder statesman, was persuaded to add his public endorsement of a measure which rumour had – accurately – suggested he deplored), and by mid-February a draft Bill had come before the Legislation Committee of the Cabinet, of which Butler was chairman. Here Redmayne (who, as Chief Whip, was the official channel for backbench complaints) spoke out strongly (in Cabinet Committees Chief Whips have a freer tongue than in Cabinet itself) about the difficulties he would have in getting the Bill through the House if it were to continue in its present form. Butler decided to refer it back to the full Cabinet, and at a prolonged Cabinet meeting on 20 February the final draft of the Bill was eventually approved, substantially unaltered, the onus of proof unchanged and the 'gateways' to exemption as narrow as ever.

On 25 February the Resale Prices Bill was published. Next day, Heath met the Trade and Industry Committee again, to explain the Bill and answer questions on it, and was actually accorded, at the end of his replies, a ration of applause. But this improved mood was deceptive. From the moment the Bill had been published, Tory backbenchers – actively assisted by the expertise of the pressure group and its legal counsel – began to breed amendments like rabbits.

The two weeks between the Bill's publication and its Second Reading on 10 March saw considerable behind-the-scenes activity. Known dissenters were seen separately by both Heath and Redmayne in a vain attempt to extract promises of good behaviour. As the number of pro-RPM amendments tabled reached three figures, it became clear that the most the Government could achieve would be to prevent a wrecking filibuster and keep at least part of the internal Party discord behind closed doors, rather than have it all publicly displayed on the floor of the House of Commons. To this end the Chief Whip suggested something of a constitutional innovation: the setting up of a backbench 'Steering Committee', representative of both pro-Bill and anti-Bill factions, to discuss and sift amendments. This would provide a private forum in which the Bill's Conservative opponents could thrash out with its supporters what the really crucial issues were and try and negotiate some form of compromise – at least on points of detail – with the Government on these issues. The idea of the Steering Committee was approved by Douglas-Home and Heath, and on 4 March it was formally proposed at a meeting of the Trade and Industry Committee by the Committee's chairman, Sir John Vaughan-Morgan, a leading advocate of compromise. (Before the Bill was published, he had unsuccessfully tried to persuade Heath to postpone it until after the General Election.) He explained that the new body would have about ten members, of whom three would be the officers of the Trade and Industry Committee (himself, the somewhat pro-RPM vice-chairman, Mr John Hall, and the secretary, Mr Leonard Cleaver) plus seven others chosen by him to provide a balance of opinion within the Party – but with Ministers firmly excluded. The proposal was supported without enthusiasm, but no decision was taken.

On 10 March Heath formally moved the Second Reading of the Resale Prices Bill. At the start of his lengthy speech he declared that : 'I begin by putting the Bill in its proper perspective. It is one element, and an important one, in a comprehensive policy. The object of this policy is to promote more competition throughout the economy.' This was the voice of the department. He concluded:

> The Bill will be a means of adding to the consumer's freedom of choice and of assisting with the stabilisation and reduction of prices. But, much more even than that, it is part of a policy to make the economy more dynamic for producing the sustained expansion on which depend all the programmes for modernisation which the country so much desires, and by which the whole country can contribute by greater enterprise whether in the economy as a whole or in the distributive trades.

That was the voice of the Minister – and of the *Zeitgeist*.

The outcome of the vote was far worse than the Government's gloomiest expectations. A bad result was inevitable, given that the Labour Opposition had boldly decided to abstain, thus assuring the pro-RPM Conservatives that they were free to rebel without risking a Government defeat. Nonetheless, 20 Conservative votes against the Bill and a further 30 or so deliberate abstentions made it the biggest Tory revolt since the vote that led to the fall of the Chamberlain Government in 1940. (At Suez there had been 15 deliberate abstentions; over the Profumo affair, 27.) The unforeseen scale of the rebellion can be attributed to three factors: opposition to the Bill itself, serviced and fanned by the pressure group; the habit that some Tory backbenchers had acquired, in the aftermath of the crushing Labour defeat of 1959, of acting as an unofficial opposition, a tendency now fuelled by a miscellany of grievances (over mortgage rates, railway closures and so on); and deep hostility to what was seen as the high-handed attitude of Heath himself.

This last had led to a formal complaint to the Prime Minister by the influential chairman of the 1922 Committee, Major John Morrison. Even the Board of Trade officials, who had nothing but admiration for Heath's firmness and determination in the face of immense Party pressure, were sometimes puzzled by his behaviour. An example of this was seen in his response to the very large number of letters he received from MPs protesting, or enclosing protests, against the Bill, either in whole or in part. The Department prepared four draft

replies, dealing with the four principal types of letter. Heath raised
no objection to the Departmental draft replies: he simply refused to
sign them (nor would he authorise one of his junior Ministers to do
so). Despite constant badgering by his officials, he had still not replied
to a single letter from a protesting Member by the time the Bill's
Committee stage began on 23 March. No doubt he could see in the
similarity of the letters the hand of a pressure group which he regarded with some contempt. It was not, however, conducive to a
climate of goodwill.

The day after the Second Reading Debate, the Trade and Industry
Committee met again. An observer recorded at the time that it was
'a subdued, morning after, meeting ... The disgruntled predomina-
ted, and everyone considered himself to be acting from the highest
motives.' It was, however, agreed that the steering committee should
be set up and would meet daily, starting on 16 March. The other
seven members, besides the three Trade and Industry Committee
officers, would be three supporters of the Bill, (Mr Anthony Kershaw,
Heath's PPS, Mr Peter Emery and Mr Philip Goodhart), three opponents of the Bill and friends of the pressure group (Sir Hugh
Linstead, Mr Roy Wise and Sir Richard Glyn), and a representative
of the Leader of the House, Selwyn Lloyd, in the person of his PPS,
Mr Peter Walker. The steering committee, in fact, became an intermediary through which the Department and the pressure group
could and, in effect, did negotiate over the drafting of amendments.
But gains to be secured in this way, against so determined a President of the Board of Trade, were minimal: the pressure group's
main objective, given that substantial amendment was unattainable,
remained to kill the Bill.

More important, however, the Cabinet also met after the Second
Reading shock. Current legislation is, of course, one of the two
standing items always on the Cabinet agenda. On this occasion,
though, most unusually, this item developed into a fresh discussion
on the merits of the Bill itself – and specifically, on whether it might
not be right, in the face of past and future parliamentary opposition,
to abandon it. Many of the original opponents of the measure now
wanted to do just that. Butler felt that the best thing to do was to
drop the Bill, and there may well have been a majority in Cabinet
who agreed with him. But Heath – although chastened by the size
of the Second Reading revolt – was adamant, and implied that if the
Bill went, he went, too. (He had already made it clear to the Prime
Minister that if the Bill were abandoned he would feel obliged to
resign from the Government.) Heath's resignation, however much
it might have been welcome on the back benches ('Ted has a knack of
making enemies' observed one senior Party official, an opponent of

the Bill, 'but the backbenchers seem to have gone out of their minds'), was not something the Cabinet sought. The Prime Minister, while privately urging Heath to 'give some ground', and despite growing personal unease, continued to give him full public backing; and after what was in some ways an even fiercer battle than that of 14 and 15 January, the Cabinet decided to press on. 'I am sure,' wrote Home to one of his Ministers who had most strongly urged dropping the Bill rather than risking defeat during the Committee stage, 'that Ted's skill and fortitude will see us through. But,' he added, 'I sense that he has seen the light.'

To some extent, perhaps, he had. He began, with a skill he had not hitherto notably displayed, to make face-saving concessions to the pressure group, using the steering committee for the purpose – notably over the 'loss-leader' clause of the Bill. He also became the soul of courtesy in the long parliamentary haul which followed. But he was not going to yield on the heart of the matter, and the pressure group knew it.

Normally the line-by-line scrutiny of a Bill of this type would be conducted 'upstairs' in a Committee of about thirty MPs: only 'constitutional' Bills – such as those to change the composition of the Lords, or to implement membership of the European Community – and (in those days) Finance Bills would be discussed in detail on the floor of the House. There was – and is – no hard and fast rule about this: the Conservative Government decided in 1971 to take the whole of its Industrial Relations Bill on the floor, in the belief (probably mistaken, as it turned out) that Labour's furious filibuster in defence of trade union privilege would damage the then Opposition. But a measure to change the rules governing a particular retail trade practice would certainly not normally be selected by the Government's business managers to take up precious Government time on the floor of the House.

Yet in this particular instance those business managers could see no practical alternative to debating the Bill right the way through on the floor. This was because the extent and nature of the unease on the Government's back benches made the problem of selecting the handful of Conservative MPs who would serve on a committee upstairs almost insoluble. If some representatives of the rebels were selected, then there would have been the prospect of repeated defeats in committee (where Government backbenchers have fewer qualms about linking hands with the Opposition than they do on the floor of the House). But if, on the other hand, the rebels were excluded, then the Government would be accused of packing the committee, and backbench outrage would have been even more intense, leading to worse trouble than ever when the Bill returned, as it would still have to do for its final, or 'report' stages to be taken on the floor of the House.

On 23 March, at any rate, the Bill began its passage through the Committee stage on the floor of the House. The next day came the first vote on an amendment. Moved by Sir Hugh Linstead, Secretary of the Pharmaceutical Society since 1926, it sought to exempt drugs, medicines and medical and surgical appliances from the scope of the Bill. Linstead's chief supporter was another prominent 'Trade Association Tory', Geoffrey Hirst, a former vice-president of the National Chamber of Trade (and, incidentally, immediate past chairman of the Trade and Industry Committee): together they acted as the two tellers for the amendment. Voting with them were another 29 Conservative rebels plus the entire Labour and Liberal Opposition; in addition, a large number of other pro-RPM Tories deliberately abstained. In the event, in a parliament with an overall Conservative majority of 91, the Government had a majority of one: the amendment was defeated by 204 votes to 203. Heath was shattered. In a BBC television interview, broadcast three years later, on 20 January 1967, he admitted that, had the vote gone the other way, the whole future of the Bill would have been in doubt – and, with it, his own position in Cabinet.

The majority of one was to prove the pressure group's last throw. The result was as great a shock to many Conservative backbenchers as it was to the Government. However unwise Heath's Bill may have been, the repeated pleas that had been made to them by their leaders, from the Prime Minister down, not to rock the boat so near to the election, suddenly and belatedly began to register.

The Government's nerve was put to the test just once more. On 21 April (first the Easter recess, and then the Budget debate, had intervened) Mr Robin Turton, a senior Tory backbencher and former Minister of Health who, throughout the Committee stage, had acted as chief sponsor of the RPMCC-inspired amendments, moved one which sought to emasculate the Bill by widening the grounds for exemption in the most general and generous manner. After more than six hours' debate (the longest discussion on any amendment) Turton withdrew, without pressing the matter to a vote, on a promise by Heath to look at the exemption clause again in the light of the debate – a promise which he met by introducing (in the words of one of Heath's more dispassionate Cabinet colleagues) a 'rather meaningless but pretentious-sounding' amendment of his own in the place of the one Turton had withdrawn.

But in reality the near-crisis of the majority of one was the climax: from then on the revolt gradually – and, after the withdrawal of the Turton amendment, abruptly – collapsed. The Bill duly became law, receiving the Royal Assent some two months before the dissolution of Parliament. And despite various alterations of detail, it had become law essentially in the form in which the Board of Trade had submitted it to Heath, in which Heath had proposed it to the Cabinet, and in which the Cabinet had agreed it. But it had been a close run thing.

Looking back over the fifteen-year-long saga of the abolition of resale price maintenance, which reached its climax with the stormy passage of the Resale Prices Bill of 1964, one strand in particular stands out. This is the dogged persistence of the Board of Trade in pressing, on successive Governments and successive Ministers, a specific departmental policy grounded in a clear departmental philosophy. In this sense, it is a classic example of civil service power. It was largely thanks to the Board that RPM remained (if occasionally latent) an 'issue' throughout that period. It was chiefly as a result of the initiative of the Board that a succession of Presidents, of differing Parties and personalities, from Wilson to Heath, espoused that issue to a greater or lesser degree. Given this strategy, the officials might well have been excused for assuming that, sooner or later, they were bound to find a Minister who was both willing and able to carry their policy through: the only thing that was not in their power was to determine when that would be. And when, with the arrival of Heath on the scene, the hour struck, it was – as we have seen – the officials who 'sold' the idea to a minister whose mind had been on other things and who, when faced with the Departmental submission, initially viewed it with understandable misgivings.

The continuity and persistence of Board of Trade policy on RPM over so long a period, while individual civil servants – as well as individual ministers – came and went, has led us to stress the Board as an entity, and its consistent departmental philosophy, rather than dwell on the role played by specific officials in keeping the cause alive. But it would be wrong to ignore the latter altogether. Reference has already been made to Miss Ackroyd; but pride of place must undoubtedly be given to Sir Frank Lee, the Department's permanent head from 1951 to 1959, one of the more forceful civil servants of the post-war era and certainly the outstanding Permanent Secretary to the Board of Trade within living memory, and to Mr Herbert Andrew, a very able no-nonsense northerner who spent nearly all his career with the Board: he had joined it before the war, was number two to Lee, and stayed until 1963 when he left to become Permanent Secretary at the Ministry of Education.

Although both these men had left by the time Heath arrived towards the end of 1963, he had already, by chance, come to know and respect them. For during that crucial and formative period of his political career, the abortive Common Market negotiations of 1961–3, he had been backed by Lee as the head of the London end of the inter-departmental EEC 'task force' and by Andrew as the Board of Trade representative on his Brussels team. And during the crucial discussions between Heath and his officials in the winter of 1963 they inevitably made him aware of Lee's and Andrew's firm belief in the desirability of RPM abolition. One official, in particular, was well placed to do this and to plead the Board's traditional case with Heath. This was his Principal Private Secretary, Mr Peter Carey, who had joined the Board during the Lee era in 1953, and had served as head of the all-important Private Office of two previous Presidents, Maudling and Erroll, before being inherited in that capacity by Heath. (Heath clearly had a high opinion of his Principal Private Secretary. When he became Prime Minister, seven years later, and set up the Central Policy Review Staff (better known as the Think Tank), Carey was appointed one of its carefully hand-picked members. It is perhaps worth noting at this point the key role the Private Office plays in the whole complex edifice of civil service power.) There was yet another, if lower-level, link with the past that is worthy of note: the Principal with day-to-day responsibility for the RPM legislation was Miss Elizabeth Llewellyn-Smith, who had been Lee's private secretary when Lee was Permanent Secretary.

But the role of these men and women – however much they may have stood out in a department where real ability was somewhat thin on the ground – was to ensure that the Board's RPM file never gathered dust and never lacked for advocacy. They neither determined, nor questioned, the contents of the file. The institutional reasons why the Board had the classical free trade philosophy that it did are discussed in the concluding chapter in this volume. But it is also possible to provide a partial explanation in historical terms.

The Second World War changed Whitehall in many ways. One of them was the incursion of a bevy of academic economists, who fanned out into almost every conceivable Government department, with the Cabinet Office as their nerve centre. They brought with them a new intellectual consensus, whose monument is the coalition government's seminal Employment Policy White Paper of 1944 (Cmd 6527). While chiefly remembered as marking the emergence of Keynesianism (for good or ill) as official doctrine, this document contained much else besides, including a stern disapproval of price-fixing as 'a serious impediment to an expansionist economy'. When the war ended, the economists returned to their universities, leaving only a few behind at the Cabinet Office and Treasury. But at the Board of Trade they lingered for a while. Mr (now Professor Sir)

Austin Robinson was appointed Economic Adviser to the Board of Trade in 1946, and was shortly afterwards succeeded by Mr (now Sir) Alec Cairncross, until the post was abolished in 1949. Both had been members of the wartime government economic mafia, and were able to ensure that the new consensus was embedded in the Board's thinking during the transition from a war to a peace economy.

The curious exclusion of all economists from the Board of Trade throughout the 1950s may have been connected with the widespread post-war belief (still not totally extinct) that such people are experts in the arcane mysteries of things like inflation and the balance of payments, but cannot be expected to know about aspects of everyday life such as shopping. As a result, for most of the period under review, the most speculative macroeconomic forecasts were treated by Governments with wholly unwarranted respect, while elementary and limited applications of the law of supply and demand were disregarded. Be that as it may, while it is most unlikely that new economic advisers would have held any different views on RPM, they might well have questioned and chipped away at the overall departmental philosophy from which the Board's policy sprang. The total absence of economists after 1949 at least ensured that this could not occur.

But if civil service power was the prime mover in the RPM affair, it was not, on its own, as we have seen, sufficient to carry the day. To be effective, it still needed to be harnessed to the ambition and drive of an unusually strong departmental minister. It may, of course, be argued that, by the time Heath arrived at the Board of Trade the circumstances had become more favourable to the abolition of RPM; and in some ways (such as the trading stamp war) they undoubtedly had. But in other ways conditions were worse: the imminence of the General Election, for example, although helpful to a degree (the government needed something to improve its image and attract votes), on balance made things very much more difficult. In general, had conditions really been made favourable in 1963/4 than during earlier, unsuccessful, attempts, the Department would not have initially regarded it as a non-starter in the winter of 1963. Nor, although this of necessity cannot be demonstrated, is it possible to imagine a single one of Heath's colleagues in the Douglas-Home Cabinet who would have been both willing and able to carry it through at that time. 'It showed for the first time,' recalls one of Heath's most senior Cabinet opponents, 'the extraordinary resolution of Mr Edward Heath.' It was a quality that was to be demonstrated again, in a remarkably similar way, when, eight years later, Heath – then Prime Minister – successfully imposed the (far more important)

European Communities Bill, to enable Britain to join the Common Market, on a divided Conservative Party.

Nevertheless, although the passage of the Resale Prices Act of 1964 can be explained by the combination of a strong departmental policy and a determined heavyweight Minister ('Certainly', adjudged the oracularly prophetic *Annual Register* for that year, 'when the Royal Assent was bestowed on 16 July it was very much Mr Heath's hour, and, for what it might be worth one day in the party, his victory'), two other factors on the same side cannot be omitted. The first is the support Heath received, throughout, from the Prime Minister, Douglas-Home. According to Heath's most senior Cabinet colleague, 'Harold [Macmillan] would have side-tracked it'. Douglas-Home chose not to. Whatever exaggerated emphasis is placed on the fashionable thesis of Prime Ministerial power (and even if it were true – which it is not entirely – that the Prime Minister's will can prevail on *any* given issue, it would still not follow that it can prevail on *every* issue) there can be no doubt that the Prime Minister enjoys the power of veto, above all when the Cabinet is divided. If power in our political system is diffused, the power that is most notably diffused is the power of veto; and the Prime Minister's blackball is decisive. Without Douglas-Home's backing, Heath could not have done it.

The second factor, a helpful although not a necessary condition, illustrates in a capricious way the potential influence of the Opposition backbencher. This is the accident of Stonehouse's Private Member's Bill to abolish RPM. Any Member who draws a high place in the ballot for such Bills will always reveal the nature of his intended legislation to his own Chief Whip; and this invariably prevents a government from being embarrassed by a Private Member's Bill introduced from its own side of the House: the Member will have been dissuaded from introducing a Bill of such indelicacy. But there is no such control, inevitably, over Opposition Private Member's Bills. The importance of Stonehouse's Bill was not, as has sometimes been suggested, that this is what determined Heath to act; as the narrative has already indicated, its role at that stage was less significant. The real importance of the Stonehouse Bill was that it obliged Heath to take the issue to Cabinet *at that time* and thus justified his doing so even in the eyes of his opponents; similarly, it obliged the Cabinet to take a decision, one way or another, *at that time* – a point which Heath made much of.

Governments tend to shy away from controversial and divisive decisions except in time of crisis: the function of a crisis is to provide a deadline and end the procrastination. The Stonehouse Bill supplied the 'crisis' in this sense; without it, the case for procrastination would have been a strong one and might well have won the day. The

Government was unable to let the sleeping dog lie, because Stone-house had woken it up. The trading stamp war, it is true, had to some extent done this; but – crucially – it did not impose a hard and fast deadline, which the Stonehouse Bill did: 17 January 1964, the date of that Bill's Second Reading.

It is, however, misleading to write history solely in terms of the victors: the vanquished clearly possess power, too, otherwise the battle would not have been so long and so fierce. Nor was their defeat inevitable. The vanquished, in this case, were the pressure group, the dissident Conservative backbenchers, and the opponents of RPM abolition in Cabinet. Of these, the last were the least important. For Cabinet colleagues, however distasteful, this was not a resigning issue; and, once the Cabinet decision has been taken, the doctrine of collective responsibility neutralises the opponents. And, second, much of the Cabinet opposition, in both 1962 and 1964, was itself a reflection of the knowledge of the strength of opposition on the back benches and among the trading interest.

When it comes to the other two factors in the equation – the power of the backbenchers (or of 'parliament') and the power of the pressure group – analysis is more complex. This is because, while, on the abolitionist side, it is relatively straightforward to distinguish between the role of the department and that of the minister, on the other side the roles of the dissident backbenchers and of the RPM pressure group were so intertwined that it is difficult to assess the relative power of each. Yet it is of some significance whether what occurred was primarily a parliamentary veto which, when flouted, burst into open rebellion, or whether it was rather a case of a pressure group which (eventually) failed, managing only to engineer an abortive backbench revolt.

The conclusion reached by this study is that the greater emphasis should be placed on the pressure group – but see Ronald Butt, *The Power of Parliament*, ch. 9, for the contrary view. The continuing existence of this group is, in its way, as marked a feature of the RPM story as the persistence of the Board's departmental policy. Although addicted to changing its name – calling itself the Fair Trading Congress in the forties, the Fair Prices Defence Committee in the fifties and the Resale Price Maintenance Co-ordinating Committee in the sixties – it was essentially the same pressure group throughout, with the same objective and the same trade associations (in particular the Proprietary Articles Trade Association, of which Linstead's Pharmaceutical Society was a key component, and the National Chamber of Trade) as its key members.

The standard objective of all pressure groups is to influence legislation by securing a close relationship with the centre of power, in other words the department and minister (for most issues do not, in any case, involve the Cabinet), aiming specifically to acquire a *de facto* right to be consulted in the formulation of policy affecting the interests they represent. In return, they offer (chiefly) political complaisance in public. The National Farmers' Union and the Ministry of Agriculture is the paradigm case. The RPM pressure group, however, faced the particular problem that, for reasons discussed in the concluding chapter of this volume, the Board of Trade distrusted pressure group politics in general and RPM in particular. It thus never became 'recognised' by the department, and never gained the automatic right of consultation it sought; nevertheless, it did succeed in being consulted in the fifties, and it was no accident that the 1956 Act brought it a favourable compromise. In the fifties, too, it maintained close links with the FBI, one of the two great permanent pressure groups (the other being the TUC) with which, in our semi-corporate state, the government always seeks accommodation and to which neither the Treasury nor the Board of Trade can deny the automatic right of access. This gave the RPM pressure group at least a proxy channel to power and a source of inside information on the current state of Whitehall thinking. It even, as has been seen, took the trouble to woo the Co-op.

This is in stark contrast with the pressure group's behaviour in the sixties. It gave up the Board of Trade as a bad job. (It is worth noting that the cotton textile lobby, permanently worried about competition from low-cost imports, and faced with a similar lack of sympathy from the Board, nevertheless continued to knock on the departmental door and even deliberately eschewed all attempts to build up support at Westminster in order to avoid alienating Whitehall.) It neglected the FBI – an indirect route to the source of power which should have been cherished all the more in the absence of the direct route. It even ignored the Co-op: it was thus in no position to prevent the bitterly divided movement's anti-RPM resolution in 1961 which, in turn, was instrumental in determining the nature of Stonehouse's Bill. All it did do, of any significance, was to build up still further its contacts with and support among Conservative backbenchers. Admittedly, this was where the soil was most fertile. But whereas in the fifties this parliamentary strength was cultivated as a means to an end, the purpose being to demonstrate to Whitehall that the pressure group was a force to be reckoned with, to be consulted rather than ignored, in the sixties it seemed to see backbench influence as constituting almost a veto (on adverse legislation) in itself.

In any event, the upshot of the pressure group's unsophisticated strategy in the sixties was clear. It failed to keep itself informed

about departmental thinking. It failed to draw the political moral of
the trading stamp war or to calculate the possible wider consequences
of the Stonehouse Bill. It failed to assess the significance of the up-
grading of the President of the Board of Trade to Secretary of State.
Above all, perhaps, it failed to appreciate the character of Heath. It
even failed to bring the fence-sitting FBI into the pro-RPM camp (as
it effectively had been during the Thorneycroft period). It seems to
have assumed that, after eight years' respite, it was safe – at least
until the election – and that it possessed a genuine parliamentary
veto. As a result, it allowed itself to be taken wholly by surprise,
suspecting nothing until the Cabainet had already taken its fateful
decision and Heath had announced it in parliament. By the time it
woke up to the danger, the government was already fully and specifically committed. Had the pressure group been less amateurish, had it
brought pressure to bear and shown its full strength *before* instead of
after the Cabinet took its decision, events might have turned out
differently.

This is not, admittedly, it would seem, Heath's own interpretation.
Recollecting the RPM battle (which at the time had wounded and
scarred him more than he ever allowed to show) Heath subsequently
conceded, in an interview published in the *Observer*, 16 January
1966, that

> My mistake was to assume that the basic philosophy of the party,
> with its emphasis on competitive enterprise, was sufficient to en-
> sure that the great majority of the party would go along with
> RPM. I wanted to get on with the legislation; time was running
> out, the election was looming, so I set a fast pace, and did not leave
> enough time for a thorough discussion within the party.

Certainly, the lack of consultation caused great offence, which could
have been avoided. But, against this, it was the 'fast pace' – including
the absence of a preliminary White Paper – and lack of time for discussion which took the wind out of the pressure group's sails.
Although it was pressure of time, and not deliberate policy, which
shaped Heath's tactics, the resultant *Blitzkrieg* may in fact have
gained Heath more than it lost him.

The pressure group was thus left with nothing but its parliamentary friends to fall back on: it had been manoeuvred into a
position where it had to use its influence at the wrong time and removed from the source of power. It succeeded in orchestrating an
unprecedentedly large backbench rebellion, but achieved nothing by
doing so.

Of course, pressure group or no pressure group, there would undoubtedly have been some Tory rebels. But what made the RPM

rebellion significant was its unexpectedly large size and scale. The quality of the dissenting Conservatives was not (with one or two minor exceptions) impressive: their quantity was. Altogether, 40 Conservatives voted against the Government either on the Second Reading, or on the Linstead amendment, or both, and many more deliberately abstained. (Of the 40, at least nine had trade association connections.) And it would be straining credulity to believe that this phenomenon had nothing to do with the previous four years of assiduous cultivation by the pressure group, to the point where many backbenchers felt morally and politically committed to RPM, almost as an article of faith. Again, while many small shopkeepers would have written to their own MP of their own volition, many more did because they had been asked to – and been told what to say. It was the pressure group which organised the rebels as a group, which briefed them on the often complex points at issue, and whose expert counsel drafted their numerous amendments for them. The pressure group provided the expertise needed to fight the expertise of the department. Without the activities of the pressure group, it is safe to say that the Second Reading revolt would have been smaller and the Committee Stage war of attrition would have been insignificant. Throughout, nothing was more striking than the discrepancy between the Bill's reception in the country and the manufactured hostility generated in the House of Commons. This discrepancy, again, would have been less without the pressure group. It was the pressure group, too, which, on a number of hostile amendments, coordinated rebel Tory and official Opposition support.

To conclude from this that the pressure group was 'using' the backbenchers would be only a half-truth: the backbenchers were also 'using' the pressure group, in the sense that they looked to it to provide them with weapons to fight for a mixture of motives that may have been wholly their own. There is, in a sense, a parallel here with the relationship between minister and department. Each needed the other: the politician needs the expertise of the permanent body, the permanent body the legislative power of the politician. But there is one vital distinction, and it is this that brands the RPM rebellion as essentially an atypical manifestation of pressure group rather than parliamentary power. This is that while the department can only work through the minister, the pressure group need not work mainly – let alone exclusively – through the government backbenchers: indeed normally, if it is to maximise its effectiveness, it refrains from doing so.

Finally, what did all the drama lead to? As a result of the 1964 Act, RPM has disappeared, with the exception of Macmillan's books and Linstead's drugs – the only two trades which have succeeded in passing through the Act's narrow gateways to exemption. The Conservatives narrowly lost the ensuing election, but the effect of RPM abolition on that result is obscure: it was probably neutral. Heath was right in predicting that the measure would be popular and get a good press; his opponents were right in predicting that it would cause great trouble in the Party (although it is fair to add that financial contributions from industry were unaffected – the Party emerged from the election with a healthier bank balance than it had had at the beginning of 1963). The parliamentary crisis did indeed interfere with the contingency plans for a June election; but in fact the election was postponed to the autumn on totally separate grounds. And it certainly did nothing to prevent the election of Heath as leader of the Party in succession to Douglas-Home – a year almost to the day after the Resale Prices Act passed into law.

5 Faith, Hope and Parity: The Non-devaluation of the Pound, 1964–7

According to the late Mr Richard Crossman, addressing a Fabian Society meeting some three months after the fall of the Labour Government of 1964–70, 'the fact that we did not devalue for three years and then, having tried for three years not to devalue, that we were forced to, is probably the single most damaging fact about the Government.' And this political judgement is endorsed by the consensus of economic opinion: thus, for example, Professor Wilfred Beckerman, in the opening chapter of *The Labour Government's Economic Record, 1964–70*, comments that: 'There is little doubt that the decision to give absolute priority to the maintenance of the exchange rate was the one great mistake of economic policy.'

Why, then, was this crucial decision taken? For although in one sense a non-event, it clearly was a conscious decision. It was not like 1931, when Sidney Webb, a prominent member of the late Labour Cabinet, watched the new National Government abandon the sterling parity and complained that 'nobody told us we could do this'. Nor was it simply a decision not to devalue at any one particular point in time: it was a decision to rule out devaluation as an instrument of policy, come what may; in Beckerman's words, to give absolute (and continuing) priority to the maintenance of the existing exchange rate. It is, of course, true that, in an era of fixed exchange rates, any decision, however provisional, to defend a parity under pressure has to be presented for public consumption as an irrevocable commitment. The peculiar characteristic of this case is that the language faithfully reflected the reality.

Ostensibly, the decision was first taken in the immediate aftermath of the 1964 General Election, which saw a Labour Government returned to power, after thirteen years in the wilderness, with an overall majority of four. The Election took place on Thursday 15 October; but the result was not clear until after lunch the following day. Accordingly at 4 pm on Friday 16 October Mr Harold Wilson arrived at the Palace to kiss hands as Prime Minister for the first time. Shortly afterwards his first list of Cabinet appointments was announced: Mr James Callaghan as Chancellor of the Exchequer, Mr George Brown as First Secretary of State in charge of the brand-new Department of Economic Affairs (DEA), and Mr Patrick Gordon Walker (who had lost his seat at Smethwick the day before) as Foreign Secretary. That Friday evening Brown had a meeting in his London flat with a number of economic advisers, including the two top officials he had picked to head his new department: Sir Eric Roll, a cosmopolitan intellectual, at that time the Treasury's man in Washington, who was to become Permanent Secretary; and Sir Donald MacDougall, the ex-Oxford economics don, then Economic Director of the National Economic Development Office, who was to be the Director-General of the DEA.

MacDougall promptly informed his new Minister (who had summoned the meeting to work out a programme for the DEA) of the existence of a massive Treasury submission on the economy, with special reference to the balance of payments, which had been carefully prepared for the incoming Chancellor. Brown at once demanded a copy, and the Treasury (reluctantly) let him have one, informing the Prime Minister, who also demanded and received a copy. Meanwhile Callaghan, having spent the Thursday night celebrating in his Cardiff constituency, was still making his rather leisurely way back to London. On his arrival Treasury officials, worried stiff by the meeting in Brown's flat over which they had no control, and in a state of near panic about the risk of stories getting out about devaluation discussions, were at last able to give the new Chancellor his copy of the precious submission to read overnight.

Next morning (Saturday, 17 October) Brown and Callaghan met at 10 Downing Street, together with Sir Burke Trend, the Secretary to the Cabinet, Sir William Armstrong, Permanent Secretary to the Treasury (later to become the *eminence grise* of the Heath administration), Roll and MacDougall. Professor Alec Cairncross, Head of the Government's Economic Service, who should have accompanied Armstrong, had been excluded by the Treasury head in the mistaken belief that he was *persona non grata* with the new Prime Minister. (Armstrong had evidently forgotten that Cairncross had been Economic Adviser to the Board of Trade when Wilson was its President during the Attlee Government.) The Treasury's bulky submission – the 'General Brief' – formed the agenda of the meeting.

In it the Treasury gave its latest estimate of the balance of payments deficit in 1964. This was a horrifying £800m, on current and long-term capital account combined, which it was reckoned would be reduced to the still sizeable figure (for those days) of £450m in 1965. (In the event, the 1964 deficit turned out to be £695m, of which £382m was on current account.) However, the Brief suggested reassuringly that between two-thirds and three-quarters of the 1964 deficit, and roughly half the forecast 1965 deficit, could be attributed to 'non-recurring factors'.

But the heart of the General Brief was the so-called 'Armstrong Report'. This was a report by a group of officials from the Treasury, Board of Trade and Bank of England, under Armstrong's chairmanship, which had been set up in great secrecy earlier in the year by the then Conservative Chancellor, Mr Reginald Maudling, to look into the problem of the balance of payments and to make recommendations. It was not completed and submitted to Maudling until September, on the eve of the election campaign.

It began with an introduction which had been written by Armstrong himself. This estimated a 'basic' balance of payments deficit (i.e. one undistorted by special non-recurring factors) of some £200m. Various means of eliminating this were considered. Deflation of home demand should play a part, and unemployment should be allowed to rise, pragmatically and as opportunity occurred, from its then level of $1\frac{1}{2}$ per cent, to $1\frac{3}{4}$ per cent or even 2 per cent; deflation alone was rejected, since the degree of deflation required would be unacceptable (the main body of the report estimated that elimination of the entire deficit by deflation alone would require $2\frac{1}{4}$ per cent or even $2\frac{1}{2}$ per cent unemployment). Although it was clear that the deficit was too large to be financed from the UK's own reserves, it was argued that, so long as there was the alternative of international borrowing, import controls should be 'kept in readiness' rather than actually used. Devaluation was cursorily dismissed as 'a confession of failure'.

The real problem, it concluded, was the excessive absorption of the nation's advanced technical resources in defence projects. The solution, therefore, should be to buttress a gradual and modest reduction in the pressure of demand at home (the Treasury, by concentrating on the production figures instead of the unemployment trend, had erroneously concluded that the economy was not overheated as such) with immediate cuts in defence spending – notably in areas which would release 'advanced technical resources' – and any other measures to increase industrial efficiency.

The main body of the report went into all this in greater detail. Its treatment of devaluation was, for a document of its great length, almost perfunctory, although unequivocally hostile. It conceded that if the 'right steps' were not taken, or if they should prove inadequate, the Government might be 'forced into devaluation'; but it opposed this partly because world trade conditions were exceptionally favourable, which would help British exports, and partly because there was no clear evidence (it was alleged) that UK costs and prices were out of line with world costs and prices. It further argued that a devaluation would be a shock to confidence overseas, causing strained relations with other countries; that it would jeopardise the sterling area and encourage a capital outflow, thus risking making the payments deficit still worse; that it would cause uncertainty in foreign exchange markets and threaten a disruption of world trade; that it would undermine the reserve currency system, and in general was fraught with peril. The report added that, in the short term, the costs of devaluation would exceed the benefits, while in the long term it would bring about no fundamental improvement in efficiency. In conclusion ministers were told that 'fuller treatment of this subject is available if required.' No such fuller treatment was to be requested – or even permitted.

Finally, the document contained a large number of appendices. One dealt with TSR 2, Concorde and other aircraft projects that might usefully be dispensed with. Another set out possible import surcharge and quota restriction (Q.R.) schemes – and suggested that, since an import surcharge involved a breach of treaty obligations and would risk breaking up the European Free Trade Area, quotas might be better. Yet another appendix set out, with impressive confidence, the precise statistical relationship between specific increases in unemployment and corresponding reductions in wage inflation. And a further, brief appendix spelt out in neutral and elementary terms the economic theory and consequences of devaluation.

Of the four officials present at the Saturday morning meeting, only MacDougall at that time favoured devaluation (accompanied by appropriate supporting measures). But in fact the subject was not seriously discussed. Instead, the meeting was largely taken up with the measures that were to appear in the White Paper, *The Economic Situation* (Or 'Brown Paper', after its putative author), nine days later – including the import surcharge (which, despite the General Brief, Armstrong was privately advising Ministers to adopt) and a 'review' of Concorde (see Chapter 2). Roll apparently made the point that, in order to prevent damaging speculation, a decision one way or the other on devaluation should be taken at once and made known forthwith; but when, after the meeting, Wilson asked Brown and Callaghan to see him again at No. 10, at 7 p.m. that evening, with no officials present, the civil servants assumed that this was in order to discuss the allocation of ministerial portfolios. In fact, as Wilson makes clear in his memoirs, it was at this Saturday evening meeting that the new Government's decision to rule out devaluation was officially taken.

The impression has since been given that devaluation was considered on its merits at the Saturday evening meeting and deliberately rejected as being politically disastrous for a Labour Government with a majority of only four. 'There was comment,' writes Wilson in his memoirs,

> and this has been subsequently echoed, that we made an initial, even a fatal, blunder in our decision not to devalue within 24 hours of taking office, when we could have put all the responsibility on our Conservative predecessors. Politically, it might have been tempting and we were not unaware of the temptation. But I was convinced, and my colleagues agreed, that to devalue could have the most serious consequences. *The financial world at home and abroad was aware that the postwar decision to devalue in 1949 had been taken by a Labour Government. There would have been many who would conclude that a Labour Government facing difficulties always took the easy way out by devaluing the pound* ...
>
> When, three years later, devaluation was forced upon us, the whole world recognised there was no alternative – central banks and governments accepted the decision as necessary, recognising the courage and determination we had shown in our fight to hold the parity ... In 1964 there would have been no such acceptance; in 1964 the true facts of Britain's deficit were not known and politics, rather than economic necessity, would have been blamed ... So *devaluation was ruled out* by a deliberate decision. [Our italics].

While it may well be true that the 1949 devaluation was economically unsuccessful, the persistent Labour Party belief that it was politically disastrous (and indeed responsible for thirteen years in the wilderness of opposition) is curious, since in fact the then unpopular Labour Government recovered to win the 1950 General Election – although admittedly only by a very narrow margin.

However, as we shall see, the events of 1949 had a profound bearing on the case. Moreover, looking back from the changed climate of the seventies it is easy to underestimate the extent to which, in 1964, a parity change for a major currency, and particularly for a reserve currency, was still almost universally regarded as opening a Pandora's box of unpredictable, and potentially horrific, consequences. There were precious few dissenting votes, either in Whitehall or outside. In October 1964 a decision to devalue the pound would, to say the least, have been a highly unorthodox step for a new (and very inexperienced) Labour Government to have taken.

None the less, although the Treasury submission unequivocally advised against devaluation, it explicitly did not – unlike Wilson and his colleagues – rule it out. Indeed, it clearly suggested that, among the steps needed to avoid devaluation was a measure of deflation – which Wilson and his colleagues (at that time) rejected out of hand. It is true that Labour entered office committed to attempting to secure trade union agreement to an effective voluntary incomes policy, but not even the authors of the Labour manifesto claimed that this, even if ultimately successful, would deal with the immediate payments crisis: instead, the short-term problem was to be tackled by a battery of export (and import-saving) subsidies – which, in the event, were never (to any significant extent) introduced.

Moreover, despite Roll's contention, there was no obvious need for a precipitate decision. The first great run on the pound did not occur until mid-November, when it was provoked by a sequence of errors which included the mishandling of the import surcharge proposal, the delayed raising of the Bank Rate, the blazoning, in the 'Brown Paper' and against Whitehall's advice, of the secret official estimate of an £800m deficit, and the 11 November Budget, which increased both taxes and social security benefits and which, according to one eminent witness, 'appalled *all* the Treasury economists, who judged it to be wholly insufficient'. By contrast, the long-expected arrival of a Labour Government in mid-October had left the foreign exchange market unruffled. Among the civil servants, Cairncross, although at that time himself opposed to devaluation, was astonished at a decision of this magnitude being taken without any thorough discussion of the issue (and the alternatives) within the Treasury. And of the four senior pro-Labour economists in the process of being brought in by the new government to fill key advisory posts, three – MacDougall; the jolly Hungarian from Cambridge, Professor Nicholas Kaldor (Special Adviser to the Chancellor); and Mr Robert Neild (Economic Adviser to the Treasury) – were already in favour of devaluation. Even the fourth, the conspiratorial Hungarian from Oxford, Dr Thomas Balogh, for long Wilson's personal economic guru and now to become Economic Adviser to the Cabinet, although at that time still violently opposed to devaluation, sent the new Prime Minister a letter on the crucial Saturday urging him not to take any hasty decisions, since the situation had not been fully analysed.

On the face of it, therefore, it would seem that the decision was taken with unnecessary haste; and that, had more time been given for reflection, the subsequent course of events might have been different: at the very least, the degree of emotional commitment to the existing parity might have been less.

In reality, however – and it is here that most published accounts of the events of 17 October 1964, lack a crucial dimension – Wilson's and Callaghan's absolute commitment to the avoidance of devaluation significantly antedated the General Election. It thus had nothing to do with the eventual narrowness of Labour's majority, nor, for that matter, with either the scale of the 'inherited' deficit or the tone of the Treasury brief.

To find the genesis of the Saturday evening decision, and the nature of the emotional commitment to it, it is therefore necessary to look back briefly into the earlier careers of both the Prime Minister and the Chancellor. They had travelled to the same destination, but by different routes.

Unlike his two economic ministers, Wilson had personal experience of devaluation, having been deeply involved in the events of 1949. When, in the summer of that year, the financial situation had become critical, the then Chancellor, Sir Stafford Cripps, was in a Zurich clinic recuperating from a serious illness. The Prime Minister, Clement Attlee, therefore asked three ministers with economic backgrounds – Gaitskell, the Minister of Fuel and Power, Douglas Jay, the Economic Secretary to the Treasury, and Wilson, the President of the Board of Trade – to put their heads together and recommend what action should be taken. Gaitskell and Jay rapidly concluded that devaluation was essential, and said as much to Wilson, who concurred. A meeting was thereupon arranged to acquaint Attlee with the collective verdict; but after Gaitskell had spelt it out Wilson, to his colleagues' astonishment, demurred. Within days, however, the situation had worsened, and Attlee was eventually able to obtain from the three ministers the unanimous verdict on which he was insisting.

Wilson continued to see devaluation in terms of the 1949 decision which, at least after the fall of the Attlee Government in 1951, he came to regard as disastrous politically for Labour and at the same time irrelevant to the solution of the nation's economic problems. Cairncross, who had worked closely with Wilson at that time, says that, when he became Prime Minister in 1964, 'I always knew he would be dead against devaluation, from his behaviour in 1949'. Others who have known him well throughout his career all endorse the importance to Wilson of what he saw as the political and economic lessons of 1949.

Moreover this formative experience soon came to be woven into an overall approach to economic policy which was perhaps about as close as Mr Wilson ever got to a political philosophy and whose *locus classicus* is his long article in the *New Statesman*, 24 March 1961. As officials who worked with him after 1964 can testify, its chief characteristics are a belief that the nation suffers from *real* problems which require *real* (i.e. 'structural'), and certainly not market or monetary, solutions; and that, in particular, specific problems (for example, a decline in motor car exports) require specific solutions –

the more detailed the better. (Curiously, this is an approach which was to a considerable extent shared by his Conservative successor: Edward Heath bitterly opposed devaluation, when it eventually came, on very similar grounds.)

Wilson was strongly reinforced in his beliefs by the one economist who had his ear throughout the Opposition years, Thomas Balogh. In the early months of 1963 there had been a spirited correspondence in the columns of *The Times*, in which the other 'Hungarian', Kaldor, strongly argued the case for floating the pound, while Balogh (among others) fiercely attacked such irrelevant heresy, asserting that 'the disastrous consequences of the Cripps devaluation can no longer be disputed' [*The Times*, 4 February 1963], and dismissing any suggestion of devaluation or floating: 'reliance on monetary gimmicks in particular will not help.' Two years later Balogh was to join the devaluationist camp himself; but by then he had lost his influence over Wilson.

There was yet another important consideration in Wilson's mind. This is what one of the economic advisers brought in by Labour describes as Wilson's 'love affair with America'. The Anglo-American special relationship was paramount. He shared, with all British Prime Ministers of the fifties and sixties, a desire to have the ear of the most powerful man in the Western world. He shared, in common with all Labour leaders, a desire to be respected by the mighty in a land where 'socialism' was a dirty word. But in particular, he admired America's Democratic Party, then in office, which was his vision of what the British Labour Party ought to become. So devaluation was to be avoided, since it would remove the first line of defence for the dollar (as indeed, in the event, it did) and thus alienate the United States; while US goodwill was in turn essential to enable the sterling parity to be successfully defended.

Discussing the 1964 'decision' in his memoirs, Mr George Wigg, at that time Wilson's closest ministerial colleague, writes:

> I accepted Wilson's view that we should not devalue. I saw force in the argument that if we had devalued immediately many of our problems would have been transferred, without warning, to the Americans. This would have angered President Johnson and endangered future Anglo-American co-operation.

He adds, however:

> Almost the only thing that can be said with certainty is that Wilson's solicitude about President Johnson's reactions was a misjudgment. I saw no sign that President Johnson ever regarded Wilson's policies with the respect they were supposed to have

earned. We paid a high price, a very high price in economic terms, for nothing.

For the origins of the Chancellor's commitment to the existing parity we do not have to delve so far back into the past. When Gaitskell had finally managed to prize the Shadow Treasury portfolio out of Wilson's hands in November 1961, Callaghan, the successor he chose, had no pretensions to economic expertise. Gaitskell therefore asked his old friend and political sympathiser Sir Robert Hall, who had just retired as Economic Adviser to the Government and become a Visiting Fellow of Nuffield College, Oxford, to provide Callaghan with tuition in current economic problems. Hall accordingly formed a 'tutorial group', whose most prominent members were three Oxford economists, Dr Ian Little, Mr Christopher McMahon (now an executive director of the Bank of England) and Mr Richard Ross; plus Robert Neild, then Deputy-Director of the National Institute of Economic and Social Research, who had been responsible for the National Institute's highly controversial advocacy of devaluation earlier that year.

All of them were former members of the Economic Section of the Treasury: as Hall puts it, the group was deliberately chosen to provide tuition in practical economic management, not pure economic theory. In any event Callaghan, who knew nothing of either of these mysteries, duly travelled to Nuffield for a series of 'tutorials' held between May 1962 and August 1963, and the various members of the group provided papers for him, principally on incomes policy and sterling. The papers on sterling and the balance of payments were written by McMahon. An Australian by birth and now a director of the Bank of England, he published his own views in a 1964 paperback, *Sterling in the Sixties*, in which he asserted that 'as things are the UK probably should never devalue'.

However, the really important contribution of the Nuffield group was to arrange in May 1963 for Callaghan to pay a visit (financed by Nuffield College) to the United States to meet for the first time the leaders of the American financial community. He went armed with introductions and briefs from the group, and his briefs counselled the wisdom of emphasising the commitment of an incoming Labour Government to the maintenance of the sterling parity. He was entertained by, among others, Mr David Rockefeller, Mr Douglas Dillon, then Secretary of the Treasury, and Mr Al Hayes, then chairman of the Federal Reserve Bank of New York. He took a particular liking to the eminently respectable and conservative Hayes, 'a man you could trust'. He stuck to his briefs, and was gratified by the response. He came home with two entrenched convictions: that an incoming

Labour Government would be able to count on all the American help it might need to avert a forced devaluation; and that he had given his solemn word to men whom he respected that he would not devalue voluntarily. When, in the summer of 1964, Callaghan, with Maudling's full knowledge and approval, began to have private discussions with Armstrong in anticipation of a possible change of Government later that year, he left the permanent head of the Treasury in no doubt about his firm commitment to the rejection of devaluation – a commitment he knew Wilson shared.

Thus the decision to rule out devaluation had effectively been taken – and, indeed, communicated to Armstrong – in Opposition, well before the Saturday evening meeting. The true purpose of that meeting was threefold. First, the decision, although taken in opposition, had to be formalised in government. Second, Wilson and Callaghan had to commit Brown. This presented no difficulty. Although no economist, Brown had long held strongly to the traditional Labour belief that devaluation was bad for the working classes. (In the short term, when devaluation implies a shift from wages to profits, this is, judged in isolation, correct: it is perhaps worth noting that Brown, who was later to join the devaluationist camp, was the only one of the three who consciously thought in class terms.) This view was reinforced in Brown's eyes by the fact that the Labour Chancellor who had devalued in 1949, Sir Stafford Cripps, was a man he had heartily detested.

In any event, given the support of both Callaghan and Brown, Wilson knew he had no need to fear being challenged in Cabinet: indeed, given the unity of the triumvirate, he could effectively prevent the matter from being so much as discussed in Cabinet. Crossman records [*Diaries*, p. 26] that at the first full Cabinet meeting, early the following week, although the economic crisis was the main item on the agenda,

> we were told as little about it as the National Executive of the Party is ever told. It really was an absolute farce to have George Brown saying: 'Naturally you won't want to be told, for fear of the information leaking, how serious the situation is. You won't want to be told what methods we shall take, but we shall take them.'

Farce or not, it apparently went unchallenged.

But the third, and perhaps in Wilson's eyes the most important, purpose of the Saturday evening meeting was to ensure silence. From then on, devaluation became known in Whitehall as 'the unmentionable', or, according to one more colourful account [*Sunday Times*, 26 November], by the code-name 'British Railways', and all discussion of the subject was forbidden, for fear that careless talk

would start a run on the pound. There is no doubt that, on a subject
as sensitive as this, secrecy was essential; but Wilson's concern with
security rapidly became obsessive.

This soon manifested itself in a startling way. In November 1964 a
meeting was arranged in 10 Downing Street for which the various
government economists prepared papers, in the normal way, in the
expectation that the ministers concerned would debate concrete proposals for action. In particular, there was a carefully prepared paper
by the Economic Section of the Treasury which dealt with the
measures that needed to be taken *in the absence* of devaluation. As
soon as Wilson heard of this he ordered it, and all the other papers
for the meeting, to be destroyed unread, and decreed that the very
word 'devaluation' must be expunged from the Whitehall vocabulary.
Thus perished the only Treasury paper between the election of
Labour in October 1964 and the eventual collapse of the parity in
September 1967 that ever dealt with the issue of devaluation. Nor
were the alternative measures outlined in the paper ever taken. It was
not the decision not to devalue that surprised Whitehall: it was the
seemingly emotional and irrational way in which the whole subject – and hence, inevitably, the whole question of the management
of the economy – was treated at the top that gave rise to increasing
bafflement, worry and alarm.

Before leaving the October decisions, however, it may be construc-
tive to speculate whether the course of events would have been
materially different had the Conservatives narrowly won the 1964
election instead of narrowly losing it. Mr Harold Macmillan, the
then Prime Minister, had become strongly attracted to the idea of
allowing the pound to float in the aftermath of the collapse of the
original Common Market negotiations in January 1963. In the final
volume of his memoirs he quotes an aide-memoire he sent to Maudling, his Chancellor, at that time, in which he declared that 'we must
definitely make up our minds that we will not return to the defence
of sterling by the methods we have used hitherto' and canvassed the
notion of floating instead. Maudling, it seems, then broached the idea
with the Governor of the Bank of England, Lord Cromer, who was
unequivocally hostile: the Bank's traditional antipathy to floating
was, if anything, even greater than its hostility to devaluation to a
lower but fixed rate.

There the matter rested; but Maudling was generally regarded by
his Treasury officials as a 'temperamental floater'. The Whitehall
view at the time was that Maudling hoped that neither devaluation
nor floating would be necessary, but in the last resort would have
taken the plunge rather than sacrifice the 'growth experiment' on
which, at Macmillan's behest, he had embarked. And it seems clear

that, had the Tories won in 1964, Maudling would have remained
as Chancellor, continuing to be given a very loose rein by his Prime
Minister, Sir Alec Douglas-Home.

And yet one wonders. It is true that Maudling had a better grasp
of the situation than his unfortunate successor, and that he might
have received a starker presentation from a Treasury uninhibited by
the political awkwardness and hypersensitivity that characterised its
original dealings with Labour. But the IMF's abhorrence of floating
at that time was very strong, and the Conservatives would have had
to fly in the face of just that same establishment consensus whose approval meant so much to Wilson. Besides, while Wilson and Callaghan at least knew that their own backbenchers were largely in-
different to the exchange rate, there was a widely held view at the
time (shared by Maudling himself) that the Tory parliamentary rank
and file would kick up rough at the abandonment of the parity in
any form. (In fact, the 1931 National Government had slipped the
parity moorings without any trouble from its backbench Conservative supporters; and the Heath Government was to do so again, with
equal ease, in 1972 – although in fairness it must be added that by
then floating had come into fashion.) It hardly seems in character for
Maudling to have proved willing to stare down anticipated resistance
on that scale. The evidence is inconclusive, but the best guess is that
a Conservative Government would have abandoned the parity well
before November 1967, but well after October 1964.

Within a month the strength of the new Government's commitment
to the sterling parity was severely tested, as the first great run on the
pound, largely triggered by the publication (at the Prime Minister's
insistence, and after officials had persuaded the Chancellor and
Brown to delete it) of the notorious '£800m deficit' estimate, rapidly
gathered momentum. According to one well-placed witness the solidarity of the economic triumvirate behind the exchange rate very
nearly collapsed at this first test: George Wigg, in his memoirs, records that

> the reactions of the Chancellor of the Exchequer to our troubles
> at that time bowled me over. Jim Callaghan's lips quivered, his
> hands shook, he had no idea what had hit him. A gathering
> at Chequers during the November economic crisis lives in my
> memory. I remember vividly Callaghan mumbling 'we can't go on.
> We shall have to devalue.'

Perhaps they would have done. But at this point, on 25 November, Lord Cromer, the Governor of the Bank of England, and Mr

Charlie Coombs, Hayes's deputy at the Federal Reserve Bank of New York, managed virtually overnight to rustle up a $3000m international loan facility for Britain, a hitherto unprecedented amount. The sterling outflow gradually abated, and the crisis, for the time being, was over.

For one minister outside the Cabinet the appearance of that quintessential Macmillan appointee, George Rowland Stanley Baring, 3rd Earl of Cromer, millionaire merchant banker married to the daughter of the first Lord Rothermere, in the guise of fairy godmother to the Labour Government was not merely incongruous, but also a bitter disappointment. This was Anthony Crosland, Minister of State at the DEA (i.e. No. 2 to George Brown, with whom he was never particularly close). For Crosland was the only economic minister – indeed the only significant minister of any kind – who was a devaluationist from the start. As the November crisis deepened Crosland was increasingly optimistic that events would undo the 'irrevocable' commitment of the ruling trio to the existing parity. He held a meeting to discuss the situation with the three political recruits – Balogh, Kaldor and Neild – to the government's civil service economic team. Balogh, the lone anti-devaluer of the three, agreed that, failing a major international loan, devaluation would be unavoidable, and sent a minute to Wilson to this effect (recommending, in this eventuality, recourse to floating). He also reported the meeting to the Prime Minister, who flew into a rage, and reported Crosland's treachery to his departmental chief. Brown gave his subordinate a characteristically vitriolic dressing-down.

Sterling's respite following the $3000m blood transfusion did not last long. The next assault on the pound began in June 1965, reaching its peak in the traditional crisis month of July, when it was met with the equally traditional package of deflationary measures, announced by Callaghan on 27 July. Well before then Balogh had become fully convinced of the need to abandon the parity as a *pis aller*, since it was now clear to him that the government (thanks, as he saw it, to the malign anti-Socialist veto of the Treasury and Bank of England) would never resort to the full-blooded quasi-wartime siege economy which he personally preferred. But Balogh's influence on the Prime Minister had vanished very soon after Wilson moved into No. 10: within the Downing Street entourage, it had not taken the coolly professional Secretary to the Cabinet, Sir Burke Trend, long to win the battle for Wilson's ear. According to one account the Prime Minister himself had told the Downing Street staff to give Balogh 'a room, some papers, and lock him in'.

None the less, this did at last mean unanimity among the four top economic advisers brought in by Labour. Accordingly, that summer as the pressure on the pound was renewed, and talk of deflation filled the corridors of Whitehall, all four of them – Balogh, Kaldor, MacDougall and Neild – plus Crosland (now a member of the Cabinet, but in the non-economic post of Secretary of State for Education) met secretly at the country home, near Cambridge, of Lord Walston, a wealthy junior minister. They agreed on two things. First, the sooner a General Election could be got out of the way the better, since there was obviously no chance of persuading the Cabinet to agree to devaluation until the government had secured an increased majority. Second, the four advisers agreed to write a joint paper, strongly urging the case for devaluation, ready to be presented to the government for immediate action as soon as the election was won. The final draft of this paper (which Crossman [*Diaries*, p. 305] mistakenly reports as having been submitted by August 1965: it seems likely he had got wind of the completion of the first draft) was ready in February 1966 – although the ever-prudent Balogh declined to sign it until the election, eventually held on 31 March, was in the bag. His subtlety was wasted. As soon as he received the paper, Wilson refused to have it circulated to the Cabinet and – as in November 1964, with the Treasury's effort – ordered all copies to be consigned to the flames, unread.

The July 1965 run on the pound did, however, have two rather less abortive consequences. Armstrong sought, and secured, Callaghan's approval for the secret preparation of a detailed contingency plan setting out the technical steps that would have to be taken in the event of a forced devaluation. This so-called 'War Book' was in fact a revised and up-dated version of a similar contingency plan the cautious Armstrong had had prepared off his own bat, early in 1964, for use in the event of a Labour Government being returned and deciding – despite Callaghan's private assurances to Armstrong – to devalue straight away, after all. It seems that, in the summer of 1965, Armstrong omitted to tell Callaghan of this genesis, much as (at that time) Callaghan omitted to inform Wilson of the operation which he had authorised. The War Book, written under Armstrong's instructions by a small group of officials from the Treasury and Bank of England, was further revised and polished in 1966 and 1967, and eventually implemented (as Wilson records in his memoirs) in November 1967: there are mixed views as to its value when finally put to the test.

But by far the more important consequence of the July 1965 crisis was the conversion of Brown to the devaluationist camp. For some time Crosland, MacDougall and Neild had been endeavouring to persuade him that there were worse things for the working class than devaluation. But it was not until the 27 July deflationary package that he finally accepted that economic growth was being sacrificed on the altar of the parity, and that, short of a complete change of policy on the pound, his beloved National Plan, on which he had been toiling ever since Labour took office, and which was at last to see the light of day that September, was as good as dead before it was even born. (The DEA's bevy of economists, including those working on the National Plan, had for some time been taking devaluation for granted in their calculations. For example, a 'shadow' exchange rate, and not the official rate, was used to calculate the return on a projected import-saving investment. But this, of course, begged the question.)

The conversion of Brown, technically No. 2 in the government, in August 1965, only nine months after the crisis of November 1964 during which he had angrily berated Callaghan for even contemplating the very possibility of devaluation, represented the first defection of a member of the ruling triumvirate, and was to have a profound effect on the events of July 1966 – although Wilson's immediate response was to instruct Brown's senior permanent officials to keep as much sensitive information as possible from their master. It also meant that, from that time on, the 'unmentionable' was increasingly mentioned, wherever two or three were gathered together.

Indeed, a few days before Brown's conversion, the intrepid Crosland, for the first time, actually raised the subject of devaluation in Cabinet. He got no support – he had expected none, seeking simply to 'raise a standard', since it was clear that nothing could be done until after the election. However, despite the government's notorious propensity to leak, nothing of this sea-change seems to have permeated to the outside world at that time. Thus in September 1965, *The Times* felt able to begin a major article on the economic situation with the assurance that 'Devaluation is a dead issue'.

The General Election of March 1966 saw the Government enlarge its overall majority from an exiguous four to a landslide 96; but on the sterling front nothing ostensibly changed. The four advisers' paper had already been destroyed. Meanwhile, during March, while the politicians were preoccupied with the election campaign (the election was held on the last day of the month), a high-powered committee of senior Permanent Secretaries was at work, under the chairmanship of the Cabinet Secretary, Trend, preparing a post-election agenda for the government. The agenda was presented to Wilson on the Saturday immediately after the election. It identified four key strategic issues on which the government should concentrate its collective mind and on which early Cabinet decisions would be helpful. These were the Common Market, the British presence East of Suez, incomes policy and devaluation. On this last, it seems that the committee had had the benefit of a paper written largely by Kaldor and Neild positively recommending the unmentionable, but this was quickly suppressed, and the permanent officials' advice appears to have been more along 'if it were done when 'tis done, then 'twere well it were done quickly' lines. In any event, this item on the agenda was simply ignored: nothing would induce the Prime Minister to allow Cabinet so much as to discuss the subject. (According to one senior official, for four weeks nothing was done about anything. No doubt, amidst all his problems, Wilson was entitled to savour his massive electoral triumph, however disingenuously it had been won.)

By this time Roll had joined the devaluationist camp, and Cairncross (privately) was moving in that direction. Moreover, shortly after the election the government had begun to move towards the renewal of overtures to the Common Market (see Chapter 3). One side-effect of this was to encourage second thoughts about the parity among the top permanent officials of the Treasury, including Armstrong. It was not that they wished to clear the decks for Market membership: as explained elsewhere, the Treasury at this time broadly shared the scepticism of its political head about the European strategy. The Great George Street view was simply that the balance of payments was clearly far too weak to withstand the strains of entry. Hence, if the government was genuinely hell-bent on Market membership, the parity would have to go. Eventually (on the eve of the formal application in May 1967) Armstrong put the point bluntly to Wilson – not, however, as an argument *for* devaluation, but implicitly as an argument *against* applying for Market entry. The Prime Minister brushed him aside, and Armstrong continued to be baffled by the manifest incompatibility of what were to become (until November 1967, when both policies collapsed almost simultaneously) the government's two main political objectives. But he said no more, justifying his silence by the private assumption (which turned out to be correct) that the European adventure would fail anyway.

However, although Wilson and Callaghan had become increasingly isolated in their struggle to defend the parity, they were fortuitously assisted at this time by a great argument that had erupted within the devaluationist camp over whether or not it was necessary to 'dig the hole first'. The economy during the early months of 1966 was booming (a condition traditionally associated with periods in which General Elections are held) and it would obviously be necessary to accompany any devaluation – designed to bring about a dramatic switch of resources into exports – with far-reaching measures to deflate demand at home. Of the four special economic advisers, Kaldor and MacDougall argued that it was economically

sound and psychologically essential to present the two parts of the
operation as a single, simultaneous, package. Balogh (predictably)
and Neild (surprisingly) were dig-the-hole-first men, arguing for a
postponement of devaluation until the deflation had been done. To
some extent this mirrored a major departmental split: Roll, as
Permanent Secretary to the DEA, favoured the simultaneous
package, while Armstrong and the Treasury were convinced that it
would be risky in the extreme to devalue before the spare capacity
had been created. The argument raged right up to July 1966, and
was to prove of considerable assistance to Wilson when, at this point,
he was at last faced with a Cabinet revolt.

The Cabinet crisis of July 1966 had its origins in yet another great
run on the pound, which began in June and rapidly worsened.

In her memoirs, Marcia Williams, Wilson's devoted political secretary and confidante, provides a characteristically vivid account of the
atmosphere:

> Throughout July many of Harold's closest friends within the
> government would ask me round for a drink or tea. They wanted,
> yet often hesitated, to refer to the dreaded devaluation question.
> But they were anxious to transmit to Harold messages pressing
> him to take action on it ... I can remember him during that period
> walking up and down in the dining room at lunchtime. He would
> eat half his lunch and then get up from the table in a contem-
> plative way. If the dreaded word was spoken, he got up and pro-
> ceeded to walk up and down, very quickly, rehearsing the argu-
> ments for and against with all the difficulties involved, setting out
> how he saw the position.

Meanwhile, in June, the Treasury, in its time-honoured way, had
begun preparing yet another, and still stiffer, deflationary package
of July measures. But at this point events took a less conventional
course. As soon as it became clear that July measures were inevitable,
Brown, with Wilson's grudging consent, commissioned Roll and
MacDougall at the DEA to produce a paper setting out an alternative package, with devaluation as its centrepiece. Then, in the middle
of July, at the height of the crisis, just as Wilson was about to go off
on a three-day visit to Moscow, an alarming report reached him from
the most authoritative sources: Callaghan had been converted to the
DEA alternative. To Wilson, all this could mean only one thing.
Not merely the sterling parity, but his own position as Prime
Minister, was being deliberately threatened. Ever since October
1964, Wilson had relied on 'creative conflict' between the Treasury
and the Department of Economic Affairs to keep Callaghan and
Brown permanently at loggerheads, thus ensuring Prime Ministerial

ascendency not merely over economic policy but over the government as a whole – for these were the two heavyweight Cabinet colleagues who had contested the leadership with him after Gaitskell's death in 1963. For these two suddenly to form a common front, in opposition to him on the one issue on which he had irrevocably nailed his colours to the mast, could be nothing less than a plot to replace him.

In fact, the Chancellor's short-lived 'conversion' to devaluation appears to have been motivated chiefly by his fear that there would be a Cabinet revolt against the severity of the measures needed (as he saw it) to avert devaluation, and that Wilson – a great one for counting heads in Cabinet – would bow to the verdict of the majority, leaving Callaghan in an impossible position.

A worried Wilson immediately saw Callaghan, and assured him that not only would he give the Chancellor 100 per cent support in Cabinet for the necessary measures, but he was prepared, in his own words, to 'knock every nail in' himself. (He was as good as his word. The 20 July measures were announced to the House of Commons not by Callaghan, but by Wilson himself.) Callaghan then pointed out the happier way matters were conducted in Germany, where Chancellor Erhard had recently told him that he and his Finance Minister agreed matters beforehand, and then automatically had their way in Cabinet – in fact, the normal UK practice before the advent of Wilson. The Prime Minister assured Callaghan that, in future, that was just how matters would be in this country, and that, as an earnest of his good faith, he would move Callaghan to sit next to him at the Cabinet table. But Callaghan was still worried about Brown, who, he feared (not without reason), would resign if he failed to get his way, to become the hero of the back benches while Callaghan was cast as the villain, a Labour Selwyn Lloyd. 'Don't worry, I'll square George' was the Prime Minister's reassuring message. Thus ended what passed into Whitehall folklore as 'Callaghan's wobble'.

Greatly relieved, Wilson flew off to Moscow. No sooner had he arrived there, however, when yet another alarming report reached him: this time that Crossman was organising, with Brown, a pro-devaluation Cabinet cabal behind his back. His suspicions of a plot to replace him reinforced, Wilson acted swiftly. From Moscow, he ordered all copies of the DEA paper setting out the devaluation alternative to be destroyed. (One copy – Brown's – apparently survived the holocaust. That apart, this was thus the third major government paper on devaluation – one by the Treasury, one by the economic advisers, and one by the DEA – to have been burned on the personal instructions of the Prime Minister.) And, with Callaghan's 'wobble' fresh in his mind, he personally instructed Trend, Armstrong and Roll to get their heads together and work out a really tough package of public expenditure cuts and other deflationary measures to save the pound, to be announced on 20 July. Then, on the morning of 19 July, he returned to London and proceeded to give a dazzling display of his skills at Cabinet management.

The crucial Cabinet meeting at which the 20 July measures had to be agreed began at 5.30 that afternoon, which had given Wilson time to see all the key Ministers individually beforehand. It was the first (and only) time that there was to be any discussion of devaluation in Cabinet (even then it was not on the formal agenda and there were no papers on the subject); it was also the first major Cabinet conflict of the 1964–70 Labour government.

The Prime Minister was to some extent helped by the composition of the devaluationist 'cabal'. It numbered six: on the left, Crossman, with his allies, Mrs Barbara Castle and Mr Wedgwood Benn (who had only been promoted to the Cabinet that very month); and, on the right, Brown, Crosland, and Mr Roy Jenkins. Brown, in his memoirs, describes it as 'the most distinguished part of the Cabinet'; one of the others claims that 'as usual, it was the intellectuals of both the right and the left against the rest.' But it was scarcely a cohesive force. Barbara Castle, for example, was passionately opposed to the burgeoning Common Market approach, while Brown and Jenkins were its two leading proponents. As Crossman has related [*Diaries*, p. 595], the Prime Minister, although himself shifting fast into the pro-Market camp at that time, was quick to warn Mrs Castle and Crossman himself that devaluation was a manoeuvre invented by pro-Marketeers to smooth the way to Europe. Yet at the same time he was preparing to 'square George' with the prize of the Foreign Office and a commitment to Europe.

It was a further stroke of good fortune for Wilson that it was Crossman who took it upon himself to lead the attack. The author of a distinguished introduction to Bagehot's *English Constitution*, Crossman was fascinated by the machinery of government; and so, instead of confining himself to demanding a straightforward choice of the alternative – devaluation – strategy, he coupled this with a complaint about the triumvirate's monopoly of economic policy-making and proposed the establishment of a new Cabinet Committee to allow a wider cross-section of ministers to become involved in the formulation of economic strategy.

Wilson seized on the second leg of the argument, insisting that, if a wider circle were drawn in, there would be 'leaks'. Crossman was played with great finesse; and when Wilson eventually conceded the committee (having, as we have seen, already privately assured

Callaghan that, so far from broadening the economic policy power centre, he would narrow it from the triumvirate to a duumvirate), Crossman was convinced that he and his friends had won a famous victory. The Strategic Economic Policy Committee (SEP) was duly constituted, packed with such luminaries as the Secretaries of State for Scotland and Wales, and disappeared from sight. (From time to time in the year that followed Crosland valiantly attempted to raise the issue of devaluation in SEP, but no one took any notice.)

The Prime Minister was not yet out of the wood. Brown and Crosland (probably the only one of the six equipped to dissect the anti-devaluation case in depth) were less easily dazzled than Crossman by the concession on SEP. The substance of the matter could not be altogether avoided. Here, in addition to all the long-standing arguments (three Labour devaluations in a row, etc.), Wilson seized on the argument among the devaluationist economic advisers themselves over the timing. Even Neild agreed that the 'hole' had to be dug first. So obviously the right time seriously to consider floating the pound would come in the spring – not from weakness but from strength. (Crossman [*Diaries*, p. 577] records a third 'concession': '... if the level of unemployment was to rise markedly above 2 per cent (480,000), then he [Wilson] would consider devaluation. This was an assurance he gave across the table to George Brown.' The Prime Minister was on pretty safe ground: seasonally adjusted unemployment, at that time, was only 1·3 per cent; it did not rise to over 2 per cent for another nine months; and in November 1967, when the unmentionable eventually occurred, it was 2·3 per cent.)

There was one more hurdle to jump: the personal position of Brown. Crossman, as he records in his Diaries, had already discovered that neither Jenkins nor Barbara Castle was in a mood for resigning (nor, it would seem, was Crossman himself). Brown, not for the first time, very much was. Furthermore, if Crossman's account is to be believed [*Diaries*, p. 547], Brown was indeed prepared to offer himself as a replacement for the Prime Minister, and had been canvassing for support. If so, this would partially explain Wilson's suspicions when in Moscow; but it inevitably exposed the cabal's fragility, for, faced with a choice between Wilson and the parity, and Brown without it, Crossman and Mrs Castle settled unhesitatingly for the parity. Crossman tells us that Brown 'implied that there were other people prepared to go with him to the last resort'. One wonders who they were.

Brown had made it clear that, if the Cabinet decision was to deflate without devaluing, then he would resign. It was, and he did; but Wilson was prepared. After an extraordinary sequence of events he succeeded in talking Brown into withdrawing his resignation. In his

memoirs, Brown states: 'The most telling argument put to me was
that if I resigned I should have to say why I resigned, and if I said
that the government was seriously split on whether or not to devalue,
there would at once be a most devastating run on our reserves.' This
was undoubtedly Wilson's reason for wishing to avoid Brown's resignation at that time (he was happy enough to accept it in March
1968, six months *after* devaluation). But he had a still more telling
argument up his sleeve. Brown's ambition to sit in the seat once oc-
cupied by his hero, Mr Ernest Bevin, at the Foreign Office, was well
known – as was Brown's passionate devotion to British membership
of the Common Market, which he had been urging on Wilson for
the past year. So (on condition that Brown stayed at the DEA a few
more weeks, just to see the Prices and Incomes Bill, another part of
the July package, through the House of Commons) the Foreign
Secretaryship – with a Common Market remit – was duly offered,
and duly accepted. Almost a decade later, on 5 April 1976, Wilson
retired at the end of his second term as Prime Minister. Asked by the
representative of the Press Association whether, throughout his long
stint at the top of the greasy pole, there was any decision which he
now regretted, Wilson replied: 'One, possibly. Looking back, I wish
we could have devalued in 1966 ...'

The events that followed the Cabinet crisis of July 1966 were something of an anti-climax. Spring 1967 came and went, without any
move of any kind even to consider 'floating from strength'. Just as it
had previously been almost treasonable to discuss devaluation when
the pound was weak, so now it had become irrelevant when the
pound was (temporarily) convalescent. The previous winter, Balogh
and Kaldor had once again privately urged on Callaghan the importance, for his own political reputation, of devaluing as an act of
policy before he was forced into it, willy-nilly. But the Chancellor's
moment of truth was past, and his mind was closed. It was a matter
of honour, and, as he had declaimed to Cairncross a short while
earlier, 'a man can only live out his destiny'. In May 1967 came the
formal British application to join the Common Market, and almost
immediately after there began the final long pre-devaluation run on
the pound. At the end of July the House of Commons debated the
state of the economy, and both front benches once again dismissed
the idea of devaluation. Callaghan spoke in particularly forceful
tones. Armstrong, who by now had seen the writing on the wall,
urged him in vain not to commit himself so irrevocably, but the
Chancellor (who, since Brown's departure from the DEA in August
1966, had at last enjoyed the undisputed control of economic policy
for which he had always yearned – subject only to the whim of the

Prime Minister) was adamant. Devaluation was 'a flight from reality', a nostrum which had become 'very modish among a number of theoretical economists, as well as some Right-wing and Left-wing thinkers'. There could hardly be a more comprehensive anathema in Callaghan's vocabulary than that.

In September the European Commision made public its reasoned assessment of Britain's renewed application for Community membership. It stopped only just short of identifying devaluation as a precondition, not just for Market membership, but for any British economic strategy, and the message was not lost on the foreign exchange markets, where the run on the pound intensified. At the end of October the Treasury's autumn balance of payments assessment confirmed that the game was up, and Cairncross wrote a polite, and strictly personal, letter to Callaghan stating that he had supported the Chancellor all the time against devaluation, and admired the struggle Callaghan had waged, but now the time had come ... Callaghan, agreeing, informed Wilson, who seemed to accept the inevitable. The War Book was taken off the shelf, and its contingency plan put into operation.

The final denouement that November – the alarmingly unconvincing television interview given by the luckless Governor of the Bank of England, Sir Leslie O'Brien (who had succeeded Cromer in July 1966), the secret implementation of the various stages in the contingency plan, the rumours, the Private Notice Question to the Chancellor from a Labour backbencher, Mr Robert Sheldon, which the Speaker was expected, and failed, to disallow, and the ensuing disastrous run on the pound after the decision to devalue had already been finalised – has little bearing on the lesson to be drawn from this case history. There was, however, one poignant incident in the last week before devaluation which deserves a mention.

The devaluation of the pound, from $2.80 to $2.40, was announced (by Wilson) on Saturday, 18 November, with the Cabinet having been kept in the dark until two days before. On Wednesday, 15 November the BBC had carried in its evening news bulletin a report from Paris of a new $1000 million support loan for the pound. (It was this story which led to the Private Notice Question in the Commons the following day, asking the Chancellor to make a statement.) What seems to have been behind the report was a final last-ditch attempt by the Prime Minister to panic the US Government. For while the Chancellor had bowed to the inevitable, the Prime Minister had been unable to do so. Right up to the end, as officials proceeded with the pre-devaluation count-down, expecting any day to have it countermanded from the very top, Wilson continued to cling to the notion that, by threatening a really substantial devaluation which would put intolerable pressure on the exposed dollar, the Americans could be scared into rustling up yet another massive international support package. And he was right: they were, and they did. Or, at least, they tried. But this time the Prime Minister was betrayed by that shift of economic power from Washington to Western Europe which neither he nor his Chancellor had ever really understood. The European governments had had enough, and Washington could no longer carry the pound alone.

Five days after the parity had at last been abandoned, the Prime Minister allowed himself to be interviewed on television. Devaluation, he conceded, 'was a setback. The Chancellor last night in Parliament described it as a defeat. It was a defeat. The last two weeks for him, for me, and for a number of others, have been hell. I don't want to disguise that at all. They've been the worst two weeks I've known....'

A decision had been taken, unannounced, in opposition, not to devalue the pound, and in effect to rule out doing so. The formal ratification of this decision had been the new Labour Government's very first act on taking office; and for more than three years, the greater part of that Government's eventual life, while policies on a whole range of other issues, all of them far closer to the heart of the Labour Party – from the independent nuclear deterrent to the statutory incomes ponicy, not to mention such minor matters as prescription charges – were reversed, this one decision was relentlessly adhered to until, at the end of the day, it was overcome by *force majeure*.

The three-year-long non-devaluation of the pound would seem to provide a clear case of absolute Prime Ministerial power. There can be no disputing the fact that it had been uniquely for Wilson that maintenance of the parity amounted to an obsession – or, in the words of one senior Treasury official, 'a sacrament'. It was Wilson who, through Trend, successfully prevented the matter from ever appearing on the Cabinet agenda – and on the one occasion, in July 1966, when he failed to prevent devaluation from being discussed in Cabinet, it was Wilson who routed the dissentients. (This was assisted, it will be recalled, by the absence of any pro-devaluation Cabinet papers: Wilson's habit of ordering the physical destruction of Government papers that mentioned the unmentionable was more than a mere – if somewhat extreme – security measure.) And again, Treasury officials all agree that Wilson – not merely as Prime Minister, but as the proud possessor of a first-class degree in PPE from Oxford – completely dominated Callaghan, who was sadly out of his depth throughout his tenure of the Exchequer.

Yet the Prime Minister almost certainly *could* have been beaten. On this issue at least, he was extremely vulnerable either to a Brown / Callaghan coalition or to the resignation of one or other of the two senior economic ministers. The avoidance of the first had, in effect, been one of Wilson's reasons for creating the Department of Economic Affairs as a *de facto* rival to the Treasury, and putting Brown at its head; thus ensuring that Brown and Callaghan were almost permanently at loggerheads, with each side seeking the Prime Minister's arbitration in their favour (the ill-fated DEA was eventually abolished in 1968). Nevertheless, there were occasions (even before the July 1966 'wobble') when Brown and Callaghan attempted to form a common front against Wilson; but Brown's volatile nature was such that a working agreement with him seldom lasted longer than 24 hours. But if, at any time, there had been a Brown/Callaghan pro-devaluation axis, Wilson could not have prevented the issue from coming before Cabinet; in which case it seems far from clear that the Prime Minister would have won.

As for the threat of resignation, which in July 1966 was within an ace of being carried to fruition (in his memoirs Brown openly regrets not having gone through with it), Wilson was vulnerable to this in two senses. First, there was the possibility that the resignation would have led to a run on the pound greater than the parity could withstand. And, second, there was the threat to Wilson within the Parliamentary Labour Party had the First Secretary resigned in protest against the sterling parity being given priority over the fulfilment of Labour's dreams of an expanding economy. It seems hard to believe that the Prime Minister would have felt strong enough to take a double risk of this kind.

The initial rejection of the devaluation option by the incoming Labour Government in October 1964 aroused no serious controversy at the time. This is not the impression, admittedly, that has subsequently tended to be given. Thus in August 1969, for example, the *Sunday Times*, arguing that 'Sterling devaluation would have been the right course in 1964', maintained that the Prime Minister's orthodoxy in clinging to the parity had been 'strongly challenged'. In fact Professor Alan Day, who wrote in the *Observer* in November 1964 that 'it is now perfectly clear to me that the Government made a first-rate error of judgement when it decided not to devalue the pound during its first two or three weeks of power', was almost alone. The authentic voice of the consensus at that time was that of the then editor of the *Sunday Times*, Mr William Rees-Mogg, who, in the same month (November 1964) had published a signed article entiled 'Why devaluation is no solution to the crisis'. And the unequi-

vocal anti-devaluation tone of the Treasury's General Brief to the
incoming Government has already been noted.

Callaghan was subsequently to complain that 'neither the Treasury nor the Bank really set the alarm bells ringing as they should
have done'. There is no doubt that, as a new and inexperienced
Chancellor, whose highest previous office had been that of Parliamentary and Financial Secretary at the Admiralty, he was taken
wholly by surprise by the virulence of the November 1964 run on
the pound. (After he had been saved by the Governor's $3000 million
support operation, he quoted ruefully an alleged aphorism of Gaitskell's that 'the Bank has expertise without loyalty, and the Treasury
loyalty without expertise'.) The Treasury and the Bank, however,
felt that it was the Government – and in particular the Prime Minister – who had quite unnecessarily and unexpectedly set alarm bells
ringing, with the publication of the £800 million deficit figure. True
though this is, it does not invalidate Callaghan's complaint. But,
more important, there is no reason to believe that even if the officials
had, in the General Brief, given the direst warning of the pressure on
sterling that might arise at any moment, the triumvirate's rejection of
devaluation would have wavered.

What does require some explanation, however, is why the Treasury did not change its tune when it very soon became clear that,
while the Government was adamant against devaluation, it was not
prepared to take the measures necessary to avoid it. The Baloghian
alternative – the siege economy and a battery of controls – was opposed by Whitehall, and never seriously considered either by the
triumvirate or by the Cabinet as a whole. The Treasury alternative –
deflation – was rejected by the Government out of hand. (This was
in 1964; its subsequent acceptance was, in the Treasury's view, either
on an inadequate scale or reversed too soon.) Why, then, did the
permanent officials go along with a policy that amounted to little
more than faith and hope (as one of them put it, 'the parity was to
be defended by courage and moral constancy')?

A number of reasons seem to have played a part in this. In the
early days, senior Treasury officials (as one of them recalls) were
anxious not to 'come down like a ton of bricks' on a new Labour
Government, in power after 13 years in the wilderness, for fear of
being thought of as 'crypto-Tories'. Later on, and especially after July
1966, Callaghan made clear to his officials that, for him, devaluation
was a moral issue which would inevitably involve his resignation:
thus advisers felt deterred from even broaching the issue since this
would be interpreted as an open and scarcely welcome call for the
Chancellor to resign. Another, linked, factor was the feeling among
officials that the decision to rule out devaluation was essentially a

political, and not an economic one, which the Treasury had to accept as such and which it was not proper for them to question. (At the same time, to Cabinet Ministers outside the triumvirate, it was an economic matter upon which – Crosland apart – they were not competent to pronounce.)

A consideration of a wholly different kind was Great George Street's obsession – which continues to this day – with incomes policy, which they believed a Labour Government, with its trade union links, was uniquely placed to pursue, and from which an important section of the Treasury (including Armstrong) hoped for miraculous results. Finally, there was the unwritten moral law, taken for granted in the climate of that time inside Whitehall as well as outside it, that devaluation was something one occasionally did, because one was forced to, but never recommended. In the words of one of the economic advisers brought into Whitehall by the new Labour Government, the Treasury was 'like a virgin willing to be raped'. Had the incoming Government opted for devaluation, Whitehall would probably have lain down and enjoyed it.

The Bank of England was a different matter: throughout it was resolutely and professionally opposed to devaluation. This was chiefly on traditional banking grounds – as the custodians of a reserve currency, the Governor and his colleagues could not betray their clients, the overseas holders of sterling. The Bank also tended to feel (and not without reason, as subsequent events have indicated) that devaluation was a device to escape the need for proper financial discipline, notably in public spending. But at no time – either in 1964 or subsequently – did the Governor or the Bank do anything to stiffen the Government's resolve to defend the exchange rate. It had no need to.

From the Bank's point of view this was perhaps just as well. For during Cromer's time relations between the Governor and the Prime Minister of the day were worse than at any time since the nationalisation of the Bank of England.* Cromer continually urged Wilson to take deflationary and other 'confidence-boosting' measures that

---

* By contrast, Cromer's relationship with Callaghan was conspicuously cordial, although his influence, initially very considerable, gradually diminished. But it is characteristic of the protocol and compartmentalisation of Whitehall that he felt unable to have a single meeting with Brown. On one occasion Brown complained bitterly about this, only to be told that the Governor could not see another Minister (other than the Prime Minister) except in the Chancellor's (or the Prime Minister's) presence. A similar constraint prevented the distinguished American Ambassador to Britain, Mr David Bruce, himself a former banker, from ever having a private meeting with Callaghan, helpful though this might have been. The Ambassador's meetings – even if they were concerned with the US attitude to sterling – had to be either with the Foreign Secretary or with the Prime Minister.

would make his policy credible, and laid particular emphasis on the
need to restrain public expenditure. Wilson made it abundantly
clear that, as the head of a democratically elected Government, he
was not going to be dictated to by the Governor of the Bank of
England – and, as the ace up his sleeve, he had a personal guarantee
from President Johnson that the Americans would provide all the
financial assistance necessary to defend the pound. Cromer was
sceptical; and anyway pointed out that the balance of power had
changed since 1949, and that the Europeans – with whom the Bank
had the crucial contacts – would have to play a part in any rescue
operation.

This cut no ice with Wilson: both for him and his Chancellor
American opinion was all that mattered. Immediately after devaluation ultimately occurred, Callaghan revealed to the House of Commons that, a few weeks after Labour had taken office in 1964, one
'very senior monetary authority in Europe' had warned him that
sterling was in fundamental disequilibrium, and ought to be devalued by between 10 and 15 per cent. The source of this confidential
advice turned out to have been Mr Emil van Lennep, the Dutch
chairman of both the OECD's key Working Party Three and the
EEC's Monetary Committee. (Mr Thorkil Kristensen, the Swedish
chairman of OECD, who was also present at this meeting, agreed.)
But who was van Lennep compared with Al Hayes? No: for
Callaghan, and still more for Wilson, the Europeans were cast in a
different role. Talking about the 1967 devaluation with Crossman on
television in February 1973, Wilson explained: 'I fought hard to
prevent it, but we had no alternative by that time, particularly since
the French were talking the pound down all the time and succeeded
in letting the floodgates loose in the end.'

Indeed, Cromer recalls that the stormy meetings between Wilson
and himself invariably ended with the Prime Minister demanding
that the Governor tell him who was 'the enemy' who was 'selling
Britain short'. On more than one occasion in 1965, Treasury officials
had to restrain the Prime Minister from setting up a tribunal to
arraign 'anti-patriotic City wreckers'. But this attitude effectively
drew Cromer's teeth. For the last thing the Governor wanted was to
allow the Bank of England – or indeed the City establishment
generally – to be held responsible for any harm that befell the pound.
In the last resort he could be counted on to put all the resources of
the Bank at the Government's disposal, whatever the shortcomings
as he saw them of its policies, simply to avoid any repetition of the
post-1931 accusations of a 'bankers' ramp'.

The tension ended with the replacement in July 1966 of Cromer
by O'Brien, a career Bank of England official who was at once more
flexible and less independent. If the Labour Government had been

determined on devaluation in 1964 or 1965, Lord Cromer could not
have stopped it. But it would certainly have had a bumpier ride than
it was likely to have under his successor; and, indeed, at the end of
the day, having got the message from his Continental counterparts,
O'Brien accepted the inevitable without demur.

Thus whatever else the three-year non-devaluation saga may have
been, it was not a case of mandarin power. The Bank and its Governor undoubtedly enjoyed an unusual importance during this period;
but this was a direct result of the extent to which the Government,
by insisting on defending the parity, had of its own volition made
itself very much more vulnerable to financial pressures. At any time
the Government could have cut the Gordian knot, and it is hard to
see what the Bank could have done about it. As for the Treasury, its
high command meekly accepted the unmentionability of the unmentionable, acquiesced in the brief to work within an impossible
framework, and marvelled at the foolishness of politicians.

But what of the great extra-parliamentary economic interest
groups, to whom it is nowadays said that real power has shifted?
Like Brown before July 1965, Mr George Woodcock, the then
General Secretary of the TUC, was opposed to devaluation on the
traditional Labour grounds that it was a backdoor way of depressing
wages: indeed, at an early date he had warned Brown that there
could be no deal on incomes policy if the pound were devalued.
And throughout, the TUC remained solidly behind the parity. Yet
the CBI and other employers' organisations were even more strident
in their wholehearted opposition to devaluation – despite the fact
that according to all orthodox economic theory this was directly
opposed to their members' interests. Moreover, at no time did either
the trade union movement or the employers' organisations exert any
perceptible influence over the course of events on this, the central
issue of economic policy at that time. Nor, perhaps equally telling,
were they able to hold up the devaluation by so much as a day when
it eventually came.

The truth is that the TUC and the CBI, along with the Prime
Minister, the Treasury knights, the Bank and the City, were all part
of an establishment consensus which transcended normal interest-
group and party politics. (In Parliament, devaluation was opposed
by the Opposition front bench with at least as much fervour as it was
by the Government itself. Its few backbench advocates represented a
disparate alliance of younger right-wing Labour MPs such as Mr
David Marquand and right-wing Tories such as Mr Hugh Fraser,
and both groups were regarded by their own party leaderships with
equal disfavour.) It is the existence and persistence of this consensus
which, as much as anything else, helps to explain why, despite his
'U-turns' on so many other issues, Wilson stuck to his original de-

cision on devaluation through thick and thin, as his economic policy collapsed about him and the Government's popularity plummeted.

The unanimity of this consensus also helps to explain the impotence of the pro-devaluation political appointees within the Government machine. As has been seen, at Wilson's one great moment of weakness, in July 1966, they lost their opportunity through the divisions within their own ranks over timing. Moreover, it is a mistake to see them (except very occasionally) as an independent force: according to the rules of Whitehall, they had to be 'integrated' into the official departmental view of the ministry to which they had been seconded – a system which ensures that ministers are presented by their officials with a carefully worked out range of options, and are obliged to choose from within that preselected range.

But, from within their Whitehall cocoon, the pro-devaluation advisers looked desperately to the outside world for succour. They hoped at least that their fellow-academic economists, from the freedom of their universities, would launch an attack on the consensus that would at least make the unmentionable mentionable. They hoped in vain, and became increasingly bitter about what they saw as a *trahison des clercs*. The then influential National Institute, which during the previous Conservative Government's sterling crisis of 1961 had set the cat among the pigeons by suggesting devaluation, blandly declared during the crisis of 1965 that action on the exchange rate was 'politically excluded'. As Professor Harry Johnson was later to record in *Encounter* (May 1968), 'though from the autumn of 1964 on, more and more economists came to regard devaluation as a prerequisite to solution of the country's problems, this was revealed to the public only after devaluation was forced on the government'.

There is no doubt that, on this issue, the economists *were* out of step with the consensus. As late as June 1967, for example, Granada TV conducted a poll on a number of current economic issues among what it called 'selected groups of influential people'. On devaluation, the poll showed a three-to-one majority against; but the professional economists included in the sample had voted two-to-one *for* devaluation. And there is equally no disputing that, with one or two notable exceptions, they declined to stand up and be counted. This may be partly explained by the fact that most academic economists, and a still higher proportion of those favouring devaluation, were Labour sympathisers, and did not want to embarrass the Government; if so, it was a sensibility that the pro-Labour economists within the Government service did not appreciate.

But even those pro-devaluation economists who did have the temerity to try and publish their views did not find it easy. Towards the end of 1964, a young Oxford economist submitted an article

setting out the case for devaluation to a leading bank review. The
editor replied that, much as he would like to publish so well-written
and well-argued an article, he could not do so because 'it advocates
something that at the moment can hardly be advocated in a clearing
bank review'. Rather like the editor of a Victorian literary journal
confronted with a contribution on sex, he could not even bring himself to mention the offending word in the rejection slip.

Nor was this self-censorship confined to the arcane columns of the
bank reviews. Throughout the press, from *The Times* to the *New
Statesman*, the Government's determination to defend the parity was
applauded. There appear to have been only two exceptions. The
contribution by Professor Day to the *Observer* in November 1964
has already been mentioned; this brought its editor, Mr David Astor,
a summons to Downing Street where he was given a severe dressing-
down by the Prime Minister for his lack of patriotism. The paper
returned to the topic, however, in July 1966 with a defiantly pro-
devaluation leading article, which this time prompted a public
attack by Wilson on 'the defeatist cries, the moaning minnies, the wet
editorials – yes, the Sundays as well – of those who will seek any
opportunity to sell Britain short at home and abroad'. The other
exception was the *Spectator*, which argued the case for devaluation
consistently both before and after the July 1966 crisis. When the
paper's then editor declared in March of that year that the question
was not whether the pound would be devalued but when, and that a
planned devaluation would be better than one imposed by the pressure of events, the article was promptly denounced at great length by
the then financial editor of the *Guardian*, as 'drivel, and dangerous
drivel at that.... We are already well on the way towards a balance
of payments surplus, and strong government will enable us to make
substantial further progress.' Thus spoke the authentic voice of Fleet
Street.

It is, of course, easy to mock the prudery of the press and its determination not to rock the boat from the standpoint of the permissive
70s. It has to be remembered that, under the Bretton Woods regime
of fixed but adjustable parities, those buying or selling currencies
were often in the happy position of enjoying a two-way option. If
they sold a weak currency (or bought a strong one) forward, they
knew that it would either be forced off its 'peg' by the weight of
money, in which case they would make a handsome profit, or the
narrow parity limits would be preserved by intervention buying, in
which case their loss would be minimal.

So it was not altogether fanciful for both the Government and
Fleet Street to believe, as they did, that loose talk – whether from
within Whitehall or from any other quarter which overseas opinion
might regard as authoritative – could be self-fulfilling. And, particu-

larly given the enormous short-term indebtedness of the UK, there
were some who genuinely feared that a 'disorderly' forced devaluation might produce, not merely complete chaos in the foreign exchange markets, but a complete collapse of the entire world
monetary system, with untold consequences for world trade and
prosperity. Even for those who were far from convinced of this doom-
watch scenario, it was easy to slip into the automatic, though sadly
misplaced, assumption of the time that the reserve currency status
of the pound was one of the few remaining outward and visible signs
of Britain's greatness, that the parity was a national virility symbol,
and that to question it was unpatriotic. Publicly to defy this climate
of opinion risked instant ostracism by the establishment.

Nevertheless, Wilson's ban on all discussion of the issue in Whitehall, and the supporting self-denying ordinance of the press, were to
cast a long shadow. For they prevented the emergence of that tide of
opinion which is so often instrumental in causing British governments to change the course of policy. The opinion in question is not,
of course, mass public opinion: throughout the saga devaluation
remained, inevitably, an argument among the *cognoscenti*. But the
influence of elite or establishment opinion – especially perhaps on a
Labour government, only lately emerged from thirteen years of
Opposition, imbued with a deep desire to be considered respectable
– cannot be dismissed.

Initially, as we have seen, what was of paramount importance to
both Wilson and Callaghan was the good opinion of the Americans.
In this, if in few other respects, the Labour leader resembled his
predecessor and rival, Gaitskell. Perhaps the transatlantic embrace
has replaced the aristocratic embrace among the hazards to which
British Labour leaders are subject. In any event, Wilson was more
than anxious to warm himself at the dying embers of the Anglo-
American special relationship. Informed Continental opinion was
sceptical about the parity from the start; but if anything this scepticism served only to reinforce the dedication of the Prime Minister and
Chancellor to the *status quo*. Both men (but especially Wilson) easily
succumbed to visions of themselves as latter-day knights in armour,
defending the virgin pound against the brutish assaults of the
gnomes of Zurich and Paris.

As for the Chancellor, while he did not share the francophobia
into which the Prime Minister, well tutored by Balogh, so easily
lapsed, he still infinitely preferred the company of solid no-nonsense
citizens like Secretary of the Treasury Henry ('Joe') Fowler to that
of sharp young intellectuals like the French Finance Minister M.
Giscard d'Estaing, with their depressing propensity to relapse into
foreign tongues. For almost the whole of the period under review

there were many in the US administration who (understandably) saw the pound as the dollar's first line of defence; and Washington was usually prepared to lay on the flattery with a trowel (see, e.g., President Johnson's extraordinary speech of 29 July 1966) for a British Prime Minister who would continue, against all odds, to hold that redoubt.

But while this explains the initial position taken on the pound, it does not really answer the question of why the Government persisted in its increasingly costly decision right up until November 1967. No Government, of course, likes admitting failure or even mistakes; but that particular government was conspicuous for the number of reversals of policy in which it indulged. It may be argued that every government tends to become publicly committed to one supreme objective, to which all other ends are subordinated, and that the more U-turns there are elsewhere the greater the determination to hold fast to that one supreme goal. Certainly the usually ultra-flexible Wilson nailed his personal colours to the parity mast with quite remarkable firmness, and increasingly saw it as a war situation, in which discussion of the very possibility of defeat could not be tolerated because it would sap morale. His former colleagues comment, too, on his endemic Micawberism: he was always expecting something to turn up to transform the situation, once the immediate sterling crisis was overcome.

All this is true – yet almost incidental. It is hard to escape the conclusion that this dogged persistence throughout three traumatic years was, more than anything else, a consequence of the curious climate of the time, in which there was no Keynes to challenge the prevailing orthodoxy, and in which various pressures (most forcibly though by no means exclusively from the Prime Minister) prevented the public emergence of a tide of informed opinion in opposition to the establishment consensus. Wilson himself points out in his memoirs that 'As we entered November (1967), sterling was still under pressure but, unlike July 1966, there was hardly a serious commentator pressing for devaluation'; while Callaghan has subsequently contended that it was impossible to devalue in 1964, since 'public opinion' was not ready for it and the Government would have been 'crucified' by the press, and that a period of 'education' was needed. Equally, the almost unchallenged persistence of the establishment consensus on devaluation must surely help to explain the supine role of the Treasury throughout this period. It requires more than the failure of a policy to bring about its reversal: it also requires – in practice – the development of an uninhibited public debate. This, in the case of devaluation, uniquely failed to occur.

6 Dimensions of Power

The world talks much of the powerful sovereigns and great ministers; and if being talked about made one powerful, they would be irresistible. But the fact is, the more you are talked about, the less powerful you are.

B. Disraeli

Six years ago Ian Gilmour, a distinguished journalist and politician who was later to be a leading member of the Heath Administration, depicted modern British government as hag-ridden by secrecy and chronically indecisive. Today it is more fashionable to believe that the nation is exhausted by governmental passion for change and innovation in a world where the disappearance of traditional landmarks has proceeded at a pace calculated to produce disorientation. Metrication and decimalisation, the 'reform' of local government, the abolition of traditional patterns of education, even an abortive attempt to change the clock, have all been rushed through Parliament with scant regard for public sentiment and little evidence of resultant satisfaction. A sudden fashion for industrial amalgamations, which reached its climax in the activities of the Industrial Reorganisation Corporation at the end of the 1960s, has given place to an almost equally prevalent conviction that 'small is beautiful'. The same authorities who had predicted disaster from the abandonment of fixed exchange rates revealed that floating currencies were indispensable for the avoidance of world slump within twenty-four hours of the unpegging of the pound.

Anyone who contemplates the fallibility of past judgements must be wary of generalisations about the real nature and distribution of power in the British polity. Even written constitutions are subject to dramatic shifts of balance, as the current reassertion of Congressional authority in the United States after forty years of Presidential aggrandisement reminds us. A portrait of the functioning of an unwritten constitution is more akin to a study by one of the early impressionists: it can only hope to capture a pattern of light and shade at a particular hour of the clock. Since the events discussed in our four case histories occurred, two successive governments have confronted the barons of the trade union movement, and on each occasion it was the government which retired hurt. This has led many commentators to conclude that the nation has become 'ungovernable', and others to think in terms of some new corporate power-structure for decision-making, embracing the TUC and the CBI as well as Cabinet and Whitehall. Thus the balance of forces has to some extent shifted since the end of 1967, just as it was evolving while the events we have analysed were taking place.

Furthermore, as noted at the outset, all four of our case histories have one thing in common, that they belong essentially to the economic dimension of Government. This is a crucial dimension – some would say *the* crucial dimension: but it is not the whole. In a subsequent volume we hope to subject some major non-economic decisions to similar scrutiny, at which point some further and perhaps rather different conclusions may emerge.

So here we see British government chiefly in its economic aspect roughly a decade ago. It has aged, and perhaps withered, in the ensuing interval. Some preliminary conclusions nevertheless do suggest themselves from the four preceding studies: their durability may be uncertain, but even where they no longer precisely reflect the living reality they may yet help to explain how the British political system arrived where it is today.

1 The Grand Arbiter: Prime Ministerial Power

The thesis of presidential government in Britain has taken a few knocks in the past decade. Harold Wilson was obliged by his colleagues to abandon trade union legislation to which he had committed his personal prestige. Even Edward Heath, arguably the most dominant Prime Minister within his own administration since the war, was eventually persuaded to seek a dissolution in the spring of 1974 against his own inclination. British Prime Ministers face none of the constitutional restraints upon their freedom of action imposed by written constitutions on the Presidents of the United States or France; yet they can be overruled within their own Cabinets in a way that no French or American President could experience.

Of our four case histories only one – devaluation (or rather non-devaluation) – was truly dominated by the personality and policy of the Prime Minister. Yet while Harold Wilson could have frog-marched his Chancellor into devaluation at any time had he been so minded, the reverse is also true, certainly from July 1966 onwards. Had Mr Callaghan decided that the parity could no longer be sustained eighteen months before it was abandoned, the Prime Minister

would have been obliged to yield to the combined weight of his two
senior economic Ministers, just as he was obliged to yield to the
Cabinet revolt on 'In Place of Strife' three years later. Even if George
Brown alone had stuck to his determination to resign unless the
parity were abandoned in the July 1966 crisis, this might well have
been sufficient to overcome the Prime Minister's resistance.

The other instance where the role of the Prime Minister was
decisive – the relaunching of the drive for Europe in 1966–7 – leads
to a similar conclusion. Several other Ministers – Roy Jenkins,
Michael Stewart, Anthony Crosland, above all George Brown – were
far more committed to the crusade for membership of the European
Community than was their leader. Yet it was his suddenly-discovered
enthusiasm and determination which carried all before it, sweeping
aside the irrefutable evidence of France's intention to exercise the
veto once more. It is hard to believe that the passionate dedication
of George Brown and his allies would have carried away the resistance of the majority of hostile and doubting opinion in the Cabinet
in the face of the inherent improbability of the whole adventure if
the Prime Minister had been neutral or only lukewarm.

On the other hand Wilson could not have imposed this choice
without the enthusiastic support of the 'Europeans' in his Cabinet
and the energetic proselytising of the civil servants at the Foreign
Office. Indeed he would hardly have tried – for not least among the
reasons for his sudden conversion was the need to sidetrack one of his
leading Europeans from the intention to resign over economic policy.

In all our other case histories the Prime Minister played a crucial,
though by no means a dominant, part. The scheme to abolish RPM
would probably have been abandoned before it ever came to second
reading in the Commons in response to the strength of opposition
on the Government's back benches and the manifest lack of enthusiasm of the departmental minister's colleagues, had the minister
not enjoyed the loyal support of his leader. He would hardly have
received the same backing from Harold Macmillan, with his family
commitment to the Net Book Agreement. So while the Bill was a
departmental measure, and its midwife the departmental minister,
one must wonder whether, for all his enthusiasm, it would not have
been still-born but for the change of tenant at No. 10 in the autumn
of 1963 – or indeed whether the departmental minister would ever
have embarked upon it at all under Harold Macmillan.

Concorde was similarly a departmental brainchild, and the attitude of the Prime Minister towards it was one of remarkable detachment almost to the last moment. But when the Prime Minister did
intervene, his intervention clinched the matter. True, there can be
no certainty that the aviation lobby would have been defeated by

the Treasury without his backing: the Treasury's record of success in its running warfare with the aerospace industry in the 1950s had been distinctly patchy. But with Harold Macmillan aligned on the other side of the argument Great George Street did not stand a chance.

When it came to the abortive attempt to kill Concorde in the winter of 1964, however, the Prime Minister took a back seat. He readily endorsed the Treasury-promoted plan to call for a 'review' of the programme. But when trouble immediately blew up both in Cabinet and outside, he kept aloof. None of his famed skills of Cabinet-management were summoned up to outmanoeuvre the opponents of cancellation. No doubt the sheer pressure of events was a factor here: the fate of Concorde was decided in the midst of the November 1964 sterling crisis, and the Prime Minister had more important matters on his mind.

This leaves the initial approach to the European Community in 1961. The popular account identifies this as a classic example of Prime Ministerial initiative. Commentators like Ronald Butt and Ian Gilmour have described for us a determined Prime Minister dragging a reluctant Cabinet and Party kicking and screaming to the gates of Europe. Not so. Certainly Harold Macmillan, having seen his grand summiteering strategy wrecked in Paris, and his attempts at 'bridge-building' between the Community Six and the Free Trade Seven almost contemptuously brushed aside by both the Americans and the French, came eventually to the conclusion that there was no alternative to an outright bid for full membership of the Community. Yet he felt in his bones that it was not going to succeed, and he dreaded the impact of a rebuff on the flaking morale of his Party. His instinct was to seek a bilateral deal with the French leader; but by this stage he lacked the resolution to overcome the passionate resistance of the Foreign Office and the suspicion of the United States. In the end he found that he had set in train a mobilisation of key civil service and ministerial opinion which, rather like the mobilisation of the armies in July 1914, developed a momentum of its own. Thus the decision to launch the first Brussels negotiations was an illustration of the limitations to, rather than of the extent of, Prime Ministerial power.

One paradox about this catalogue is worth a moment's digression. A foreign diplomat who had followed Harold Wilson's career at fairly close quarters all the way from the Board of Trade to 10 Downing Street once commented to one of the authors that he had never known him take a decision. He was exaggerating, of course: but his assessment reflected a widespread feeling in Whitehall that here was one Prime Minister who instinctively preferred to allow

events to mould his choices for him. Yet of the three Prime Ministers
under scrutiny it was he, rather than either of his predecessors, who
twice made a personal choice, first over devaluation, and then over
the Common Market. On closer scrutiny, however, the paradox is not
too difficult to resolve. For the devaluation choice was essentially
negative: it was the rejection of a course of action, and – as his civil
servants soon discovered with dismay – it was unaccompanied by any
commitment to an alternative strategy to re-establish the viability of
the existing exchange rate. As for the Common Market, this should
be seen as what Mr Crossman called 'one of his stunts': more
momentous in its implications, no doubt, but not essentially different
in kind, from other initiatives like the abortive Commonwealth
Prime Ministers' peace mission to Vietnam.

The common theme that emerges is one of the Prime Minister as
arbiter of choice in government, rather than the preselector of decisions. His acquiescence is a necessary (though not a sufficient) condition for decision on major policy issues – even if that acquiescence
has sometimes to be extracted by something akin to *force majeure*.
Hence a strong Prime Minister is not an indispensable precondition
for decisive government in Britain. The lack of a dominant lead
from the top results in paralysis of Government in genuine Presidential constitutions such as those of France or the United States (or
even in hybrids such as that of Federal Germany). In Britain the
Queen's government was carried on effectively enough under Sir
Alec Douglas-Home; and history may well conclude that the relaxed
– not to say negligent – style adopted by Harold Wilson during his
second term of office proved more rewarding than the frenetic acti-
vism of his first tenure of the Premiership.

The evidence of our case histories sheds light, however, on other
aspects of Prime Ministerial power apart from its crucial influence
at the moments of decision. There is the power of suppression. The
control of Cabinet minutes means that under the British system the
Prime Minister, like the snark, has often been found by his colleagues to have

> summed it so well that it came to far more
> than the witnesses ever had said

– or rather, more usually, to far less. Sometimes the editing of the
minutes at No. 10 is little more than a matter of face-saving, as when
Crossman recorded in his diary how all reference to an abortive
attempt by Harold Wilson to extract some more cash from the
Treasury for Barbara Castle's department was expunged. Sometimes
more is at stake. Crossman, in his *Inside View*, commented ruefully
that 'sometimes as a member of Cabinet you don't realise that you

lost the battle; it was not your impression of what happened. But once it is there, written in the minutes, it *has* been decided against you.' That is a passage which must have struck an answering chord in the memories of many who had served in Cabinets of all political colours.

Another priceless Prime Ministerial asset is control of the Cabinet agenda. In Crossman's words 'there is nothing decided at Cabinet unless the PM specifically wants to have it discussed'. He implies that there was something uniquely Wilsonian about this situation, whereas in fact it is an accurate description of the *normal* situation under all Prime Ministers. The importance of this control is revealingly demonstrated by the incident of the suppression of the Transport House paper attacking the Common Market in the winter of 1966–7 (although its author was surely incorrect in attributing this suppression to the Cabinet secretariat rather than to the Prime Minister). Another instance we have witnessed was the repeated suppression of papers advocating devaluation in the period 1964–7.

Yet Crossman's generalisation, although it describes the normal situation, was too sweeping. Indeed he himself went on in later passages in his diary to describe how during the July 1966 economic crisis the Prime Minister was powerless to prevent the argument regarding devaluation coming out into the open in Cabinet, much as he would have wished to do so (even if he could still keep it off the actual agenda). The control of the agenda is thus not an absolute power. But it does take considerable determination on the part of a Cabinet minister – or more likely, several – to overcome it and force discussion of an item against the Prime Ministerial will.

Crossman commented that 'this PM [Wilson] very much likes fixing things up privately with Ministers by bilateral discussions if he can'. Once again, Wilson was certainly not unique: as we have seen, Harold Macmillan was careful to smooth the way for the endorsement of the Concorde decision by calling in other ministers of the great spending departments to assure them that they would not suffer. Indeed this is the way the Cabinet system is designed to function: as Harold Wilson rightly asserted [*A Personal Record*], 'Cabinets do not proceed by the counting of heads.'

Yet, *pace* Harold Wilson, the evidence of his colleagues is virtually unanimous that this is indeed the way that his own first administration came to proceed. Crossman even records one instance when the counting of heads led to a tie, and the Prime Minister (according to this account) was left asking his colleagues what to do then. This was undoubtedly a constitutional aberration, and one which Mr Wilson's successors are unlikely to follow. It reflected his instinctive preference for implicating colleagues in responsibility for decisions which might subsequently turn sour: but to most Prime Ministers the resulting loss of authority would be far too high a price to pay.

What, then, of the legendary 'ultimate deterrent' of the tenants of Downing Street: the power to seek a dissolution of Parliament? Under certain circumstances this can have an inhibiting effect on the Opposition: thus it was the fear that Harold Wilson might immediately seek a dissolution which scared the Conservatives off from trying to defeat the Government immediately, in the debate on the Queen's Speech, following the February 1974 election. (This occasion produced another constitutional curiosity. Suggestions circulated in the highest echelons of the Tory Party that if the Government were beaten, and the Prime Minister were to ask for a dissolution, the monarch would be duty bound to refuse the request and invite the Opposition to try to form a government. By all accounts word went went out from the Palace that this was an unfounded assumption.) But the circumstances of March 1974, when the opposition parties combined had a majority over the Government of 32, were wholly exceptional. Whatever the future may bring, it has hitherto been generally true that the Opposition has no more prospect of beating the Government in the lobbies unaided than the American Congress has of unseating a President in mid-term (which, as we have seen, can also happen).

This is not the context in which the 'ultimate deterrent' is usually referred to. The power to seek a dissolution is seen as the vital cement for party discipline within the *governing* party. The argument is that if rebel backbenchers carry their dissent to the point of voting against the government, and thereby secure the government's downfall, then they will, in Harold Wilson's notorious phrase, 'have their dog licences withdrawn' by being refused renomination by their local parties at the ensuing General Election.

No doubt that is what would happen – if it ever came to the point. But a moment's reflection shows that this 'ultimate deterrent', like the military one, suffers from its suicidal nature. Backbenchers rarely feel inclined to rebel when the Government is riding high in popular esteem: rebellions reflect the existence of dissatisfaction at the grass roots. (And if Government supporters do become rebellious in periods of ministerial popularity, the Opposition can be trusted to read the signs, and to ensure that the Prime Minister is given no excuse to seek renewal of his mandate. A rare and possibly instructive – if speculative – exception to this rule concerns the Conservative Government's Common Market approach in 1971. The Prime Minister faced a backbench rebellion within a year of taking office. It did not matter, for a number of Opposition backbenchers came to his support. Had they not done so, and had he been defeated on the floor of the House, it would have been in character for him to have demanded a dissolution. Which is why it would never have happened.) But when the government is unpopular the dissolution which might deprive backbenchers of their 'dog licences' would also presumably deprive the ministers of their portfolios.

So it is largely a myth; but none the less potent. It should be seen as one of Ibsen's 'saving lies' – indispensible to the happiness of Prime Ministers, their colleagues and their Whips, but also of backbenchers as well.

There remains what to many observers seems the most crucial weapon of all in the Prime Ministerial armoury: the weapon of patronage. The history of modern British government is full of instances of the draconian nature of the power to hire and fire departmental ministers: Baldwin's decision to appoint Churchill, an object of contemporary loathing to large members of his backbenchers, as his Chancellor of the Exchequer; Macmillan's breezy parting first with Lord Salisbury and then with his entire Treasury team. Once again there is a need for caution. Harold Wilson felt safe to part with George Brown in the spring of 1968; but he went to very considerable lengths to hang on to him eighteen months earlier. The 'night of the long knives' in the summer of 1962 did not strengthen Harold Macmillan's position: it gravely weakened it. Nor is the power of appointment by any means untrammelled. The way in which Lord Home waited to see whether key figures such as R. A. Butler would agree to serve before accepting the invitation to form a government in 1963 has often been noted. We have also seen that ministerial reshuffles seldom reflect anything much in the way of a conscious policy strategy: men like Christopher Soames, Roy Jenkins and Anthony Crossland were not recruited to Cabinet to swell the ranks of pro-Europeans, they commanded promotion on merit.

All British Prime Ministers take office with an ample stock of political capital to draw upon. Their security of tenure is almost absolute (far more so than they themselves imagine it to be: Harold Wilson's obsession with palace revolutions in the period 1964–70 had plenty of precedents). If like Harold Macmillan in 1959, or Harold Wilson in 1964, or Edward Heath in 1970, they have an election triumph under their belts, their authority is enormous. Yet it wears with use, and still more with abuse. Harold Macmillan's troops were grumbling within eighteen months of the 1959 Election, and Harold Wilson faced an admittedly half-baked Cabinet revolt within six months of his 1966 victory. Edward Heath survived for nearly four years after his election victory without a single significant rebellion, it is true; but within the life-span of a normal parliament from the time he entered No. 10 he was out on the back benches. So long as a Prime Minister delivers the goods of electoral esteem his power, uninhibited by a written constitution, is indeed greater than that of Presidential counterparts overseas – if he wishes it to be. But let his government run into serious electoral trouble and he will swiftly discover, as Mr Nigel Birch icily informed Harold Macmillan in the Profumo debate in the summer of 1963, that it is 'never glad confident morning again'.

2 The Departmental Minister: Baron or Buttons?

The story of RPM abolition should be enough to dispose of the *canard* that the departmental minister, under the modern British Cabinet system is – or at any rate needs to be – the Prime Minister's poodle. He can have a mind of his own, and he can exert a decisive influence of his own – indeed of all our four case histories it was that of the RPM battle where the influence of one personality was most clearly portrayed. Most departmental ministers, unlike their leader, have the weight and expertise of a massive civil service machine behind them. The popular notion that the independent authority of a departmental minister in Cabinet stems essentially from his Whitehall power-base is exaggerated: for example William Whitelaw, as Lord President and Leader of the Commons, and hence without a major Whitehall department, nevertheless played a key role in the shift of Government strategy which occurred in the winter of 1971–2. Access to the Prime Minister's 'ear' is indubitably a great asset: Julian Amery, not even a Cabinet minister, smoothed the flight-path of Concorde from his vantage point as son-in-law to the Prime Minister. But a recognisable constituency on the back benches is equally valuable.

Macmillan was right to worry about the impact of a revolt by Mr Butler or Lord Hailsham over the Common Market (even if he was wrong to worry that it was likely to happen); and he dangerously underestimated the repercussions of his dismissal of Selwyn Lloyd in 1962. Harold Wilson was rightly scared of the consequences of a resignation by George Brown in the summer of 1966. Edward Heath, alone among modern British Prime Ministers, arguably confronted a Cabinet without barons (and here the conviction that he had created a Cabinet of 'yes men', whether justified or not, was one of the charges which ultimately led to his downfall).

If they need not be Prime Ministerial poodles, however, departmental ministers can easily become the captive balloons of their Whitehall offices instead. The burden of departmental work is daunting: Harold Macmillan settling down to the housing files during Cabinet discussion of Europe in the early 1950s was following a well-trodden path (twenty years later a senior minister in the Heath Administration subsequently admitted that he had been only too happy to stifle his occasional qualms about the way the economy was being managed by reading reassuring notices in *The Economist*). Many men in high office display an almost instinctive adaptability to departmental priorities: Peter Thorneycroft, Michael Stewart and George Thomson are examples drawn from our case histories. The business of 'fighting one's corner' in Cabinet and Cabinet Committees easily becomes all-engrossing. Besides, that is how reputations are made: it was by building 300,000 houses that Harold Macmillan opened his approach road to No. 10; and similarly Edward Heath convinced his colleagues that he was the man to do battle with Harold Wilson by the nerve he had displayed over the abolition of RPM and the Brussels negotiations (however much many of them had deplored his tenacity at the time).

Yet the influence of ministers – particularly that of senior ministers with an independent backbench power-base – is not *necessarily* confined to their own direct departmental responsibilities. Butler, Hailsham, Thorneycroft, Jenkins, Crosland and Castle all played significant roles in the Common Market debate in their respective epochs, notwithstanding the fact that their departments were at best peripherally involved; and George Brown ran something like a private Common Market training camp at the Department of Economic Affairs. Crosland was the first to broach devaluation in Cabinet as Secretary for Education while the (admittedly unsuccessful) pro-devaluation lobby eventually included the Home Secretary, the Secretary for Social Services and the Minister of Housing. It may be legitimately argued that the Common Market and devaluation were bound to transcend narrow departmental demarcations; but then Denis Healey led the rearguard action in favour of Concorde cancellation from the Ministry of Defence (where the departmental interest was, if anything, *against* cancellation); James Callaghan took charge of the resistance to 'In Place of Strife' from the Home Office; and Lord Hailsham emerged as the foremost opponent of RPM abolition from the Ministry of Science, Technology, Sport, Education and the North-East – in fact virtually anything *except* retail trade.*

One of the features of the British Cabinet system which differentiates it from the American Presidential system is that every Prime

---

* One member of a recent Cabinet whose departmental responsibilities had little to do with economic policy even went to the lengths of registering a formal complaint with the Chief Whip about a particular item of economic legislation. This was a curious instance of 'the usual channels' (as the Whips are known) flowing uphill.

Minister confronts a number of potential successors across the Cabinet table. American Cabinet members have been known to reach the White House: but it has invariably been an achievement which owed little to their previous Cabinet service. British Prime Ministers are surrounded by men who want their job, usually including one or two who have already challenged them for it.

This benefits the Prime Minister, not his colleagues. Rivalry for the succession creates an uneasy balance which underpins the sitting tenant. The ambitious minister on the way up may be too busy carving out his departmental reputation to spare a thought for the wider scene, where ambition also incites caution. Leaders of putative palace revolutions soon discover that dissatisfaction with the existing leadership is far from implying agreement about its replacement. Apart from anything else the man who fancies his own chances for the succession knows that changes occur infrequently, and so he is not going to risk the interposition of another if he can avoid it. George Brown had powerful allies in his fight for devaluation in the summer of 1966. But as soon as he talked of unseating the leader, they melted away.

What, then, of the weapon of ministerial resignation? Ian Gilmour [op. cit.] argued that it was no longer even two-edged: 'the only edge which is sharp is the one turned towards the resigner'. Yet Edward Heath was the first Prime Minister since Clement Attlee without a major rebellion on his Commons record-sheet; and Anthony Eden and Harold Wilson could be said to have paved the way to the top for themselves with a strategic resignation. The political extinction of men like Lord Salisbury, Ray Gunter, Christopher Mayhew and Lord George-Brown through resignation has tended to obscure the dividends reaped by others.

Timing is important. Eden caught precisely the turn of the appeasement tide; Wilson the moment when the ship he left was already within sight of the rocks. Thorneycroft, by contrast, walked out over state profligacy just as the tide of fashion was turning to public largesse.

Timing is not all, though. It takes a Cabinet minister of substance to stage a successful resignation. Mayhew chose the moment when 'East of Suez', over which he resigned, was going out of fashion. Yet outside the Cabinet his resignation was not even a nine days' wonder. Perhaps there is another lesson here: the wise resigner picks his subject to suit his Party. Resignations from the Ministry of Defence make sense under a Tory Government, not a Labour one; whereas resignations from the Department of Social Security are for periods of Labour rule (and if Callaghan had carried out his intention to resign had Harold Wilson proceeded with his *'In Place of Strife'* legislation, he would surely have done himself a power of good – because of the subject, rather than because of his office).

There is also the impact of the *threat* of resignation to be considered – after all, it is much commoner. Here again, much depends on the man, the time, and the issue. Mackintosh [op. cit.] quotes the story of the row between the Treasury and the Admiralty over cruisers in the Baldwin Government of 1925. Churchill, as Chancellor, was refusing to find the money the Admiralty wanted. Baldwin, on inquiry, found that for the First Lord of the Admiralty this was a resigning matter; whereas for Churchill it was not. So he plumped for the Admiralty.

This account leaves much to be desired. Large sections of the Tory Party would have heaved a sigh of relief if Churchill had resigned, as he himself must have been well aware. The resignation of the First Lord would have been a very serious matter. Churchill lost the argument because he was dispensable, whereas the First Lord was not – and both men knew the odds. From our case histories the contrast between the strength of George Brown's threat to resign in 1966, and the irrelevance of his eventual resignation in 1968, is similarly indicative. Perhaps the ideal moment to threaten resignation comes when a General Election is imminent – particularly as, for the Prime Minister, re-election is vital, whereas for his rivals electoral defeat may be a positive blessing.

It may be instructive, to conclude this section, to see what impact a resignation – or the threat of it – might have had on the course of one of our case histories: Concorde. There is no suggestion that either Selwyn Lloyd or his successor, Reginald Maudling, ever contemplated backing up his departmental brief with a threat of resignation: the impact of the Concorde spending programme was no doubt too remote and too uncertain. Nevertheless, would it have made any difference had they done so? The answer, as usual, must depend on which one it had been, and when.

A Selwyn Lloyd resignation, or serious threat of resignation, over the failure to include the axing of Concorde in the July 1961 economy measures would probably have left the Prime Minister cold: he was increasingly out of sympathy with what he regarded as his Chancellor's excessive deference to Treasury caution, and underestimated the size of Lloyd's back bench constituency. A Maudling resignation, or serious threat of resignation, over the final clearance of Concorde in the winter of 1962 would have been a different matter. Not because the Chancellor had a larger power-base in the Party: on the contrary, he had nothing to compare with his predecessor's retinue. No, it was the Prime Minister's position which had changed. With 'the night of the long knives' he had shot his bolt. He could risk no more resignations. Fortunately Maudling was hardly the Chancellor to resign in protest at the prospect of excessive expenditure. Which was, of course, why he had been chosen in the first place.

3 The Civil Service: Treasury, Foreign Office and the Rest

A coherent view is nearly always a view dominated by Treasury thinking.   R. H. S. Crossman, *Diaries*

Most politicians with experience of the workings of Whitehall, and most outside observers, would probably agree that if the Prime Minister is *primus inter pares* among ministers, the Treasury is *primus inter pares* among Whitehall departments. The ambitious candidate for the Home Civil Service, with an Oxbridge First (or better still a Fellowship of All Souls) under his belt, pays the Treasury the tribute of his first preference. Amidst the 'magic circle' of the Permanent Secretaries in Whitehall the former Treasury men are rightly regarded by the rest as almost a mafia – a 'family' whose members are to found at the key points in the whole civil service network.

Yet what is striking about our case histories is the chequered record of Treasury achievement. Admittedly the Treasury could always have been counted on to support RPM abolition if its opinion were asked; but it was a peripheral departmental interest. Not so the other three decisions. Devaluation was pre-eminently a Treasury issue. Adaptation to the Common Market's agricultural support and trading systems had vital implications for sterling. As for Concorde, the Treasury's hostility was unwavering.

It is true that the departmental attitude towards devaluation – unlike that of the Bank of England – was surprisingly unemotional, given the climate of the time. The Treasury was chaste; but if, in the autumn of 1964, the incoming ministers had been intent on rape, the department was in no mood for a struggle. When, instead, it transpired that ministerial intentions were honourable to a fault, the officials responded accordingly. If Ministers subsequently complained – as they did – that they had never been properly alerted to the full deflationary implications of the attempt to defend the parity, the civil servants' answer was that any new ministerial team needed time to accommodate itself to the facts of life.

Maybe. But in three long years of education the Treasury failed to persuade its political masters to adopt a sustainable alternative strategy. One after another the sacred cows of Labour's public spending priorities were slaughtered. But they were always too few, and always too late.

No doubt this was all inevitable. According to the conventions of the epoch, devaluation was not a conscious choice. It was something imposed by *force majeure* when all the other choices were exhausted.

There was also the incidental advantage (identified, perhaps, with benefit of hindsight rather than consciously planned in advance) that if in the end devaluation had to come the steady accumulation of deflationary 'packages' unwrapped in the pound's defence would have created the spare capacity in the domestic economy which the hoped-for boost to exports would then be able to absorb without 'overheating'.

So there were logical grounds, of sorts, for the Treasury's slide to devaluation. Concorde and the Common Market are less easily disposed of. Throughout the 1960s Great George Street dreaded the impact of Community membership on the pound. It was sufficiently realistic to plan ahead against the day when ministerial stomach for the battle for the parity might be exhausted. But it rationally objected to a strategy calculated to put the pound in jeopardy embarked upon by ministers who were still dedicated to its defence.

It was strikingly unsuccessful in impressing its anxieties on the politicians in 1961 and again in 1966-7, notwithstanding the fact that on both occasions the Chancellor himself was at best an agnostic on Europe. Admittedly in 1961 its anxieties were much less acute than they later became. Indeed on that occasion the prime mover in the Whitehall drive for Europe was the Treasury's own – albeit imported – chief civil servant, Sir Frank Lee. But in 1966, with no such complications, and a vastly enhanced awareness of the risks involved for the currency, it was unable to dissuade the Government from capping a determined rejection of the devaluation option with a decision to renew the Market application. The Treasury knights were powerless to prevent the adoption of what they knew to be a hopelessly contradictory strategy.

As for Concorde, this was a saga of unrelieved humiliation for the Treasury. Twice it made a major effort to kill the whole enterprise, in the summer of 1961 and again in the autumn of 1964, and twice it failed; while in its rearguard battle to block a decision to go ahead with the aircraft in the summer and autumn of 1962 it was beaten at every stage. That the Treasury should have failed in its perennial resistance to open-ended forward spending commitments when the economy was in recession, and pump-priming of the order of the day – as in the autumn of 1962 – may not be surprising. That it was equally successful when the economy was booming – as in the summer of 1961, or the autumn of 1964 – is significant.

The Treasury had its victories, of course, in many day-to-day struggles during the period covered by these case histories. It is also important to remember that over both the Common Market and Concorde it was in conflict with the Foreign Office, a department whose 'in house' expenditures are too modest to give the Treasury much leverage. Yet when every allowance is made our case histories hardly bear out the reputation of the 'over-mighty subject', the 'abominable no-man' of popular legend. Part of the explanation must lie in the character and attitude of the Prime Minister. Harold Macmillan viewed the Treasury with profound distrust. He saw himself as a lone Cassandra forewarning of the slump into which the Treasury was determined to plunge the nation, and indeed the whole Western world (though a distinguished classicist, he was unperturbed by the fact that the prophetess whose example he invoked was celebrated for her accuracy as well as her pessimism). Hence he was determined to look outside the ranks of the Treasury knights whenever the senior civil service post in the department fell vacant during his tenure of office. It is perhaps not surprising that they sometimes lost heart. Yet they did not fare notably better under Harold Wilson, whose decision to defend the parity at all costs played straight into their hands.

Perhaps the answer is that in Whitehall, as in other spheres, nothing succeeds like success, or fails like failure. The performance of the economy during the 1960s left much to be desired in the eyes of politicians and the public at large. Whether fairly or not, the Treasury took the rap, and its power and influence dwindled with the purchasing power of the pound.

Its reputation, though, endured. Ministers continued to stand in awe of, or to fret at, the imagined influence of the Great George Street mafia. The witch doctor promises rain; the rains do not come. But still the natives bow before him.

Only one other department in Whitehall rivals the Treasury in prestige: the Foreign Office. The significance and scope of British diplomacy has waned with the end of Empire and the long decline of British power. Still, in the 1960s, the social status of the Foreign Office survived more or less intact. Most politicians continued to regard the Foreign Secretaryship as the acceptable climax to a ministerial career if No. 10 were not available (and in the 1970s, during the Heath administration, it was for some years adorned by an ex-Prime Minister).

Indeed in many ways the record of the Foreign Office during the period under scrutiny was almost the antithesis of that of the

Treasury. Commentators at home and abroad tended to dismiss the prestige it still enjoyed as a typically British exercise in nostalgia. Yet in the Whitehall cockpit the Foreign Office's departmental triumphs were almost as consistent as the Treasury's rebuffs.

This may seem a perverse judgement. Was not the principal international strategy of British governments in the 1960s – accession to the European Community – contemptuously frustrated, not once but twice, by General de Gaulle? The answer is that although accession to the Community was certainly *the* external objective of governments, the primary departmental interest was somewhat different.

Throughout the 1960s British diplomacy had two closely connected professional purposes: to cling to what was left of the 'special relationship' with the United States, and to block the ambitions of the President of France. History will surely concede that it succeeded in both. Of course it is true that de Gaulle excluded us from the European Community throughout the decade. But the Foreign Office was a belated convert to Europeanism; and if membership of the Community was to be incompatible with the preservation of the remnants of the 'special relationship' – as it was – then there was never any doubt which the 'Office' put first. What really mattered to our diplomats was the prevention of de Gaulle's grand design for a third-force Western Europe. And the grand design was prevented – and much of the credit, or at any rate the responsibility, for this must accrue to the way in which the Foreign Office persuaded its political masters to go on thumping in applications for membership of the Community regardless of the certainty of their rejection. Whether such a policy was in Britain's best interests is a matter for conjecture; but that it achieved its purpose is hard to dispute.

Furthermore if departmental achievement is judged by ministerial conversion to a departmental angle – and for the professional civil servant this must be as good a yardstick as any – then the Foreign Office's record in the 1960s is impressive indeed. Every Foreign Office Minister, without exception, endorsed the departmental strategy, even though two at least – Michael Stewart and George Thomson – took office resolutely opposed to it. Each of the ministers primarily concerned with relations with the Community – Edward Heath, Michael Stewart, George Thomson, above all George Brown – swiftly accepted that the departmental tactics of isolating France and relying on the 'friendly five', and particularly Germany, were shrewd and correct.

Yet not only did these tactics repeatedly fail, their compatibility with natural British priorities was by no means apparent – as Harold

Macmillan and Harold Wilson both, in turn, instinctively recognised. After all it was the French, and not the 'friendly five', who shared the British preoccupation with global relationships; and it was the French, and not the 'friendly five', who shared British distaste for supranational adventures.

Not only did the two Prime Ministers recognise this fact, they also tried to do something about it. Both found themselves in conflict with the Foreign Office as a result, and both of them bit the dust. Indeed it is perhaps not too much to detect the influence of Foreign Office thinking in the curious failure of Wilson and Callaghan to grasp the extent to which financial power had shifted from Washington to the Community by 1967.

How are we to explain this display of civil service virtuosity? Certainly the instinctive preferences of the Foreign Office coincided with those of many of the politicians. Wilson and Callaghan were no less attached to the remnants of the 'special relationship' than were the diplomats; and while Macmillan longed for an *entente* with de Gaulle, he also basked in the rays of Washington's favour. The fact that French politicians regard it as a matter of honour always to speak French, even when, like Couve de Murville, they can speak near-perfect English, while British politicians rarely speak any other language than their own, is not conducive to a close cross-Channel relationship.

Another factor which works in favour of the Foreign Office is the remoteness of modern diplomacy from the hustings. Gone are the days when the Opposition could sweep to power on a campaign of denunciation of Bulgarian atrocities. Prime Ministers still hanker after the world stage, and therefore like to interfere. But even the most avid summiteers among them never lose sight of the fact that summits will not save them from the electoral consequences of economic disappointment. Nor is the Foreign Office a great spending department, its energies constantly dissipated in the battle with the Treasury for a place in the sun.

None of this suffices to explain the almost instant alignment of the politicians with departmental plans for renewal of the Community membership application when such plans were so obviously doomed to failure. The truth is that the Foreign Office has always had a 'way' with politicians, and particularly Labour politicians. Most Labour MPs continue to harbour preconceptions of diplomats as toffee-nosed Tories in Old Etonian ties. Then, on appointment to the Foreign Office, they suddenly find themselves surrounded by bright and deferential young men who sometimes even turn out to have voted Labour. They are swept off their feet.

Once again it is instructive to point a contrast. Under the Heath administration the thrust of British diplomacy underwent a dramatic (although not an enduring) transformation. For a brief period something remarkably like an *entente cordiale* with Paris was established. Admittedly the old Foreign Office bogeyman had left the scene. Nevertheless there was more than a whiff of Gaullism in the air – relations with the United States swiftly sank to their lowest point since Suez. The Foreign Office was aghast; but it was powerless to stop it.

What had happened was that the Foreign Office was confronted with an unusually dominant Prime Minister with formative personal experience of diplomacy. Macmillan longed to play a grand role on the world stage; so did Harold Wilson. Edward Heath, by contrast, was in many ways much more preoccupied with domestic economic policy. But apart from Sir Alec Douglas-Home (a Prime Minister *pas comme les autres* – non-executive chairman rather than managing director) he was the first Prime Minister since Anthony Eden to have made his name at the Foreign Office. It is no coincidence that Eden, too, had constructed his own foreign policy.

The Treasury and the Foreign Office have been worth a special detour because of the exceptional spread of their respective influences throughout Whitehall. But the case history of RPM abolition justifies its place in this volume not least because of the particular light it sheds on the nature of the interplay of influences between politicians and civil servants over the more mundane issues which make up the bread-and-butter of British political life. It is time to return to it.

The popular conception of politicians as creatures of Party, and civil servants as open-minded individuals is, operationally, if anything the reverse of the truth. It is ministers who tend to think and act as individuals (the isolation of ministers from each other in modern government, the type of man who chooses politics as a career, and personal ambition all play a part), while it is the civil servants who (in general) acquire power by sinking their individuality in a corporate ethos: in this way they both build up a departmental *esprit-de-corps* and limit the range of policy options from which ministers are invited to choose.

It is, on the face of it, surprising that the Board of Trade had the particular, classical liberal, departmental philosophy that it did have. In general – as, say, with the Ministry of Agriculture and the farming industry – departments tend to develop a symbiotic relationship with their clients. (This is generally explained by the government's need, in a managed yet free economy, to gain the acquiescence of those it seeks to regulate. There are, however, other factors.) For the Board of Trade to have had a philosophy (and thus embrace policies) totally opposed to that of the bulk of the trading interest would seem anomalous. The likeliest single explanation is that the Board of Trade, partly for historical reasons, saw itself as, and in a real sense was, not a normal specialist department like agriculture, labour or transport, but a second economic ministry, after the Treasury.

Two consequences stemmed from this. First, rivalry with the powerful Treasury (as the ill-fated experiment of the Department of Economic Affairs was later to demonstrate) was suicidal; the keynote would have to be co-operation. This meant operating within the framework of public interest politics (as the Treasury, in its own eyes at least, did) and not that of pressure group politics, as other departments by and large did – and rare indeed was the pressure group that was not seeking, in some way or other, usually through government expenditure, to frustrate Treasury policy. The second consequence of the Board's perception of its role was that it saw its task as formulating policies (largely in the microeconomic field, while the Treasury was concerned principally with the macroeconomic) that were economically right, leaving political considerations to the politicians.

There *is* an economic consensus, as Samuel Brittan has pointed out [*Is There an Economic Consensus?*] and the abolition of RPM would undoubtedly, according to this non-partisan consensus, be in the overall public interest. The problem was the classic political one that, while the benefits would be spread thinly among the consuming public (plus various supermarket groups and other would-be price-cutters who were politically insignificant), the cost would be concentrated on a well-organised and vocal minority ('the trading interest'). But the political problem was for the politicians to weigh up; the Board saw its own task as that of putting the objective economic case that might otherwise go by default – not that officials in the Board of Trade, any more than in any other department, would refrain from tactfully suggesting to ministers how a recommended policy might best be presented politically.

From this it is also clear that the acceptance of departmental policy on RPM by sucessive Presidents of the Board of Trade does not imply that ministers are necessarily the puppets of officials (although weak ones, of course, usually are). Admittedly, it was helpful that abolition could be presented to Labour Presidents as an attack on wicked businessmen and to their Conservative counterparts as a practical demonstration of the party's oft-proclaimed faith in competitive enterprise. But much more important than this, ministers accepted the official line because it was objectively right in terms of orthodox economic analysis – and most British ministers, of either party, prefer to think in terms of public interest rather than pressure group politics. For those who despair of rationality in politics, this may, perhaps, offer some comfort.

But if the persistence of the Board of Trade in campaigning for the abolition of RPM so relentlessly, until it was eventually crowned with success, is evidence of civil service power, it is equally evidence of civil service weakness. For the fact is that, despite all the Board's efforts, until the abolition of RPM in 1964, the proportion of goods sold subject to price maintenance had, if anything, increased over the previous fifteen years. The Wilson/Shawcross attack on the practice in 1949/51 had come to nothing; the Thorneycroft Act of 1956 had resulted in a compromise which (although it was not so clear at the time) proved wholly in favour of the practitioners of RPM; Maudling had filibustered and Erroll had been crushed in Cabinet. Heath alone succeeded where all his predecessors had either failed or, sensing failure, declined to try. In this, important, sense the story of RPM abolition is an example of ministerial power; not the power of any minister or even of the average departmental minister, but the power of a strong and determined minister to overcome all opposition to a strictly departmental but highly controversial measure.

When, in a subsequent volume, we shall hope to examine the evolution of departmental attitudes on some other issues of domestic policy, involving other departments of state, it will be instructive to compare them with this example. Meantime the exceptional nature of the RPM affair needs to be underlined.

4 The Bank of England: Montagu Norman Lives On

According to an agreeable piece of Treasury folklore there was an occasion during the last war when General de Gaulle visited the Bank of England to collect some gold reserves deposited by the Bank of France at the outbreak of war. The Governor met him with a polite but unyielding refusal. De Gaulle, furious, took his case to the Prime Minister. Churchill was full of sympathy but unable to help; explaining that: 'devant la vieille dame de Threadneedle Street je me trouve impotent'.

So much for ancient folklore. Now for modern history. On 2 July 1975 the *Evening Standard* carried a brief item in its '*Londoner's Diary*'. Two days before, it reported, as the Prime Minister was on his way by helicopter to the Royal Show in Warwickshire, the Governor of the Bank of England was demanding, and obtaining, an

urgent interview with the Chancellor. He 'warned Mr Healey that
the slide [in the pound] could not be stopped other than by severe
and immediate measures.' At the Royal Show, meanwhile, the Prime
Minister was tucking into strawberries and cream and talking bravely
about the rejection of 'panic measures'. Twenty-four hours later the
Chancellor presented his 'panic measures' to the House of Commons.

This incident must be immensely reassuring to those who may have
feared that the days when Montagu Norman was supposed to sway
the nation's destiny from Threadneedle Street, were long forgotten.
Yet closer analysis of the course of events in the 1960s hardly bears
out the agreeable vision of Ministerial impotence. Of our four case
histories one – RPM abolition – was right outside the Bank's territory; and while the long-term implications of the Concorde programme might have been a matter of concern to Threadneedle
Street, it would hardly have been expected to adopt a 'departmental
view'; nor did it. The Common Market applications were much
nearer the Bank's heartland, for both the role of the City as an international financial centre and the parity of sterling were intimately
affected by the way the decision went. These two considerations
pulled in opposite directions: the Bank's clientele in the City was
fiercely in favour of early membership of the Community; whereas in
1961 the long-term implications of membership, and in 1966 the
short-term implications, for the pound parity, were ominous.

Characteristically it was the Bank's clientele which emerged vic-
torious from this potential conflict of interests. The Bank was solidly
pro-Europe. Not that it mattered: neither the Tory Government in
1961, nor the Labour Government in 1966, lost a night's sleep about
the views of Threadneedle Street on Europe. There was no reason
why they should have done.

Devaluation was a different matter. In the days of fixed exchange
rates the Bank stood sentinel over the parity as over nothing else. On
the face of things it did a pretty impressive job under the 1964
Labour Government. For more than three years the parity was held
against mounting odds; and when it eventually went the Bank had
already given it up for lost. It is true that Sir Leslie O'Brien, the
Governor, had flown to Basle the weekend before devaluation to test
the climate for one more support package: but his heart was not in
it, and he needed little convincing that the game was up. Furthermore during the intervening period the rising tide of public spending which Labour had interited and initially swelled, and which the
Bank consistently identified as the main threat to the parity, had
been gradually contained and reversed in the face of the natural
preferences of ministers and backbenchers. Many Labour politicians

firmly believed in retrospect that their government had been led by the nose by the Bank of England.

The reality, as we have seen, was more complex. Arguably the Bank's job was done for it when Callaghan was sent to the United States in the summer of 1963 with a brief comprehensively rejecting devaluation; and the author of that brief, Christopher McMahon, earned his subsequent preferment at the Bank. Yet there was an element of sheer chance to this: if McMahon had not been on hand at Oxford when James Callaghan embarked upon his 'teach-in' there the draftsman of his American brief might easily have been someone like Ian Little or Robert Neild, in which case it would have read very differently.

Nor was the Bank in any way responsible for the Prime Minister's passion for the sanctity of the parity. To a large extent it had Thomas Balogh to thank for this – an improbable concordance if ever there was one.

Contrast the Bank's success in assisting Labour to hang on to the parity for three years with its failure to prevent the Tories floating sterling in the summer of 1972. It is true that the climate had changed by then; things could never be the same after the wholesale abandonment of fixed parities which preceded the 'Smithsonian Agreement' in the winter of 1971–2. Nevertheless the Bank *did* resist the pressures to float, and continued to do so right up to the morning of the day the Chancellor's decision was announced. Its advice was simply brushed aside.

In 1972 the Bank was dealing with an unusually dominant Prime Minister who had largely taken over the Treasury's responsibility for economic management. Moreover it was, for once, out of step with the Treasury. In 1964–7 Treasury and Bank moved in tandem from wholehearted commitment to the parity to the conviction that it was lost (similarly in the summer of 1975 Bank and Treasury were at one in believing that the Government must be obliged to accept control of incomes). In 1972 the Treasury had served notice of its intention to abandon the parity peg in the spring Budget: the Bank was on its own.

Still the Heath administration was not the only recent Tory Government to spurn the Bank. Macmillan's did the same (even if not as often as the Prime Minister would have wished). Moreover while the Bank's counsel was ignored in 1972, other sources of external advice were not. It only took a telegram from the Chief Constable of Glasgow warning of bloodshed in the streets if the Government declined to bail out Upper Clyde Shipbuilders to reverse the entire contemporary industrial strategy.

The truth is that modern British governments quake before

pressures of which their members feel themselves to lack personal experience. The Governor of the Bank can frighten Labour governments, whereas Tory ministers think they know all about the foreign exchange markets. It takes a factory sit-in to scare a Tory administration whereas Labour ministers will be likely to dismiss this as a harmless piece of union 'aggro'. Here we see another fantasy at work: modern Tory ministers often have no more first-hand experience of the exchange markets than their Labour rivals, who are equally lacking in personal experience of the picket-line. But fantasies are all-important in politics: which is why the Bank of England has no cause to weep over a Labour victory at the polls (even though it invariably does so – in private).

5 Parliament: Back Benches and Opposition

Over the past ten years three successive governments have won elections on programmes which pledged themselves and their parliamentary supporters always to eschew statutory control of wages, only to introduce such controls within months. With only minor ructions the backbenchers have then marched obediently into the lobbies in support of that which they had sworn to eschew. A Tory government, elected on a ticket of disengagement, nationalised Rolls-Royce and passed an Industry Act with open-ended powers of interventionism; a Labour government, elected on a platform of extending the 'social wage', promptly reimposed prescription charges and slashed state spending (and another is now treading the same path). There were rumbles; but most MPs followed their leaders when the division bells rang. It is not surprising that the public looks on the backbenchers as marionettes.

Yet their leaders do not. Harold Macmillan was genuinely scared of a backbench revolt over Europe; and the backbenchers came within one vote of wrecking the RPM Bill; later on they successfully killed Labour's plans for Trades Union legislation, and then went on to kill a scheme for the reform of the House of Lords endorsed by both the front benches.* The backbenchers may be docile; but they are not toothless.

---

* Harold Macmillan went to exceptional lengths, by modern standards, to keep his backbenchers happy. His distribution of political honours far surpassed anything seen since the days of Lloyd George. On one occasion, when his fortunes were particularly bleak, in the summer of 1963, he perpetrated a most unusual act of Prime Ministerial patronage. A senior member of the Executive of the 1922 Committee – the Tory equivalent of the Labour NEC – had been worsted by the Board of Trade in a wrangle over protection for a local industry. The day before the resulting Parliamentary Order was due for publication, he obtained an inter-

We have studied the course of the RPM revolt in some detail. Let us now look at three other backbench rebellions, two of which succeeded, while one failed: the way in which Harold Wilson was obliged to drop his trade union legislation to which he had committed his personal prestige to a dangerous extent; the way in which the Heath administration was induced to abandon its plans to control the ownership of firearms; and the way in which it crushed the opposition within the Party to its Industry Bill.

The story of the 'In Place of Strife' débâcle is told in graphic detail by Peter Jenkins in *The Battle of Downing Street*, and this is not the place to go over the ground again. But the similarities with Edward Heath's RPM Bill are striking. In both cases the government was planning legislation with proven popular appeal in the run-up to a General Election; and in both cases it was defying a powerful and articulate lobby with privileged access to its own backbench supporters in the Commons. In both cases popular support for the proposed legislation ruled out any question of an outright alliance between government rebels and the opposition. In both cases the Cabinet was more or less publicly split. An important difference was that whereas the Prime Minister simply gave his blessing to the abolition of RPM, his successor virtually took the 'In Place of Strife' legislation over from the departmental minister. Yet it was the former which went through; and the latter which was abandoned.

No doubt this tells us something about the personalities of the two Prime Ministers involved. Sir Alec Douglas-Home had given his word to Edward Heath, and whatever his subsequent second thoughts, 'his word was his bond'. To Harold Wilson, by contrast, as Enoch Powell has pointed out in a perceptive sketch [*The Director*, September 1975], 'the U-turn is [the] normal method of progression'.

But the contrast also tells us something important about the distinctive traditions and styles of the two main political parties. Labour MPs spend their days and their evenings at Westminster when Parliament is sitting. They have nowhere else much to go. Not so Tories. They have dinner engagements to fulfil, clubs to visit, houses and flats to retire to. They are perfectly prepared to keep a Labour government and its supporters out of bed. But they draw the line at being kept at the House by a rebellion by some of their own colleagues.

This was arguably of crucial importance in the case of 'In Place of Strife'. The Cabinet was never in any danger of defeat on the substance of the legislation, for the Opposition could not afford to

___

iew with the Prime Minister. The Order was scrapped – and the Minister responsible at the Board of Trade very nearly resigned.

vote against it. The real threat it faced was that it would fail to carry
the procedural motion to send its Bill for detailed scrutiny to a small
committee of MPs 'upstairs', and hence would have to conduct all
stages on the floor of the House. Then the Labour rebels could have
filibustered it to death – as they and their colleagues had just succeeded in doing to the House of Lords legislation – wrecking the rest
of the Government's legislative programme in the process.

Some contemporary Labour MPs – notably Mr Woodrow Wyatt –
fiercely contested this assessment at the time. They argued that if
the Government had stuck to its guns it would have carried its legislation, and probably gone on to win the 1970 General Election. We
shall never know: but these MPs undoubtedly underestimated the
effectiveness of the procedural threat.

The Tory government of 1964, by contrast, itself decided to take
the RPM Bill on the floor of the House: it was scared of trouble in a
small committee upstairs, whereas – aided admittedly by the unusual device of its backbench 'steering committee' – it had little fear
of a filibuster on the floor. No wonder Labour Chief Whips sometimes look with envy at their opposite numbers.

Nor is it just a question of MPs' nocturnal habits. In the Labour
Party the rebel is a hero to a substantial section of his Parliamentary
colleagues and in the constituencies. In the Tory Party he is at best
a nuisance, at worst a traitor. It is the loyalist who has to fight for
survival in the Labour Party, whereas it is the rebel who has to do so
among the Tories.

The two Tory backbench rebellions of the Heath administration
are instructive in a different sense. The Industry Bill introduced in
the spring of 1972 was an astonishing *volte-face* by any standards.
Here was a Secretary of State who little more than one year earlier
had scrapped investment grants and denounced the 'soft sodden
mass of subsidised incompetence' suddenly announcing the reintro-
duction of investment grants, and taking power to subsidise on a
hitherto unprecedented scale. There was considerable unhappiness
in the Tory ranks. The chairman of the 1922 Committee, always a
formidable figure for a Tory government to tangle with, himself
spoke to a critical amendment and reminded the front bench that it
had attracted the signatures of the chairmen of several backbench
committees. But though the government threw a few sops to the
critics, who kept the House sitting on a Friday night until 10.30 p.m.
for the first time since 1912, there were only a dozen backbenchers
willing to vote against the government when the time came. The
government had nothing to fear.

The Home Office's scheme for restricting the ownership of shotguns in the summer of 1973 was picayune by comparison with this.

The police were worried by criminal use of shotguns; so the Home Office decided to require shotgun owners to prove their right to shoot game. A number of field sports societies were outraged. They circularised their members. Tory MPs began to get letters – hand-written – not just from random constituents, but from heavyweights in their local Parties. Soon a steady stream of them were making tracks for the Chief Whip's office. When MPs returned to West-minster after the summer holidays it was discovered that the pro-jected legislation had got lost somewhere. No doubt it was a measure of marginal significance, lacking in political content; still, it *was* a firm departmental objective, and one which had been cleared by the legislative committee of the Cabinet, and it *was* abandoned.

What are the conclusions to be drawn from all this? First, success-ful backbench rebellions are about interests and not about ideo-logies. Perhaps a majority of Tory MPs were against the Industry Bill in 1972. But it was designed to give a lot of their constituents cash (and the fact that the same constituents would have to provide the cash in the first place never seems to worry the modern MP). Besides, in a genuine, 'constitutional' sense, Parliament *should* rebel on behalf of interests: ideologies are for governments to determine.

Second, Labour is the Party of rebellion, the Tories the Party of conformity. Rebellions can occur under Tory administrations, and can succeed. But the odds are much more heavily loaded against the rebels.

Third, rebels should strike before the iron is hot. Once the Government has published its Bill, it cannot abandon it without painful loss of face. True, Harold Wilson could obtain only the flimsiest of figleaves from the TUC to cover his retreat from 'In Place of Strife'; nevertheless his humiliation would have been even worse if he had published his Bill. Edward Heath was probably right to believe that the passage of a wrecking amendment against his RPM Bill would have necessitated his resignation.

Finally, there is no substitute for Ministerial 'bottom'. Labour might have carried its trade union legislation had it tried, and the Conservatives would surely have succeeded in restricting the owner-ship of shotguns. On the other hand it is not easy to think of other contemporary politicians who would not have quailed and drawn back when confronted by the rage of backbenchers and the distaste and hostility of Cabinet colleagues as Edward Heath was over RPM in 1964.

If our case histories provide plenty of evidence of ministerial sensitivity to the views of government backbenchers, evidence of sensitivity to the views of Opposition MPs is hard to come by.

Contemporary legend decrees that Labour's decision to apply for
membership of the European Community in 1967, by contrast with
the Conservative decision in 1961, was facilitated by advance assurance of bipartisan support. In fact the 1961 decision enjoyed Labour's
goodwill: but Harold Macmillan and his colleagues lost no sleep
over whether they had it or not. Their preoccupation was exclusively
with responses within the Conservative Party.

Labour's decision to defend the parity between 1964 and 1967
enjoyed the vociferous support of the Opposition front bench; but
the desire to retain this support did not enter into ministerial
motivations, nor is there any reason to suppose the Government's
attitude would have been different had that of the Opposition been
different. Julian Amery certainly believed that hostility to his role
in government played a part in the subsequent attempt by Labour to
scrap Concorde, but the evidence is against him. If support from the
Opposition benches were an asset to government Mr Heath, knowing
that he faced powerful resistance to his plans for the abolition of
RPM on his own benches, might have been expected to make overtures to Labour. He never did, because in fact it would have proved
counter-productive.

Indeed there was only one occasion in the course of the events
described in our case histories where Opposition attitudes played a
significant, if subordinate, role. This was when Harold Wilson's
enthusiasm for Europe was unexpectedly kindled, at least in part, by
the thought that a Labour application for membership of the Community would steal the Tories' clothes.

To balance this there should be some reference to a more recent
occasion when, in the eyes of many observers, the attitudes of Opposi
tion MPs *were* of significance in shaping government policy: the
Heath administration's successful bid to join the European Com
munity in 1971-2. Undoubtedly the Prime Minister at that time
attached great importance to securing the support of most Liberal
and some Labour MPs: it was for this reason – at least in part – tha
he abandoned plans he had adumbrated in Opposition for nuclea
collaboration with France. Yet the knowledge that there were pro
European rebels on the Labour benches swelled the ranks of th
anti-Europeans on the government back benches. Moreover it woul
be a complete misreading of Mr Heath's character to imagine tha
he would necessarily have drawn back from Europe even if he ha
been faced by a united Opposition and had rebels behind him.

But if Opposition attitudes rarely influence the choices c
ministers, the desire to change the attitudes which Parties may b
expected to assume in Opposition is a constant preoccupation of th
civil servants. If *only* Labour governments can be committed t

Europe, or Tory governments to price and income control, then
when eventually they are shown the door, as no doubt they will be,
and their successors are persuaded to take up the same policies in
their turn, the 'parliamentary dog-fights' will be averted, and the
long hours they have toiled under one government will not be
cancelled out by their own efforts under the next.

For a body which lives in perpetual contact with Parliament the
civil service is sometimes surprisingly naïve about the working of the
political system. Successful conversions wrought on ministers rarely
survive the reversion of their Parties to opposition. Ministers, armed
with the sweetener of patronage, can always force-feed the majority
of their backbenchers with unpalatable legislation. But once the
sweetener is withdrawn, the diet is usually regurgitated. Labour soon
ditched its commitment to Europe after June 1970; a united Conservative Party could never have been mustered in support of an
incomes policy after February 1974.

Nor is it necessarily true that Opposition support facilitates the
task of government in mustering its own troops. The fact that a
course of action is endorsed by the Opposition is calculated to en-
hance the suspicions about it on the government benches. Perhaps
the purest example of bipartisanship in recent years was the Labour
Government's scheme to reform the House of Lords in 1969. This
emerged from detailed consultation with the Opposition, and carried
the specific endorsement of both front benches. It was promptly
destroyed by an unholy alliance of the backbenchers. It is true that
it was the stratagem of a government running out of ideas, and that
there was not much ministerial capital behind it. Nevertheless the
successful blocking of legislation by backbench filibustering was a
considerable humiliation for the government. It does not appear to
have taught the civil servants anything at all.

Before we leave Parliament a word should be said about the role
of the individual backbencher. For most of the time the backbenchers are privileged spectators, members of the club from which
the rulers are drawn, awaiting the call which, for most of them, will
never come. Yet they are part of the company, and from time to time
they have a walking-on part: we have seen how a Conservative backbencher, Peter Kirk, played a minor but not insignificant role,
through his European contacts, in nudging the Macmillan government towards the point of opening negotiations with the European
Community. Given perseverance the backbencher can change the
Statute Book through time: the achievement of Sydney Silverman in
the fifties in undermining the principle of the death penalty, or of
Eric Heffer in pushing hare-coursing beyond the law in the seventies,
are cases in point. But the strongest weapon for a private member is

the Private Member's Bill. The MP who wins a high place in the annual ballot for Private Member's Bills can, if he is so minded, set in train a course of events with far-reaching consequences for Government policy. John Stonehouse's part in launching the RPM Bill on its way to the Statute Book is a striking, but by no means unique, example. A backbencher who wins a high place in the ballot, provided he chooses a Bill acceptable to the Opposition (and as most Private Member's Bills involve extra expenditure by the taxpayer, this endorsement is seldom hard to obtain), is unlikely to have his Bill sidetracked except by positive government action against it. Yet very often such positive action would get the government a bad press. It is hardly surprising that the Whips' offices are well stored with innocuous subjects for private members' legislation to sell to the more malleable members of the flock.

6 The Interest Groups: the Unions and the Business Lobbies

In the autumn of 1972 Edward Heath told his Party Conference that he had made 'an offer to employers and unions to share full with the Government the benefits and obligations involved in running the economy'; and two and half years later a former senio Cabinet Minister who had spent long years in the Commons, Lor Watkinson, found nothing incongruous about referring to the CB and the TUC as 'the representative institutions' with which th government needed to establish a permanent dialogue. If the 197 Labour government was in the habit of enlisting the aid of the TU in drafting its legislation, it was not without precedents to cite.

Anybody reading our case histories and comparing the evidenc they offer of the role which the CBI (and its predecessor the FBI) an the TUC played in decision-making in the 1960s might be forgive for concluding that the constitution has undergone a sea-chan? since the end of the 1960s. Certainly both bodies were regularly co sulted about the evolution of policy towards, for example, th European Community. Anxieties about TUC reactions played part in the Cabinet debate about the attempt to cancel Concorde the autumn of 1964. But there was only one occasion thrown up our four case histories when either employers or unions played an thing approaching a dominant role in policy-formulation, and tl was when the FBI masterminded the creation of the ill-fated Eur pean Free Trade Association following the breakdown of t' Maudling negotiations in 1958. And that was generally regarded Whitehall as a regrettable and not-to-be-repeated aberration.

Has the pattern of events really been as discontinuous and asy metrical as this bald account suggests? Is it not at least arguable tl what was at stake in the great conflicts which led first to the abandonment of Labour's plans for trade union law reform in 1969, then the frustration of the Conservatives' Industrial Relations Act in 1971–3, and finally to the demolition of the Conservative Government in 1974 at the hands of the miners, was the very *raison d'être* of the trade union movement? Whether legitimately or not, the union leaders undoubtedly felt that their status as negotiators for their membership was threatened by the attempts to change the laws under which they operated; while the successive attempts to restrict the scope of wage bargaining by law did indisputably conflict with the primary purpose for which the unions had first come into existence. Can it be asserted with confidence that the NFU would have knuckled under to an attempt to scrap the annual farm price review?

The truth is that 'In Place of Strife', the Conservative Industrial Relations Act, and successive Acts to limit the scope for wage-bargaining, were, like the abolition of RPM (which provoked a similarly emotional response), departures from the normal incestuous relationship between the interest groups and Whitehall. This is a relationship built on compromise. Whitehall's instinct is to invent a lobby where none exists; it feels the need for a recognised intermediary between itself and the economic groupings on whose responses it relies. The lobby is accorded the privilege of prior consultation; in return it is expected to help sell the eventual bargain – a bargain struck somewhere in the no-man's land between the most the interest group will swallow and the minimum the department is determined to have.

In the case of RPM abolition the lobby had neglected its channels of communication through complacency (after all, it had successfully emasculated the 1956 restrictive practices legislation). But in all these cases the departments concerned, or their political masters, were braced for confrontation, and the scope for compromise did not really exist.

There is no reliable general principle to the art of successful lobbying in the British system. Influencing policy in gestation is crucial; but while some lobbies consciously eschew appeals to the parliamentary dimension – the CBI, the textile lobby at most times, the TUC under George Woodcock's leadership – others have found it advisable to cultivate politicians to the point, if need be, of promoting backbench rebellion: the TUC under Vic Feather, for example, or the NFU at all times. The commonest line is to treat the MPs as the last resort, to be appealed to only when the possibilities of negotiation with the civil servants has been exhausted. Yet on occasion the approach direct to the Minister can work wonders, as in the case of the launching of EFTA.

It is a matter of horses for courses, at any rate where the politicians are concerned. It is no use rallying the Landowners' Federation to wring the withers of government backbenchers under a Labour administration, or enlisting the Co-op to stir up trouble in the 1922 Committee (although the canvassing of support on Opposition benches is not to be ignored, if only because Governments have little to fear from rebellions behind them which do not have Opposition support). For the conscientious lobbyist detailed knowledge of the constituency power structure in the two main parties is invaluable. In the words of the old military adage, 'time spent in reconnaissance is seldom wasted'.

7 The Popular Dimension: Press and Public Opinion

At indeterminate intervals our warring politicians descend from the rarified atmosphere of Westminster and fight for ascendancy in the sand and dust of the public arena.

> *The accursed power which stands on privilege*
> *(and goes with Women, and Champagne, and Bridge)*
> *Broke – and democracy resumed her reign –*
> *(which goes with Bridge, and Women, and Champagne).*

What would Belloc have said today? Not one of the major decisions examined in these pages was ever put to the electorate at election time. The issue of devaluation was about the last thing that governments would have dreamed of discussing with the electorate: it was far too delicate for that. Nor would it have entered the heads of politicians to discuss with their electors the wisdom of spending their money on the building of supersonic transport (unless, that is, they happened to be standing for constituencies with aircraft factories, in which case they would always be ready to pledge themselves to secure the contributions of other taxpayers for the support of the local industry).

Our other two case histories are in a different category, however. The preservation of RPM is precisely the sort of issue that Conservative candidates (and Labour candidates too, for that matter, albeit with little or no prospect of influencing electoral support) are liable to be pressed for their views about at election time. That they were not so pressed during the 1959 election campaign once again reflected the complacency of the Fair Prices Defence Committee. Had they been pressed, they would without doubt for the most part have given the reassurances requested; but whether this would have affected their votes when the moment came almost five years later is another matter.

As for Common Market membership, this was an issue which had already entered into public debate by the time of the 1959 election, and remained there with increasing prominence in 1964 and 1966. In 1959 the overwhelming majority of candidates had no qualms about following their leaders in discounting any possibility of British membership; while in 1964 the official line of both the major parties was that it was what Sir Alec Douglas-Home called 'a dead duck'. By 1966 the large majority of Tory candidates had joined the large majority of Liberal candidates (and some Labour candidates too) in calling for early British entry into the Community. But nobody un-acquainted with the significance of the small print in Harold Wilson's speeches could have guessed from his speech in Bristol in the middle of the election campaign that he was less than six months from leading the next assault on the European citadel.

The contrast between electoral promise and ministerial perform-ance – the course of incomes policy is the classic case – has power-fully contributed to popular cynicism about politics and politicians. Yet it would be quite wrong to deduce from this that modern British government ignores the electorate and public opinion. Noth-ing shakes the morale of ministers more than a series of by-election reverses, for they know that as each new hostile replacement for a Party faithful takes the oath before the assembled Commons, their backbenchers are rudely reminded of their own survival prospects. Nowadays it goes even further down than this: the capture of two Scottish local authority seats in Bo'ness and Bishopbriggs led directly to the wholesale reversal of Government industrial policies with the rescue of Chrysler in the winter of 1975. Economic policy, most of all, is dominated by the evidence of popular sentiment.

Nor is it only by-elections, nowadays, which keep ministers in touch with movements of popular opinion during the lifetime of a parliament. However much they may affect to ignore them, all Governments pay close attention to the findings of the opinion polls. Ian Gilmour [op. cit.] argued that public opinion was chiefly effective as one more dimension to the chronic reluctance of modern British government to make positive decisions. Yet on at least two occasions described in our case histories the evidence of the opinion polls acted as a positive spur to action. The consistent showing of the polls that the abolition of RPM would be popular with the electorate helped to make up Edward Heath's mind to tackle it, and – even more important – helped to enable him to persuade the Prime Minister to back it. Two years later the fact that, for the first time since the beginning of the decade, public opinion, as measured by the polls, showed a balance in favour of Common Market member-ship was a not insignificant motive for Harold Wilson's dramatic change of front.

The paradox between Ministerial preoccupation with 'public opinion' and the consistent failure of the politicians to parade their major intentions before the electorate, or to be bound by those they have paraded, is more apparent than real. For a General Election – or, for that matter, a by-election – is a post-mortem, and not at all the horse-trading for votes that it often appears to be. This is why, for example, the Labour Party could win four out of five General Elections between 1964 and 1974 on a programme of more and more sweeping nationalisation at a time when all the evidence showed that the large majority of the electorate was profoundly antipathetic to nationalisation in any shape or form. The Party manifestos are important because of the use that incoming ministers can make of them in Whitehall: but in electoral terms they are no more than ritual, like the rosettes worn by the candidates. No doubt the electorate would feel deprived without them. But the non-fulfilment of election pledges will not be held against a government which has satisfied the electorate's expectations in other ways, any more than the ability to tick off the performance of a manifesto will save a government which has disappointed.

Nor is the fashionable cynicism about the relationship between MPs and their constituency interests well founded. It is no doubt true that they often find a constituency motivation for personal prejudices, like R. A. Butler worrying over the impact of Common Market membership on the barley-farmers of north-west Essex. Nevertheless the single-member, single-ballot method of electing MPs, and the fact that in every government most senior ministers are MPs, mean that Labour Prime Ministers and Secretaries of State have to face the wrath of their local trades councils, and their Tory opposite numbers that of local farmers and shopkeepers, come the weekend. There is little danger of MPs losing touch with the grass roots.

Baldwin depicted his backbenchers consulting their local station-masters in the twenties, while in the late fifties and early sixties Macmillan was renowned for his propensity for picking the brains of gamekeepers about the state of the nation's housekeeping. But it was not the gamekeepers (a class of men not perhaps given to enthuse about the nostrums of 'The Middle Way') who cropped up in Macmillan's Cabinet table-talk, so much as his unemployed constituent in pre-war Stockton-on-Tees. George Brown's faith in the validity of the reactions of the citizens of Swadlincote as a litmus-test of the nation's feelings became something of a byword in Whitehall.

This is of the essence of the British political tradition. It has contrary consequences on occasion: thus the tendency of modern Conservative Cabinets to be dominated by the representatives of the south ern commuter constituencies has probably weakened their ability to resist the notions of civil servants who are as ignorant as they themselves are liable to be about what is happening north of Watford Gap. And since ignorance can breed alarm, the imagined views of voters in Scotland and the North tend to have more influence on Tory Governments, not less.

The tide of opinion in the world outside Westminster thus constantly makes itself felt by our rulers. But often it is 'opinion' as reflected through the distorting glass of the newspaper editorials: the view of elites rather than masses. We have witnessed how important the endorsement of what had recently been so conveniently christened 'the Establishment' was in stiffening Harold Wilson's commitment to the parity. In a subsequent volume we hope to look at the evolution of policy towards immigration, a classic example of an issue which was stirring the grass roots for several years while Westminster and Whitehall largely ignored it because opinion in the editorial offices was almost solidly hostile to any form of control. But the dominance of elite opinion is perhaps nowhere more clearly demonstrated than in the matter of capital punishment. All the evidence suggests that public opinion has remained solidly in favour of the death penalty. The elite has begged to differ; and it is the elite which has – so far – consistently prevailed at Westminster.

The attitude of our rulers to Fleet Street is perverse. Editorials do not sell newspapers (in fact they are probably about the last section of a newspaper most readers turn to), nor do newspapers achieve mass conversions. When a great crusading polemicist like Beaverbrook went into newspaper proprietorship to promote his favourite causes, fully prepared to lose money in the process, his newspapers flourished and his causes collapsed. Yet the politicians continue to act as if the editorials both mould and reflect public opinion: Edward Heath, for example, attributed his discomfiture at the hands of the miners in the spring of 1972 to the fact that the editor of the *Sun* was a miner's son, who therefore told the government to 'give them the money', and other popular newspapers felt bound to follow this lead. The majority opinion of Fleet Street editors in favour of wage control (motivated, perhaps, by the apparent helplessness of their own proprietors in a situation of untrammelled wage bargaining) has played its part in overcoming the reluctance of successive governments to bow to similar advice from Whitehall and the Bank of England. Similarly the solidarity of Fleet Street – with rare and largely 'non-elite' exceptions – behind the European crusade in the 1960s assisted the conversion of first a Conservative and then a Labour Government. Provided they speak more or less with one voice on an issue (discord between them is self-cancelling) the editors wield considerable influence. It is an influence grounded in illusion, but it is no less powerful for that.

Deference to elite and press opinion strengthens the popular conviction that governments ignore the views of the mass electorate. Often they do – as is their right, just as it is the right of the electorate to punish them for so doing when election time comes round. But there is another dimension of which the public is usually and largely unaware. All governments are continuously influenced by *anticipated* public opinion. The act of deference, however, occurs within the secrecy of the Cabinet room, so the people never learn of the triumphs they have won. The people complain that their opinions are ignored, while ministers are frustrated by the constraints of (real or imagined) popular sentiment.

8 The Residual: Chance and the Zeitgeist

Interest groups cajole, the Bank of England warns, the civil servants guide, the backbenchers plot, the departmental ministers propose, and the Prime Minister disposes. But so often it is pure hazard which tips the scales of decision in the end. Concorde might never have been embarked upon had de Gaulle staged his most celebrated press conference two months earlier; and it would probably never have got to the point of Cabinet discussion but for the replacement of Mr Georges Hereil by General Puget as chairman of Sud-Aviation a few months before that. Edward Heath would surely have stuck to his initial preference for regional development initiatives at Christmas 1963 if John Stonehouse had not won first place in the ballot for private members' motions. And on the crucial night when the government survived the key amendment to the RPM Bill by one vote two Conservative MPs (one of them a Cabinet colleague of Mr Heath's) who had been dining nearby ran their timing so fine that the door to the division lobby slammed shut on their backs. One set of adverse traffic lights might have cost Mr Heath not only his Bill, but also his portfolio. After which the future might have been very different. If Gary Powers had not lost his way over Russian Central Asia the 1960 Paris Conference might have been more nearly the triumph Harold Macmillan dreamed of, and the *pis aller* of a bid for the Common Market might have stayed in the pending tray.

But not, surely, for very long: which brings us to that second great influence which neither ministers nor civil servants can ever be wholly immune to: the *Zeitgeist*. Patrick Gordon Walker [*The Cabinet*], reflecting on his own experience as a Cabinet Minister, concludes that the search for the course and causes of any specific decision must distort reality. It presupposes the isolation of an issue from its background: an isolation of which no Cabinet or any other decision-making apparatus is capable.

This judgement is too sweeping. The origins of a particular decision may run back ten years or more, as they did in the case of the RPM Bill. But they can be traced, and provided they *are* placed against their background, reality is not necessarily distorted thereby. But it would be fatal to ignore that background.

The trading-stamp war, and the advance of the cut-price retailers, proclaimed the march of the *Zeitgeist* against RPM. The financial plight of the aircraft industry, and jealousy of the Americans, might well have tipped the scales for Concorde without any need for Harold Macmillan's great aunt's Daimler. Moreover the early 1960s marked the first fine careless rapture of faith in state entrepreneurship among the elites. France's *Commissariat au Plan* was thought to have discovered the secret of perpetual growth. The notion of Whitehall launching the age of supersonic travel would have seemed incongruous in the 1950s. Not so in the early 1960s. Again, Harold Macmillan's doubts and hesitations might have postponed the moment of decision to bid for membership of the Common Market, but they would not have averted it. The fears of British industry – very largely unfounded fears – about the impact of exclusion from the Common Market tariff wall were too strong to be denied for much longer.

In the case of devaluation it was essentially the *Zeitgeist* which enabled ministers to cling to the $2.80 exchange rate for as long as they did. From the safe distance of the 1970s we can afford to laugh at the treatment of a particular exchange rate as a war situation, in which 'careless talk costs lives', and the gnomes of Zurich might be dropping from the skies at any moment to stab the pound in the back. But the metaphors of the politicians were only an exaggerated reflection of the elite opinion of the epoch. (The Bank of England's rearguard action against floating the pound in 1972, by contrast, was a forlorn attempt to buck the *Zeitgeist*. For between 1967 and 1972 floating had suddenly become not merely forgivable, but positively fashionable.)

Epilogue: Towards the Eighties

The events described in detail in this book took place in the 1960s. All contemporary history lacks perspective. Half-way through the ensuing decade we can identify subsequent apparent modifications to the power balance of the British political system without being certain about their significance or their durability. There are three of these which seem to call for preliminary comment to round off the portrait we have attempted to draw. These are the transfer of civil service patronage from the Treasury to the Civil Service Department; the invocation of the device of the referendum; and the apparent trend towards corporatism to which reference has already been made earlier in this chapter.

Of these it is the first, the emergence of the Civil Service Department, about which a preliminary judgement can be most confidently advanced. In October 1965 an exasperated Crossman reported to his diary how he had told his Departmental Permanent Secretary, Dame Evelyn Sharp, 'How deeply I resented people in my Department leaking ... to the Treasury.... All my key officials,' he went on,

> know that promotion comes to them not from the Minister ... but from the standing which they have in the eyes of the Treasury and of the head of the Civil Service, Helsby. It is this relationship which makes so many higher civil servants willing to spy for the Treasury and to align themselves with the Treasury view even against their own Minister [Crossman, *Diaries*, pp. 342–3].

There was an element of Ministerial pique about this outburst; but there was also an element of reality. Constitutionally the most senior posts in the Civil Service are at the Prime Minister's disposal; and both he and the departmental ministers can and sometimes do black-ball senior nominations. George Brown vetoed the appointment of Sir Con O'Neill as Ambassador to Bonn, and Crossman refused to accept Sir Bruce Fraser as Permanent Secretary of the Ministry of Housing. A known Prime Ministerial prejudice will always be respected: it was no use putting forward the names of Treasury knights to Harold Macmillan for promotion to the top jobs at the Treasury itself. But given the crushing pressure of business on the modern Cabinet Minister and Prime Minister it is inevitable that a considerable degree of autonomy should be left to the civil service's own patronage machine. (For an interesting, if highly discreet, picture of the way this operates in practice the reader is referred to Heclo and Wildavsky, *The Private Management of Public Business*.)

At the time of which Crossman was writing, and to which all our case histories refer, the head of the Civil Service and the senior Joint Permanent Secretary of the Treasury were one and the same person. So the senior civil servant with ambitions working in a spending department had a delicate path to tread. If he became identified by his departmental Minister as a Treasury fifth columnist his promotion prospects might be damaged at the margin by Ministerial animosity. But were he to overstep the limits of Treasury patience in the pursuit of Ministerial favour he could be sure that he would discover, like Belloc's Godolphin Horne, that his name had been erased from the list, when it came to the distribution of Whitehall's most glittering prizes.

The establishment of the Civil Service Department at the end of the 1960s subtly changed all this. Henceforth the Head of the Civil Service no longer lodged at Great George Street. It is true that the first two incumbents were themselves former heads of the Treasury; nevertheless the nature of their allegiances, and the pressures upon them, were bound to change with their address. Sir Douglas Allen, the second incumbent, commented with characteristic caution

> In the old days of the combined Treasury several opinions could be obtained very readily from other departments. Now there cannot be so many people in contact when decisions are taken on the staffing function [*The Director*, September 1974].

Notwithstanding its dominant role in the 'staffing function' we have watched the Treasury lose some major Whitehall battles in the 1960s. The creation of the Civil Service Department was arguably the most decisive rout of all. Perhaps it was not entirely coincidental that by the mid-seventies public expenditure appeared to be out of control.

Much greater caution is required in assessing the consequences of the Labour Government's invocation of the referendum over the Common Market issue in the summer of 1975. Except in countries such as Switzerland, where it is a matter of routine, or the United States, where the voters are given an opportunity to pass a verdict on a range of specific issues of purely local significance on their ballot papers at election time, the referendum has most frequently been used by governments of an authoritarian character to secure a well-rehearsed popular endorsement of decisions already taken. The outcome of the British referendum had something of this appearance. It is as well to remember, though, that it was a device promoted by those who believed it would result in popular rejection of Community membership; and that up to six months before it occurred most supporters of British membership feared precisely that result.

Maybe what matters for the future is that the government did obtain the response it desired. Of course it also repeatedly insisted that this was a unique device for a unique occasion. Well, we shall see. If, however, the referendum does establish itself as a new feature of the evolving constitution it is surely more likely to do so because of the outcome of this first exemplar rather than because of its genesis. Had the precedent then existed, it must have been tempting for the Heath government, for example, to invoke a referendum rather than a General Election to secure popular endorsement for its stand against the miners at the end of 1973. And that endorsement would no doubt have been forthcoming (although whether that would have swayed the miners or their leaders is another question). But if this were to become the pattern, then of course it would be quite wrong to view the referendum as constituting a new dimension of public participation in decision-making. Rather it would be a useful adjunct to the means already available to Government to secure the enactment of decisions already reached.

The trend towards corporatism which has developed since the occurrence of the events discussed in our case histories would, by contrast, if confirmed, modify profoundly the interplay of influences and pressures we have described. As we have seen, it is not entirely a new phenomenon. Nevertheless the manner in which the Heath administration offered specific concessions on such matters as the rates of VAT, the terms of its Industrial Relations and Fair Rents Acts, the level of pensions, and even to reveal the contents of the Treasury's jealously-guarded medium-term economic assessment, during the course of its 'tripartite talks' with CBI and TUC in the autumn of 1972 did break new ground. This was a precedent consolidated by the detailed prior negotiation of Labour's legislative programme with the moguls of the TUC in 1974 and carried still further, in form if not in substance, by the 'conditional' Budget of 1976.

Much will depend on the evolution of counter-inflation policy. At the time of writing the issue is finely balanced. Faith in the potentialities of wage and price control in Whitehall seem undimmed by the harsh lessons of experience. Yet governments will still presumably have to secure popular endorsement from time to time at the hustings: and if past experience is any guide the accolade of endorsement by TUC or CBI – or even both together – is no guarantee of electoral success. Thus so long as Britain remains recognisably a democracy, with a directly-elected parliament, the representatives of corporate power could at best (or worst, according to taste) only constitute an adjunct to the existing power structure we have been discussing, and not a replacement for it.

If, on the other hand, the increasingly articulate body of opinion which regards the corporatist trend as a barrier to the resolution of the very inflation problem it is supposed to cure, and also – more relevantly to our present purposes – a passing fashion which will not survive the abatement of inflation by more orthodox remedies, then presumably the TUC and the CBI will in due course revert to their traditional role: that of the most prestigious, if by no means always the most influential, of our domestic lobbies.

These are all features about which it may be possible to pass some tentative judgements at a later date. Another is the extent to which membership of the European Community has begun to restrict the freedom of choice of the civil servants and their 'masters'. Notwithstanding the flood of Community secondary legislation which has preoccupied anti-Marketeers – and others – in the House of Commons, it was, at the time of writing, much easier to point to instances where major decisions had been taken in defiance of Community obligations than in deference to them. Perhaps the Chrysler rescue operation at the end of 1975, when the anxiety of the 'pro-Europeans' in the Cabinet to avert the threat of a collision with the Community over import controls on cars seems to have been an important factor in the way the decision went, marked a change of trend.

There is only one certainty, and that is that both the true nature of the distribution of power and influence in the British polity, and our understanding of it, are constantly evolving. There will never be definitive conclusions. Those we have advanced in the preceding pages make no pretentions to such status. If they have shed some extra light upon the processes at work and the interplay of men and institutions at a particular moment in the recent past, they will have served their purpose.

Select Bibliography

MEMOIRS

Ball, George, *Discipline of Power* (Allen Lane, 1968)
Butler, Lord, *The Art of the Possible* (Hamish Hamilton, 1971)
Crossman, Richard H. S., *Diaries of a Cabinet Minister*, vol. 1, 1964–6 (Hamilton/Cape, 1975)
de Gaulle, Charles, *Memoirs of Hope*, vol. 1, *Renewal, 1958–62*; vol. 2, *Endeavour, 1962–* (Weidenfeld & Nicolson, 1971)
George-Brown, Lord, *In My Way* (Gollancz, 1971)
Gladwyn, Lord, *Memoirs* (Weidenfeld & Nicolson, 1972)
Gore-Booth, Paul [Lord], *With Great Truth and Respect* (Constable, 1974)
King, Cecil Harmsworth, *The Cecil King Diary, 1965–70* (Cape, 1972)
Kipping, Sir Norman, *Summing Up* (Hutchinson, 1972)
Macmillan, Harold, *Pointing the Way, 1959–61* (Macmillan, 1972)
—— *At the End of the Day* (Macmillan, 1973)
Wigg, George [Lord], *George Wigg* (Michael Joseph, 1972)
Williams, Marcia [Lady Falkender], *Inside Number 10* (Weidenfeld & Nicolson, 1972)
Wilson, Harold, *Labour Government, 1964–70: A Personal Record* (Michael Joseph, 1971)

CONSTITUTIONAL STUDIES

Bagehot, Walter, *The English Constitution* (1867: with an introduction by R. H. S. Crossman, Collins, 1963)
—— —— *Collected Works*, vols 5, 6, 7 & 8: *The Political Essays*, with an introduction by N. St John-Stevas (Economist Newspaper, 1974)
Berkeley, Humphry, *The Power of the Prime Minister* (Allen & Unwin, 1968)
Birch, A. H., *The British System of Government* (Allen & Unwin, rev. ed., 1973)
Bray, Jeremy, *Decision in Government* (Gollancz, 1970)

Butt, Ronald, *The Power of Parliament* (Constable, 2nd ed., 1969)
Crossman, Richard H. S., *Inside View* (Cape, 1972)
Gilmour, Ian, *The Body Politic* (Hutchinson, rev. ed., 1971)
Gordon Walker, Patrick, *The Cabinet* (Fontana, rev. ed., 1973)
King, Anthony (ed.), *The British Prime Minister* (Macmillan, 1969)
Mackintosh, John, *The British Cabinet* (Stevens & Sons, 2nd ed., 1968; Methuen paperback, 1968)
Rose, Richard (ed.), *Policy-making in Britain* (Macmillan, 1969)

CONCORDE

Costello, John, and Hughes, Terry, *The Battle for Concorde* (Compton Press, 1971)
Davis, John, *The Concorde Affair* (Frewin, 1969)
House of Commons, *Second Report of the Estimates Committee, Session 1962–3: Transport Aircraft* (HC 42 : HMSO, 1965)
International Air Transport Association, 'Technical, Economic and Social Consequences of the Introduction into Commercial Service of Supersonic Transports' (Document 8087 c/925, 1960)
Report of the Committee of Inquiry into the Aircraft Industry (the Plowden Committee) (Cmnd 2853 : HMSO, 1965)
Technology, Ministry of, *Report of the Steering Group on Development Cost Estimating* (HMSO, 1969)
Wilson, Andrew, *The Concorde Fiasco* (Penguin, 1973)

THE COMMON MARKET

Beever, R. Colin, 'Trade Union Re-thinking', *Journal of Common Market Studies*, November 1963
Beloff, Nora, *The General Says No* (Penguin, 1963)
Camps, Miriam, *Britain and the European Community, 1955–63* (Oxford, 1964)
Heath, Edward, *Old World, New Horizons* (the Godkin Lectures, March 1967 : Oxford, 1970)
Kitzinger, Uwe W., *Second Try* (Pergamon, 1969)
Lieber, Robert J., *British Politics and European Unity* (California University Press, 1971)
Nordlmyer, Eric, *Britain and the Common Market: the Decision to Negotiate* (Prentice-Hall, 1968)

RESALE PRICE MAINTENANCE

Andrews, P. W. S., and Friday, F. A., *Fair Trade: RPM Re-examined* (Macmillan, 1960)
Final Report of the Committee on Consumer Protection (the Molony Committee) (Cmnd 1781 : HMSO, 1962)

Haley, G., 'Politics of Resale Price Maintenance' (University of Sheffield, 1968, unpublished)

Report of the Committee on Resale Price Maintenance (the Lloyd Jacob Committee (Cmd 7696: HMSO, 1949)

Yamey, B. S., *RPM and Shoppers' Choice* (Institute of Economic Affairs, 1960)

DEVALUATION

Beckerman, Wilfred (ed.), *The Labour Government's Economic Record, 1964–70* (Duckworth, 1972)

Brandon, Henry, *In the Red* (Deutsch, 1966)

Brittan, Samuel, *Steering the Economy* (Penguin, rev. ed., 1971)

Hirsch, Fred, *The Pound Sterling: a Polemic* (Gollancz, 1965)

McMahon, Christopher, *Sterling in the Sixties* (Oxford, for the Royal Institute of International Affairs, 1964)

THE CIVIL SERVICE

Hecclo, H., and Wildavsky, A., *The Private Government of Public Money* (Macmillan, 1973)

Lee, Sir Frank, *The Board of Trade* (Stamp Memorial Lectures: Athlone Press, 1958)

Thomas, Hugh (ed.), *Crisis in the Civil Service* (Blond, 1968)

CONCEPTS OF POWER

Bachrach, Peter, and Baratz, Morton S., *Power and Poverty: Theory and Practice* (Oxford University Press (New York), 1970)

Polsby, Nelson, *Community Power and Political Theory* (Yale University Press, 1963; paperback, 1966)

MISCELLANEOUS

Brittan, Samuel, *Is there an Economic Consensus?* (Macmillan, 1973)

Bruce-Gardyne, Jock, *Whatever Happened to the Quiet Revolution?* (Charles Knight, 1974)

Butler, D. E., and King, A., *The British General Election of 1964* (Macmillan, 1965)

—— —— *The British General Election of 1966* (Macmillan, 1966)

—— and Pinto-Duschinsky, M., *The British General Election of 1970* (Macmillan, 1971)

Foot, Paul, *The Politics of Harold Wilson* (Penguin, 1968)

Hutchinson, George, *Edward Heath: a Biography* (Longman, 1970)

Jenkins, Peter, *The Battle of Downing Street* (Charles Knight, 1970)

Sampson, Anthony, *Macmillan: a Study in Ambiguity* (Penguin, 1968)

Index

Ackroyd, Dame Elizabeth, of the Board of Trade: appointed first Director of the Consumer Council, 96–7

Adenauer, Konrad, Chancellor of the German Federal Republic 1949–63: agrees to bilateral negotiations with the British at official level in the autumn of 1960, 54; successfully wooed by President de Gaulle (qv), 45

Amery, Rt Hon. Julian, MP for Preston North 1950–66, Secretary of State for Air Oct 1960–July 1962, Minister of Aviation July 1962—Oct 1964: constituency interest in TSR 2, 23–4; as Aviation Minister not a member of Cabinet, 25; 'abused relationship' with father-in-law Macmillan, 26, 158; meets Buren (qv), 27; signs Concorde agreement with de Courcel (qv) 28; 'target of Tory extravagance' for Labour, 30

Andrew, Sir Herbert, Second Secretary, Board of Trade 1955–63, Board of Trade member Heath negotiating team, Brussels 1961–3: strong advocate of RPM abolition, 109–10

Armstrong, Sir William (subsequently Lord Armstrong of Sanderstead), Third Secretary, Treasury 1958–62, Jt Permanent Secretary, Treasury 1962–8, Permanent Secretary, Civil Service Dept, and Head of Civil Service 1968–74: believes Sir Alec Cairncross (qv) *persona non grata* with Labour Government, 119; chairs committee on balance of payments, 120; told Labour ruled out devaluation in Opposition, 127; drafts devaluation 'War Book', 131; argues Common Market membership will mean devaluation, 133; believes deflation must precede devaluation, 134; prepares July 1966 deflation package, 136; recognises inevitability of devaluation, 138

Astor, Hon. David, Editor of *Observer* 1948–75: dressed down for lack of patriotism, 147

Attlee, Rt Hon. Clement (subsequently Earl), Prime Minister 1945–51: 1949 devaluation, 124

Aviation, Ministry of: and Concorde, 12–37 *passim*

Ball, George, Assistant US Secretary of State 1960–6: opposes nuclear deal with French, 48; gives green light for British Common Market membership, 56; accuses Macmillan of crablike vacillation, 61

Balogh, Thomas (subsequently Lord), Economic Adviser to Harold Wilson in opposition, and the Cabinet 1964–7; consultant to Prime Minister 1968: opposes Common Market, 66; argues against hasty decision on devaluation, 123; opposes Kaldor (qv) on floating pound, 125; discusses devaluation with Crosland (qv), 130; joins in writing devaluation memorandum, 131; advises Callaghan to devalue in winter 1966, 138; favours siege economy, 130, 142; Francophobe, 148

Bank of England: has 'expertise without loyalty', 142; professionally opposed to devaluation, 143, 169–72 *passim*

Barclay, (Sir) Roderick, Ambassador to Denmark 1956–60, adviser on European trade questions at Foreign Office 1960–3, Ambassador to Belgium 1963–9: significance of 1960 appointment, 49

Messmer, Pierre, French Defence Minister: reputed to have told Healey (qv) of French willingness to see Concorde cancelled, 33–4

Mills, Lord: relationship with Macmillan, 21, 34; backs Concorde, 25; opposed to RPM abolition, 91

Mills Committee: established, 21; backs Concorde, 25

Ministerial Action Group on Public Expenditure (Magpie): set up, 26

Molony Committee on Consumer Protection: reports, 91

Monopolies Commission: instructed to look into RPM, 84; reports, 85

Morgan, Morien (subsequently Sir), Deputy Director, Royal Aeronautical Establishment 1954–9, Scientific Adviser, Air Ministry 1959–61, Deputy Controller of Aircraft (R & D), Ministry of Aviation 1960–3: launches work on SST, 10–11; in charge of STAC (qv), 12; on BOAC's attitude to Concorde, 23; on technological 'fall-out' and employment implications of Concorde, 24

National Chamber of Trade: organises nationwide campaign against RPM abolition, 101

National Farmers' Union (NFU): relations with FBI, 43; attitude to lobbying of, 57, 179; shift in attitude to Common Market, 70

Neild, Robert, Deputy Director, National Institute of Economic and Social Research 1958–64, Economic Adviser to Treasury 1964–7: anti-Common Market, 66; 'excluded' from committee of officials on Market, 67; favours devaluation, 123; member of Callaghan's 'tutorial group', 126; helps to draw up pro-devaluation paper, 131

Net Book Agreement: significance of, 87

Nield, William (subsequently Sir), Labour Research Department 1937–9, Under Secretary, Ministry of Agriculture 1959–64, and DEA 1964–5, Deputy Under Secretary of State, DEA 1965–6, Deputy Secretary, Cabinet Office 1966–8, Permanent Secretary, DEA 1968–9: brings pro-European bias to Cabinet Office, 66

1922 Committee of Conservative backbenchers: 102

Nuffield College, Oxford: 'tutorial group' established for Callaghan, 126

O'Brien, Sir Leslie (subsequently Lord), Governor of Bank of England 1966–73: and devaluation, 139, 144–5

O'Neill, Hon. Sir Con, Ambassador to EEC 1963–5, Deputy Under Secretary of State, Foreign Office 1965–8; reputedly likens de Gaulle to grouse, 75; appointment to Bonn vetoed, 186

ONERA: attitude of, to Concorde, transformed, 17

Ormsby-Gore, Sir David (subsequently 5th Lord Harlech), MP for Oswestry 1950–61, Minister of State, Foreign Office 1957–61, Ambassador to Washington 1961–5: warns Macmillan of Kennedy suspicion of de Gaulle, 55

Osborn, John, MP for Sheffield, Hallam 1959– : introduces and carries Trading Stamps Bill, 94, 96

Padley, Walter, MP for Ogmore 1950–70, Minister of State for Foreign Affairs 1964–7: left-wing supporter of Common Market, 59

Page, Graham, MP for Crosby 1953– , Vice-President, National Chambers of Trade: opposes RPM abolition, 116

Pagliero, Leonard: becomes Chairman of RPMCC (qv), 88, 101

Palliser, Michael (subsequently Sir), Head of Planning Staff, Foreign Office 1964–6, Private Secretary to Prime Minister 1966–9, Minister at Paris Embassy 1969–72: significance of appointment to 10 Downing Street, 66

Plowden Committee on the Aircraft Industry, 1965–6: highlights Whitehall origins of Concorde, 16; on employment case for sustaining aircraft industry, 23; on 'technological spin-off', 24

Powell, Sir Richard, Permanent Secretary, Ministry of Defence 1956–9, and Board of Trade 1960–8: fervent convert to Europe, 50

Press: influence of, and Common Market, 53, 54, 61, 78; and RPM